Part of the Family

Part of the Family

Christadelphians, the Kindertransport, and Rescue from the Holocaust

Volume 2

JASON HENSLEY

"Part of the Family" is an ongoing project attempting to catalogue the lives and experiences of the Jewish refugees who lived with Christadelphians during the 1930s and 1940s. To that end, if readers know of anyone who could possibly be included in a further work, or if they or their family were Jewish refugees who were sheltered by Christadelphians and would like to have their story published, please contact the author at iwaspartofthefamily.com

Copyright © 2017 Jason Hensley
All rights reserved. No part of this publication may be reproduced in any form or by any means, electronic, mechanical, photocopying, recording or otherwise, without the prior permission of the author.
Published in the United States of America 2017

Grateful acknowledgment is made to the following for permission to reprint previously published material:

Excerpts from the Glossary in *Echoes and Reflections Teacher's Resource Guide* (New York: Anti-Defamation League, 2005, 2014), www.echoesandreflections.org. All rights reserved.

Photographic credits can be found at the end of this volume.

To Allyse, Cole, Hannah, Jamin, Kalyn, Laura, Mia, and Noah

Another report tells of the establishing of a 'Death House' in the village of Treblinka in Poland. To these death chambers the men, women, and children are beaten, whipped and driven; the cells are filled to capacity, the doors are hermetically sealed and the process of asphyxiation by liquid gas begins. What is to be our attitude to this state of things? We can assist Israel in two directions. The first and most potent is the continual approach by prayer to the throne of grace; the second, and also important, is that of personal sacrifice in the contributing of funds to the alleviation of the condition of these people.

H.P. M<small>ANSFIELD</small>
"Debtors to Israel," *Logos Magazine*
December 1943

Contents

Preface	iii

Part I

A Distinct Community	3

Part II

Netty Gladstone	35
Rudi Hart	77
Susan Clapper	119
Rudi Weil	143
Inge Beacham	179
Ben Weiss	199
Max Harper	247
Rita Devletian	283
Rita Glanz	317
Ernst Billig	335
Appendix - Elpis Lodge	369
Glossary	428

Part of the Family
Volume 2

Preface

This project has gone well beyond anything I had ever imagined. Former refugee families have been connected with the Christadelphians who sponsored them; letters, documents, and fates of family members that had remained largely unknown for decades were unearthed; and stories of hope, love, and faith that would otherwise have gone untold have been unveiled. In this way, it has shed light on the significance of the individual and their story in the midst of the enormity of the Holocaust. Each individual has a unique story, and each unique story bears its own value in being told. Sharing these stories has been a primary goal of this project.

Additionally the project has brought to light the story of a group of people, the Christadelphians, which believed fervently in the inspiration of the Bible, and thus the promises made to Abraham and in the hope of Israel contained therein. In this way, it has served as a reminder of the crucial role that doctrine plays and the impact it can have on actions. Beliefs affect behavior. Acknowledging this relationship has been another major goal of this project.

Unlike the first volume, this one features a much shorter introduction. It is assumed that in going through these pages, the reader already has knowledge of the Christadelphians and their unique beliefs. To ensure that this volume's introduction builds upon that of the first, this introduction specifically portrays the Christadelphians' apolitical stance and its connection to the Holocaust and considers the relationship of the Christadelphian community with the Jews from 1940 to 1945. This latter component helps to complete the record of the history of the Christadelphian Church and its connection to Jewry during era of the Third Reich, as the first volume's introduction focused on Christadelphian history and the Christadelphians and the Jews up until around 1939.

The bulk of this book comprises ten individual stories; their details help convey the sheer magnitude of the Holocaust. Six million Jews perished at the hands of Hitler and his followers. So, too, did six million stories. Each person murdered was an individual: a father, a son, a mother, a daughter. Each had hopes, goals, dreams, and fears. These were all destroyed in the Holocaust.

I hope that the sharing of this handful of individual survivor stories will serve as a vivid reminder that each person who perished also had a story—and that these stories taken together, *six million of them,* could fill countless pages.

The stories herein can be told because a small Christian group, the Christadelphians, was moved to act on behalf of Europe's Jews.

This second volume, in contrast to the first, which focused nearly wholly on children who lived with Christadelphians families, tells the stories of five refugees who came to live in Elpis Lodge: Rudi Hart, Ben and Heinz Weiss, and Max and Rolf Koenigsbuch. Consequently, it seemed appropriate to include an appendix of primary sources about Elpis Lodge. I hope those sources will help create a picture of Elpis Lodge and of the collaboration between the Christadelphian community and the wartime Jewish community. These sources can also build a clearer understanding of why the Christadelphians jumped in wholeheartedly to help save Jewish children from annihilation.

Just as with the first volume, the stories included in these pages were both read and approved by the refugees and/or their families before being printed. The chapters are named after the

Preface

refugees with whom I have been in contact. As such, the experiences are told from their respective points of view. Max Harper's biography is a notable exception—I named the chapter after Max and have been in contact with him, but relied on his deceased older brother Rolf's memories of growing up in Hamburg, which were recorded in 1955, to provide the details of the brothers' early life.

May these stories bear out the care shown by Christadelphians to the Jews in their time of distress. In so doing, may these accounts serve as a source of inspiration: despite the darkness that enveloped Europe more than 70 years ago, some sparks of light shone, lit by the fervent beliefs of the Christadelphians, bringing hope to those who otherwise would have been crushed by the darkness.

Part I

The Christadelphians and the Jews

A Distinct Community

Unlike many historical events, the Holocaust presents a powerful dichotomy: on one hand, the sheer evil of our nature and its capacity for ill is readily apparent.[1] On the other hand, through the darkness shone events and actions that went against the tide: individuals—and sometimes groups of people—chose to risk their lives or give of themselves for the sake of the Jewish people. These events demonstrate that although the mass of humanity may choose the "broad" way, there are those who will defy that well-traveled path and will choose to rescue. In the dedication to *Voices and Views*, a history of the Holocaust, Rabbi Harold Schulweis describes the latter path this way:

> From the behavior of thousands of non-Jews who risked their lives and those of their families to rescue Jews from the Nazi predators, we learn that goodness existed even in the face of indescribable evil, that passive complicity was not the only alternative to totalitarian oppression and murder.[2]

Indeed, if it were not for these acts of rescue, the judgment upon humanity might be absolute.

Thus, the Holocaust becomes an essential topic of study for those who desire to better understand humans and their behavior. Ephraim Kaye, the director of the International Seminars for Educators Department at Yad Vashem, states:

> The Holocaust is an irrational human event. It doesn't make sense. So what does that mean for humanity? Germany was the seat, the epic center of European culture. How could this country perpetuate the

Holocaust? . . . The other side is the conspiracy of goodness. Peripheral to the entire story, but important. There were people who were willing to save Jews. How is it possible to become a perpetrator and how is it possible to put everything in danger to become a righteous gentile? What does that say about human behavior? Studying the Holocaust is a place to study human nature.[3]

A study of the Holocaust becomes vital for those longing to understand why humans make the choices they do—and why, in the midst of the travesty of the Holocaust, darkness was overshadowed by light. In studying the way in which many groups—including countries—confronted the Holocaust, we see that the reverse is more generally the case: darkness often overpowered light. For instance, although some German Christians attempted to shelter and rescue Jews, most did not. As stated in the United States Holocaust Memorial Museum's Holocaust Encyclopedia, "In 1933 . . . almost all Germans were Christian"—with one-third of the population belonging to the Roman Catholic Church and two-thirds belonging to Protestant churches.[4] It was in that overwhelmingly Christian country that the Holocaust began. What happened to the Christian values of love, kindness, and peace? The majority of German Christians found themselves supporting a regime that set about eliminating the Jews. In the United States, again, a country some consider to possess a strong moral compass, the State Department ignored and stifled news of European Jewry's destruction,[5] and American newspapers gave such news little coverage.[6] Therefore, the United States, in a sense, became a bystander. And within the Catholic Church, a number certainly attempted to rescue Jews, but the vast majority stood on the sidelines. Susan Zucotti, in her study of the Catholic Church in Italy's reaction to the Holocaust, explains:

> There were in Rome in 1943 and 1944 hundreds of parish churches, 1,120 religious institutions for women, and 152 for men. Given that surprisingly large number, the statistics of 100 female convents and 55 male institutions (including eleven parish churches) that sheltered Jews become less impressive. Most Catholic institutions, after all, took pride in their reputation as dispensers of hospitality and succor. It should have been the norm rather than the exception for them to shelter Jews and others in distress.[7]

Yet, it was not simply that many in the Church did not act, thereby becoming bystanders—but some of its members were either complicit with the Nazis or were even *worse* than the Nazis were to the Jews. Croatia, a nation allied with Nazi Germany, was led by Ante Pavelić, a staunch Catholic whose regime promoted Catholicism because it was part of the Croatian heritage.[8] This Catholic regime began to eliminate its Jews even before Nazi Germany did: "Before the death camps in Poland were operative, thousands of Croatian Jews were herded into concentration camps. By the end of 1941, approximately one-third of the Jewish population had died or were murdered in these camps."[9]

In fact, at the Wannsee Conference in 1942, where top Nazis met to determine how to carry out the destruction of European Jewry, it was declared, "[In] Croatia the matter is no longer so difficult, since the most substantial problems in this respect have already been brought near a solution." In another instance, when Pavelić met with Hitler in Berlin, the former reprimanded the latter for having not yet solved the Jewish question, whereas the matter had already been solved in Croatia.[10] Croatia was also the site of the notorious Jasenovac concentration camp—staffed by Catholic priests and led by a priest called "Brother Satan" by his victims.[11]

5

Indeed, the Holocaust offers an opportunity to see glimpses of human nature—both the brutality with which it is capable and the love and compassion with which it can combat the brutality. Tragically, in nearly every instance and every group—including religious groups whose principles should have compelled them to act on behalf of the Jews—many acted as bystanders, collaborators, or perpetrators. Though some sought to effect rescue, the majority almost never did.

The Christadelphians, a small Christian denomination whose members were mostly concentrated in Great Britain at the time, remain an exception—among a few others, such as the Quakers and the nation of Denmark. Chana Kotzin, in her thesis on *Christian Responses in Britain to Jewish Refugees from Europe, 1933–1939*, writes the following:

> A pattern seen in other Christian groups serves as a contrast and comparison for the Christadelphian fellowship. Responses within Unitarianism, Methodism and Anglicanism were often initiated by fairly high-ranking or high profile individuals who raised the refugee cause, and through their efforts (as opposed to leadership directives) managed to elicit interest from the laity of their respective movements. This support was never truly widespread but it was significant. Within Christadelphianism it was traditional for an interested individual to initiate a programme of aid and gain support from other brethren within his own ecclesia and beyond through word of mouth and a notice in the main journal. At least half of the wider fellowship were at one time or another actively involved in fundraising efforts and a proportionately large number of children were given hospitality in Christadelphian homes. Thus, although initiated by 'low-ranking' individuals, the loose network of ecclesias and members took up the cause

through their biding and this effectively became a movement wide programme.¹²

When studying the Christadelphian response to Jewish refugees, Dr. Kotzin recognized that unlike many other Christian groups, the Christadelphians' efforts to aid Jews became a community-wide effort. The majority of Christadelphians attempted to aid the Jews and resist the Nazis—making the Christadelphians a distinct community amongst the various religious groups, cultural groups, and nations that were confronted by the Nazi terror. The introduction to this second volume will attempt to demonstrate that, indeed, Dr. Kotzin's analysis of the Christadelphians' behavior toward the Jews is correct—looking at specific ways in which the Christadelphians refused collaboration with the Nazis and helped the Jews. It will then consider *why* it was that Christadelphians took a difference stance towards the Jews than many other Christians did.

Avoiding Collaboration

Rather than referring to their congregations as "churches," Christadelphians use the word "ecclesias"—each church is called an "ecclesia" (based on the Greek word translated as "church"). In the 1930s, when the Nazis came to power, it would appear as though there were four Christadelphian ecclesias in Germany: one in Berlin, one in Stuttgart, one in Esslingen, and one in Bonn.¹³ It is difficult to assess how many Christadelphians made up these four ecclesias at the time, but it seems there were approximately one hundred Christadelphians in the entirety of Germany.¹⁴ Nevertheless, this small group of Christadelphians did indeed suffer for their faith at the hands of the Nazis.

Christadelphians fervently believe in the coming Kingdom of God. They see Jesus Christ as their king, and they expect him to one day return from heaven and rule the world from Jerusalem (Luke 1:31-33). It is to this Kingdom that Christadelphians pledge their allegiance (Philippians 3:20). Thus, Christadelphians refrain from political involvement—doing what they can to spread the love of God and His message personally rather than politically. This belief, along with the conviction that Jesus charged his followers to live at peace with everyone (Romans 12:18) and to love their neighbors as themselves (Matthew 22:39), has also caused Christadelphians to take the stand of conscientious objectors. Following Jesus's words to Pontius Pilate, Christadelphians will not fight in the wars of this world (John 18:36).

Therefore, Christadelphians essentially do not collaborate with *any* government. They are not against the governments of the nations of the world, but they are not for them either. Instead, Christadelphians remain apolitical and follow the biblical dictum to pray that the leaders of the government will continue to allow them to practice their faith in peace (1 Timothy 2:1-2).

Nevertheless, the story of the Christadelphians in Germany is exceptional—specifically because not only did the Christadelphians avoid involvement with the Nazi government, but also this specific stance—in particular, the choice to be conscientious objectors, put the Christadelphians in an incredibly dangerous position with the Third Reich.

In 1934, the changes that had been brought about by the Nazis were initially minimal. Spreading "propaganda" was forbidden, so the Christadelphian ecclesias in Germany were prevented from holding public lectures and passing out handbills.[15] By 1935, letters were being censored, so Christadelphians in England were warned that "any innocent

Some of the members of the Stuttgart Christadelphian ecclesia on the occasion of Stanley Ramsden's visit in 1934. An arrow is pointing to Albert Merz.

communication might be misunderstood and cause our brethren in Germany much trouble."[16]

However, by 1937, life had become considerably more difficult. L. A. Ramsden, a Christadelphian from England, visited the ecclesias in Germany and wrote of their troubles:

> It is still possible to hold meetings in private, but these are subject to periodical inspection and, it appears, suffer no ill so long as the Jewish aspect of the Truth does not happen to be the topic on these occasions. The houses of private citizens too are visited, and specimens of their reading matter taken away.[17]

Meetings could no longer occur publicly, and individual houses were searched for any type of literature that could be considered propaganda.[18] However, the major issue that confronted the brethren in Germany was their conscientious objection to military service. Unlike the United Kingdom and the United States, the Third Reich had no provision for conscientious objection. In the same letter, L. A. Ramsden described what had happened to one of the members of the small German Christadelphian community. He states, "One young brother was recently sentenced to a term of 18 months for refusing to accept military authority. His present whereabouts are unknown to his anxious brethren."[19]

In October of the same year, another English brother, Guy Joint, visited the Christadelphians in Germany and brought back news of the young brother who had been sentenced for his conscientious objection—and noted ominously that surely this young brother will not be the sole member of the German Christadelphian community to be targeted in such a way:

> The relatives of the young brother mentioned by Bro. L. Ramsden in the August *Fraternal Visitor,* have now had news of him: he is working in a stone quarry for the duration of his sentence. There are other young brethren likely to be called to the colours during the next year or so, who will probably share a similar fate.[20]

Less than two years later, in July 1939, the ominous warning did in fact come to pass. The young man who had been sentenced to 18 months in the stone quarry had a brother who had met with an identical fate.[21] In August of the same year, a German Christadelphian was able to visit England—and there he conveyed to the brethren the worsening situation for conscientious objectors,[22] and thus for Christadelphians, in Nazi Germany: "The mildest form of punishment is prison labour, while in some cases a number have been summarily shot.[23] Where possible a few brethren meet in their own houses to comfort and exhort each other."[24]

After August 1939, with the war's arrival, the Christadelphians in England were cut off from those in Germany—and the next communication received from the latter came in December 1945. There, the fate of the two brothers referred to in July

A Distinct Community

Top: Rudolf Merz, 1960.
Bottom: August Merz and his wife Ida in Schwerin, 1947.

1939 was provided: "One of the brethren from Stuttgart was shot in Berlin because he refused to be a soldier; another was sent away to a lunatic asylum."[25]

Eventually, more details were revealed about these two brothers—and a third sibling, too. The first, but the youngest out of the three, Rudolf Merz, just as the magazine had initially declared, had been sentenced to 18 months of hard labor. But his suffering did not end there—he was the brother who had been sent to the "lunatic asylum." After serving his sentence for over a year, in May 1938, he was instead sent to the Psychiatric Detention Center in Bruchsal because he had displayed signs of mental illness—likely due to the treatment he had received in the course of his term of hard labor. When he had completed his sentence, he was released and returned to his work as a miller. Nevertheless, on January 15, 1940, he was again called to military service—and again refused. With his refusal, he was sent to trial, and his signs of mental illness

Albert Merz (far left).

returned. Because of this illness, he was acquitted by the court, but he spent the next 10 years, until 1950, in various hospitals, health centers, and psychiatric institutions. After his release, he found employment as a crane driver—supporting the idea that he was capable of normal work and that the mental illness was related to the stress brought upon him by the Nazi regime.[26]

August Merz, the middle brother of the three—and one not mentioned in the communication to the English brethren in December 1945, had been sent to Sachsenhausen concentration camp in December 1940.

Built in 1936 by prisoners who had been transferred to the region from Ems, Sachsenhausen was the main concentration camp for the Berlin area. By 1938, the camp was still under construction, and 900 prisoners were brought from the Esterwegen concentration camp to continue the building work. As a result of their circumstances at Sachsenhausen—both the lack of food and the barbarity of the SS—the majority of these 900 died within a month or two of their arrival.[27]

An industrial yard lay outside of the camp's western boundary—inmates were forced to work in the yard, and those who could not were required to stand at attention for the entirety of the workday. The *Jewish Virtual Library* describes Sachsenhausen in this way: "Like all other **Nazi concentration camps**, the conditions of life in **Sachsenhausen** were incredibly barbaric. There were daily executions by shooting or hanging, and many more died as a result of casual brutality and the poor living conditions and treatment."[28]

In its early stages, Sachsenhausen held a number of political prisoners and either real or perceived criminals. Some of the more well-known prisoners include Pastor Martin Niemöller, who is perhaps best remembered for his "when they came for me"[29] quotation; Yakov Dzhugashvili, Joseph Stalin's son; and Herschel Grynszpan, the young Jewish man whose murder of Ernst vom Rath preceded *Kristallnacht*.[30]

In Sachsenhausen, August Merz became prisoner number "34590." During his time in the camp, he was sent to the *Krankenrevier*, or the hospital of the camp, from March 4, 1941, to March 15, 1941. No other records of August Merz exist in the Sachsenhausen archives.[31] He did, however, survive the deprivations of Sachsenhausen until its liberation in 1945.[32]

Tragically, the eldest of the three brothers, Albert Merz, was executed by guillotined for his refusal to serve in the German military.[33] After the war, one of the letters that his lawyer, Erich Höhne, had written to him on February 21, 1941, shortly before Merz's execution, surfaced:

> Erich Höhne,
> Lawyer and notary
> at the Landgericht Berlin
>
> Berlin, 22 February 1941
>
> To: Rifleman Albert Merz,
>
> At present
> Berlin-Tegel,
> Wehrmacht Detention Prison
>
> Yesterday's proceedings ended with the death sentence being passed on you. No other outcome was possible because you remained to deaf to all arguments. It went exactly as I told you it would at our meeting. You will have to concede yourself that the President of the court made every effort to cure you of your mistaken

attitude. The more I reflect on your attitude, the more incomprehensible your conduct becomes to me. You will remember that the President read to you verbatim the passage in the Bible which says that every soul must be subject to the higher powers and that the powers that be are ordained by God. If you yourself always say that for you as an 'Urchrist' [Christadelphian] only the Bible is authoritative, then you must recognize the force of this passage against you. You were unable to say a single word in reply to this passage. If the state authority, such as our Führer in this case, calls upon the German people to defend themselves in their struggle against the intended attacks of our envious neighbors, if necessary with force of arms, and as the legitimate authority has introduced universal military service, then in the light of this passage that is a order of which God approves too and which every subject must obey.

Everything is not yet lost for you. Although this grave sentence has been passed on you the sentence can still be rescinded if, at the last minute, as it were, you will be convinced of the error of the position that you have adopted hitherto and will declare that you are willing, without any conditions, to do military service.

I hope that in the face of death you will yet come to this wiser conclusion. Your standpoint, which you adopt so decidedly, without even considering the thoughts and arguments of your fellow-countrymen, who are only seeking your good and who are good Christians too, is not a defense of the original gospel, as you mistakenly think; in reality your attitude comes rather from the spirit of antichrist, inspired in you by the sinful pride, as though only you and the few adherents of your erroneous beliefs had rightly understood the teaching of Jesus Christ and all the rest of us offend against God's commandment. My firm opinion anyway, shared by every true German, is that the good Lord will take greater pleasure in the man who has given his life in the fulfillment of his duty towards his Fatherland than in someone who throws away his life pointlessly simply because out of pride he has refused to listen to those with greater wisdom. Such conduct can in no circumstances be pleasing to God.

As your counsel, officially appointed by the court to defend you, I have considered it my duty to urge you to consider the matter one last time. Should you come to this more sensible conclusion, you must immediately ask to be brought before the court again and make a formal statement accordingly. The matter is very urgent, however, for you have only a few days in which to do so.

Heil Hitler!
(signed)[34]

Two days later, Albert wrote to his family:

Berlin, 23 February 1941

To all my dear ones,

It is hard for me to write to you today, not on my own account but because I know that this letter will cause you grief. So I beg you not to take it too hard. You all know my faith and my hope: 'For me to live is Christ and to die is gain'. So do not weep for me even if the worst befalls me, but be strong and take courage. If I have been sentenced to death on 21 February and am to be executed, that simply means that the life which

A copy of Albert Merz's first letter to his family.

took on visible form in me will return to its source and will at the appointed time again assume this form. If my time is now at an end and I have to part, then remember that it is appointed unto men once to die and after this the judgement.

Tomorrow I shall submit a petition for clemency. Perhaps the court may yet show mercy on me, and even if not, I still hope to be allowed to write to you once more. Remember me in your prayers. And now I will close, trusting in God and His Kingdom, and greet you with all my heart.

Yours,
Albert[35]

On April 3, 1941, one day before his execution, Albert wrote again to his family:

Brandenburg, 3 April 1941

My dear ones,

I would like to use my last hours to write to you again and at the same time to ask you not to take it too hard, for it is God's will, John 19:7; Romans 14:7-12; [Romans] 8; Isaiah 59.

On Friday 4 April at 5.30 in the morning my time will be over and my struggle will be at an end.

My last wish is that you may live in peace and ensure that none is lost, 2 Timothy. O my dear friends, if only I could put on paper the thousand thoughts that I have addressing to you in silent conversation and still am.

But you can find many of them in the holy scriptures, especially in the letters of the Apostles, the farewell addresses of Jesus in John, etc, and I hope that I shall see you all again after my awaking.

I will close now, and you will understand why I have not written more, it would be too much, and I send you my sincere greetings.

Yours,
Albert

Give my greetings to all the brethren and sisters and to those who think kindly of me. The grace of our Lord Jesus Christ be with you. Amen.[36]

On the back of the letter, Albert had written a well-known poem, probably from memory:

> What you are, be that completely whole.
> Not only the bright blossom
> But also the simple leaf
> Is needed for the wreath.[37]

Such is the story of the Christadelphians in Germany. They were a persecuted people—a group that found its meetings regulated, its literature banned, and some of its members imprisoned. It did not collaborate with the Third Reich, nor did it stand idly on the sidelines as a bystander. Instead, living according to Christadelphian doctrines by remaining apolitical and refusing to serve in the military, the Christadelphians were actively persecuted, with one brother, Albert Merz, giving his life for these beliefs.

Elpis Lodge. Note that the name of the hostel can be seen faintly at the top of the doorframe.

Christadelphians and the Jews, 1940–1945

Throughout the years of the Holocaust, the Christadelphians actively supported the Jews. Before the war began, they found homes for refugee children who had fled to England on the Kindertransport and they made numerous donations to Jewish relief funds.[38] However, the years before the war will not be treated in this volume, as they were largely detailed in the first.

During the war, these donations continued, as did the Christadelphians' support of the refugee children. In 1940, solely through their own contributions, the Christadelphians established a hostel in Birmingham for Jewish refugee boys called Elpis Lodge.[39] The hostel was run upon Orthodox lines, and twice during the war years, *The Jewish Chronicle* reported on the environment at the hostel—favorably both times. An excerpt from each article gives the sense of the way in which the Jewish community at the time felt about the Christadelphian community—and reinforces that the

Christadelphians did all they could to support the Jewish people. The first article, titled "Christadelphians' Fine Gesture," is featured on the front page of the newspaper and begins with the sentence, "Christadelphians have again demonstrated their sympathy for Jewish victims of persecution."[40] The second is titled "Birmingham Refugee Hostel – Christadelphians' Continued Generosity," and it explains how the hostel was run, describes the way the boys were taught and how they were found "trainee jobs" to enhance their skill sets, and notes that the Christadelphians financed the hostel's operating costs. The article states, "No reasonable expense has been spared by them as far as maintenance is concerned, the provision of good substantial food together with some items which may be looked upon as luxuries, is one of the features of the catering."[41] Both articles have been fully reproduced, with kind permission from *The Jewish Chronicle*, in the appendix to this volume.

The hostel also received a significant amount of publicity in the Christadelphians' main publication, *The Christadelphian* (all of which has also been reproduced, with kind permission from the Christadelphian Magazine and Publishing Association, in the appendix). Every few months, an update on the hostel was published, but perhaps the most significant for this study's purposes are some of the opening remarks of Rabbi A. Cohen, who spoke at the hostel's dedication. There, he stated:

> Among those not of our own people who were conspicuous in their sympathy and their endeavour to be helpful was the community of the Christadelphians. This is not by any means the first occasion on which they have shown their interest in the welfare and fate of the Jewish people. For long years they have contributed generously to our efforts to re-establish the Jewish people in their homeland; and therefore we appreciate

> to the full the magnificent act of generosity which has found its expression in this Hostel for Refugee Boys. We of the Jewish Community feel that a sacred trust has been committed to us, a trust we shall endeavour to discharge faithfully to the utmost of our ability.[42]

Such is the relationship that the Christadelphians had with the Jewish people, both before and during the war. In fact, in 1940, when C. C. Walker, one of the former editors of *The Christadelphian* magazine, died, director of *Keren Hayasod*, Dr. Arthur Hantke, sent a touching note to *The Christadelphian* on behalf of the chief fundraising agency for Palestine:

> We have just read of the passing of Mr. C. C. Walker, the long-standing editor of your paper, a fine and upright man, a champion of the oppressed and persecuted, a true and loyal friend of the Jewish people, who will hold his name in honour. We associate ourselves with the grief felt by your community and would ask you to be good enough to convey our expression of sincere sympathy to Mrs. Walker and her family.[43]

Indeed, it would have certainly been an honor for a Christadelphian to receive such a note.

Lest, however, it appear as though the Christadelphian actions on behalf of the Jews during the war were simply the actions of a few individuals, or one ecclesia, such as the one in Birmingham, it should be noted that *all* Christadelphians were in fact encouraged to do what they could for the Jewish people. Therefore, when another Christadelphian brother died, around the time of C. C. Walker's death, it was reported, "The local Jews held him in high esteem, and prayers were made on his behalf at the synagogue during his fatal illness."[44] Approximately one year later, another event told the same story—this time a Christadelphian sister had passed away. She did not receive any type of tribute from the local Jewish community, but *The Christadelphian* magazine reported a story in her obituary:

> Like Hiram of old, she was 'ever a lover of David', and this was shown by her consistent support of the Jewish Relief Fund out of her very slender means. A touching little incident in this connection came to light after her death, when a sum of money was found knotted in her handkerchief specially earmarked for this fund.[45]

Throughout the war, Christadelphians were encouraged to support the Jews in any way they could—and those who attempted to say anything otherwise about the Jewish people were rebuked. H. P. Mansfield, one of the leading Christadelphians of the time, showed clearly that support of the Jews was the Christadelphian position—nothing else:

> Paul [the apostle] did not respond to any anti-semitic sentiments, although, to their discredit, one occasionally hears the old hackneyed mis-statements regarding Jews retailed by some Christadelphians. ... These being Paul's sentiments, would he hesitate to assist Jewry in its time of need? Would he stand back and say, 'Oh no, they are accursed of God! Let us enjoy the amenities of life to the full, but let Israel suffer the curse they so justly receive?'[46]

Throughout this intensely antisemitic period in world history, the Christadelphians stand as an outlier. As a community, the members prayed for the Jews in their suffering and attempted to alleviate that suffering in whatever ways they felt they could—most tangibly through the housing of Jewish refugees who fled to Great Britain on the Kindertransport and through the establishment of Elpis Lodge.

Asking the Question

This all seems to beg this question: *Why* did the Christadelphians take this stand? What made them act together as a community on behalf of the Jewish people? Why were they so intensely interested in Jewish affairs? The same questions were asked in the first volume—and yet their import is so weighty that they must be asked again.

Perhaps one of the reasons the Christadelphians did so much for the Jews was in hopes of somehow converting them. Specifically concerning their actions in the Kindertransport, by bringing the children in and away from their parents, into their homes, or into a hostel, the Christadelphians would have ample opportunity to indoctrinate the children. This type of activity was undertaken by a number of churches that sponsored refugees—and so in 1941, *The Christadelphian* magazine printed the following article, titled "Jewish Fears of 'Spiritual Kidnapping'":

> Vigorous protests have been made in a correspondence in *The Jewish Chronicle* against conversionist activities among refugee or evacuated children. One correspondent describes it as 'the spiritual kidnapping of children removed from the vigilance of their parents or guardians.' The position of foster-parents is a difficult one; if their faith as Christians is reflected as it should be in their own home life, the children brought into the family circle cannot be uninfluenced by it. That, of course, is not the kind of influence to which chiefly the correspondents refer, and we would agree that those who have the care of refugee children would betray a trust if they used their power to influence their

> charges against the wishes of their parents. But in cases where guardians or others responsible show no marked interest in their children's religious education, would foster-parents be doing their duty if they allowed the children to grow up without religion? There are also practical difficulties, such as that if children do not accompany foster-parents to meetings, someone must stay at home with them. Clear-cut rules cannot be made; those who have the care of refugees must judge what is right and honourable in the circumstances of each case—always remembering that with children too young to judge for themselves their primary responsibility is to the parents who are deprived for the time being of their child. More may be accomplished for the day of their acceptance of their Messiah than we may dream of if our present contacts with Jewry lead them to see Christ reflected in us; but the cause of Christ will not be served by 'compassing sea and land to make one proselyte' in circumstances which savour of betrayal of trust.[47]

Christadelphians were caring for the children on behalf of their respective parents. As such, the parents' religion and values *had* to be considered. The community advocated this stance, at least in general, and the individual stories told in both volumes 1 and volume 2 bear this out. Consistently, the children stated that they went to the meetings and did the daily Bible readings with their foster families, but did not feel pressured to become Christadelphians themselves. Elpis Lodge was run according to Orthodox principles. Consequently, this work was not done with an eye toward proselytizing or converting Jews.

Why then did the Christadelphians act for the Jewish people?

The clearest explanation comes from an editorial in *The Christadelphian* magazine, written in August 1943 by John Carter, during the midst of the war. The editorial attempts to explain the history of Christadelphian support of the Jews, and it brings the reader all the way back to 1882, around the time the Christadelphian movement was still in its infancy. Thus, as a community, one of the reasons that the Christadelphians acted the way they did was because of the power of antiquity—this was what the community had always done. But certainly there were additional reasons. The editorial went on to declare perhaps the clearest explanation: "The Jews are men: we have the opportunity afforded us. This is sufficient, were there no other reasons to justify us in what we propose to do." The proposal at hand was another collection for Jewish relief. Yet the article continues to list another reason—and here, the real crux of the Christadelphian sympathy for the Jews is explained:

> In the very place where it says, 'Do good unto all men as ye have opportunity,' it is added, 'but especially to those who are of the household of faith.' Here is an 'especially' in certain directions. We shall find there are many 'especially's' in the case of the Jews. In the first place, who are they? We cannot know the truth and be ignorant of this. We have to use Paul's words, and say 'Whose are the fathers, and of whom as concerning the flesh Christ came.' We have to say with him 'they are beloved for the fathers' sakes.' They are the descendants according to the flesh of him who was called 'The friend of God', to whom the promises were made, and to whom we have become related as his seed and heirs according to the promise, if we walk in the steps of that faith which our father Abraham had. . . . They are the nation of whom Jehovah himself has said 'He that toucheth you toucheth the apple of His eye,' and 'cursed is he that curseth thee.' There is

> not a nation in the civilized world but what is cursed under this clause. True it is, that Israel has been scattered among them for their sins; and they (the Gentile nations) have been made use of as God's instruments to punish them; but this does not alter the fact that the nations, in ill-treating Israel, have offended against Israel's God. . . . [The believers] will never be found lifting a foot against them so far as it is left to their voluntary action. Rather will they reverence, and pity, and pray. Israel is the holy nation in the earth. The [believers] have nothing but blessings for them.[48]

The editorial continues, undeterred, giving reason after reason for the Christadelphian brethren to act on the Jews' behalf—this understanding of the Jewish people is indeed a central tenet of Christadelphian doctrine. "We cannot know the truth and be ignorant of this." In other words, Christadelphian teaching concerning the Jews was considered such a priority, that those who did not understand it were considered to not truly know the gospel.

This is the reason the Christadelphians acted, and acted so strongly, on behalf of the Jews: the Christadelphians believed that they were commanded to do so by Scripture. The Bible noted the Jews as a special people to God, Jesus stated that "salvation is of the Jews," and even the apostle Paul explained that they are "beloved for the fathers' sakes." In a Christadelphian's eyes, anyone who read the Bible and who truly believed what it said, would *have* to do what they could to help alleviate Jewish suffering. Just as their beliefs prevented Christadelphians from collaborating with the Nazi regime, it was their beliefs that led them to aiding the Jews.

Again and again, the pages of *The Christadelphian* echo this message—not only during the six years of the war, but from the magazine's very beginnings in the 1800s. Since that time, the Christadelphian message regarding the Jews has been consistent—and that consistency resulted in rays of hope during the darkest days of the Holocaust. Because of this teaching, approximately 250 refugee children found comfort and safety in Christadelphian homes.

These are some of their stories.

---

[1] Michael Gray, *Teaching the Holocaust: Practical Approaches for Ages 11-18* (Abingdon: Routledge, 2015), 85-86.

[2] Harold Schulweis, *Voices and Views: A History of the Holocaust*, ed. Deborah Dwork (New York: The Jewish Foundation for the Righteous, 2002), xliii.

[3] Deborah Batiste, Ephraim Kaye, and Claudia Wiedeman, "Meet the Team Behind Echoes and Reflections," *Echoes and Reflections*, September 1, 2014, http://echoesandreflections.org/uncategorized/meet-the-team/.

[4] "The German Church and the Nazi State," *United States Holocaust Memorial Museum*, accessed February 28, 2017, http://www.ushmm.org/wlc/en/article.php?ModuleId=10005206.

[5] David Wyman, *The Abandonment of the Jews* (New York: Pantheon Books, 1984), 81.

[6] Deborah Lipstadt, *Beyond Belief: The American Press and the Holocaust* (New York: The Free Press, 1986), 164.

[7] Susan Zucotti, *Under His Very Windows* (New Haven: Yale University Press, 2000), 201.

[8] Michael Phayer, *The Catholic Church and the Holocaust, 1930-1965* (Bloomington: Indiana University Press, 2000), 32.

[9] Ibid, 85.

[10] Mark Aarons and John Loftus, *Unholy Trinity* (New York: St. Martin's Griffin, 1998), 74.

[11] David Cymet, *History vs. Apologetics: The Holocaust, the Third Reich, and the Catholic Church* (Lanham: Lexington Books, 2012), 337.

[12] Chana Revell Kotzin, "Christian Responses in Britain to Jewish Refugees in Europe: 1933-1939" (doctoral thesis, University of Southampton, 2000), 153.

[13] Stanley Owen, *Into All the World* (Glasgow: Self-Published, 1998), 36.

[14] G. S. S., "News of the Brethren in Germany," *The Fraternal Visitor*, December 1945, 159.

[15] S. H. R., "The Work of the Truth in Germany," *The Fraternal Visitor*, September 1934, 238.

[16] "Ecclesial Notes," *The Fraternal Visitor*, January 1935, 27.

[17] L. A. Ramsden, "From Across the Seas," *The Fraternal Visitor*, August 1937, 223.

[18] Stanley Owen, *Into All the World* (Glasgow: Self-Published, 1998), 38.

[19] Ibid, 224.

[20] Guy Joint, "Ecclesial Notes," *The Fraternal Visitor*, October 1937, 279.

[21] "From Across the Seas," *The Fraternal Visitor*, July 1939, 195.

[22] By far, the vast majority of those who suffered as conscientious objectors were Jehovah's Witnesses.

[23] In all, there were approximately 200–250 Jehovah's Witnesses who were executed as conscious objectors.

Graham Jackman, "'Ich Kann Nicht Zwei Herren Dienen': Conscientious Objectors and Nazi 'Militärjustiz' The Undocumented Cases of Three Brothers," *German Life and Letters* 64, no. 2 (2011): 189.

[24] "From Across the Seas," *The Fraternal Visitor*, August 1939, 223-224.

[25] G.S.S., "News of the Brethren in Germany," *The Fraternal Visitor*, December 1945, 159.

[26] Graham Jackman, "'Ich Kann Nicht Zwei Herren Dienen': Conscientious Objectors and Nazi 'Militärjustiz' The Undocumented Cases of Three Brothers," *German Life and Letters* 64, no. 2 (2011): 202–203.

[27] "Sachsenhausen (Oranienburg): History & Overview," *Jewish Virtual Library*, accessed June 9, 2017, http://www.jewishvirtuallibrary.org/history-and-overview-of-sachsenhausen-oranienburg-concentration-camp.

[28] Ibid.

[29] "First they came for the Socialists, and I did not speak out—
Because I was not a Socialist.

"Then they came for the Trade Unionists, and I did not speak out—
Because I was not a Trade Unionist.

"Then they came for the Jews, and I did not speak out—
Because I was not a Jew.

"Then they came for me—and there was no one left to speak for me."

Martin Niemöller quoted in "Martin Niemöller: 'First They Came for the Socialists...,'" *United States Holocaust Memorial Museum*, accessed June 9, 2017, https://www.ushmm.org/wlc/en/article.php?ModuleId=10007392.

[30] "Sachsenhausen," *United States Holocaust Memorial Museum*, accessed June 9, 2017, https://www.ushmm.org/wlc/en/article.php?ModuleId=10005538.

[31] Monika Liebscher, archivist at Sachsenhausen Museum, e-mail message to author, September 18, 2015.

[32] Graham Jackman, "'Ich Kann Nicht Zwei Herren Dienen': Conscientious Objectors and Nazi 'Militärjustiz' The Undocumented Cases of Three Brothers," *German Life and Letters* 64, no. 2 (2011): 201.

[33] Graham Jackman, e-mail message to author, June 2, 2017.

[34] Erich Höhne, letter to Albert Merz, February 22, 1941. Translated by Graham Jackman. Copy of translation in possession of the author. Original German available in "'Ich Kann Nicht Zwei Herren Dienen': Conscientious Objectors and Nazi 'Militärjustiz' The Undocumented Cases of Three Brothers," *German Life and Letters* 64, no. 2 (2011): 214–215.

[35] Albert Merz, letter to his family, February 23, 1941. Translated by Graham Jackman. Copy of translation in possession of the author. Original German available in "'Ich Kann Nicht Zwei Herren Dienen': Conscientious Objectors and Nazi 'Militärjustiz' The Undocumented Cases of Three Brothers," *German Life and Letters* 64, no. 2 (2011): 215–216.

[36] Albert Merz, letter to his family, April 3, 1941. Translated by Graham Jackman. Copy of translation in possession of the author. Original German available in "'Ich Kann Nicht Zwei Herren Dienen': Conscientious Objectors and Nazi 'Militärjustiz' The Undocumented Cases of Three Brothers," *German Life and Letters* 64, no. 2 (2011): 216.

[37] Graham Jackman, e-mail message to author, June 2, 2017.

[38] Chana Revell Kotzin, "Christian Responses in Britain to Jewish Refugees in Europe: 1933-1939" (doctoral thesis, University of Southampton, 2000), 154.

[39] Barry Turner, ... *And the Policeman Smiled* (London: Bloomsbury, 1990), 163.

[40] "Christadelphians' Fine Gesture - Hostel for Birmingham Refugees" *The Jewish Chronicle*, May 1940, 1.

[41] "Birmingham Refugee Hostel - Christadelphians' Continued Generosity" *The Jewish Chronicle*, August 1940, 13.

[42] A. Cohen, quoted in "An Abode of Hope" *The Christadelphian*, June 1940, 258.

[43] Arthur Hantke, quoted in "Jewish Tribute to Bro. Walker," *The Christadelphian*, June 1940, 284.

[44] "Obituary - Bro. J. M. Thomas, Llanelly," *The Christadelphian*, June 1940, 285.

[45] "Intelligence," *The Christadelphian*, August 1941, 378.

[46] H. P. Mansfield, "Debtors to Israel," *Logos Magazine*, December 1943, 92.

[47] "The Jews and Palestine," *The Christadelphian*, November 1941, 516.

[48] John Carter "Christadelphians and Jewish Relief," *The Christadelphian,* August 1943, 146-147.

Part II

The Children

Introduction

1. **Netty Gladstone** - Rheydt, Germany - October 1924
2. **Rudi Hart** - Zinten, Germany - December 1925
3. **Susan Clapper** - Bad Salzuflen, Germany - June 1926
4. **Rudi Weil** - Vienna, Austria - April 1928
5. **Inge Beacham** - Forst, Germany - October 1928
6. **Ben Weiss** - Berlin, Germany - August 1929
7. **Max Harper** - Hamburg, Germany - December 1931
8. **Rita Devletian** - Forst, Germany - January 1932
9. **Rita Glanz** - Vienna, Austria - March 1933
10. **Ernst Billig** - Vienna, Austria - March 1935

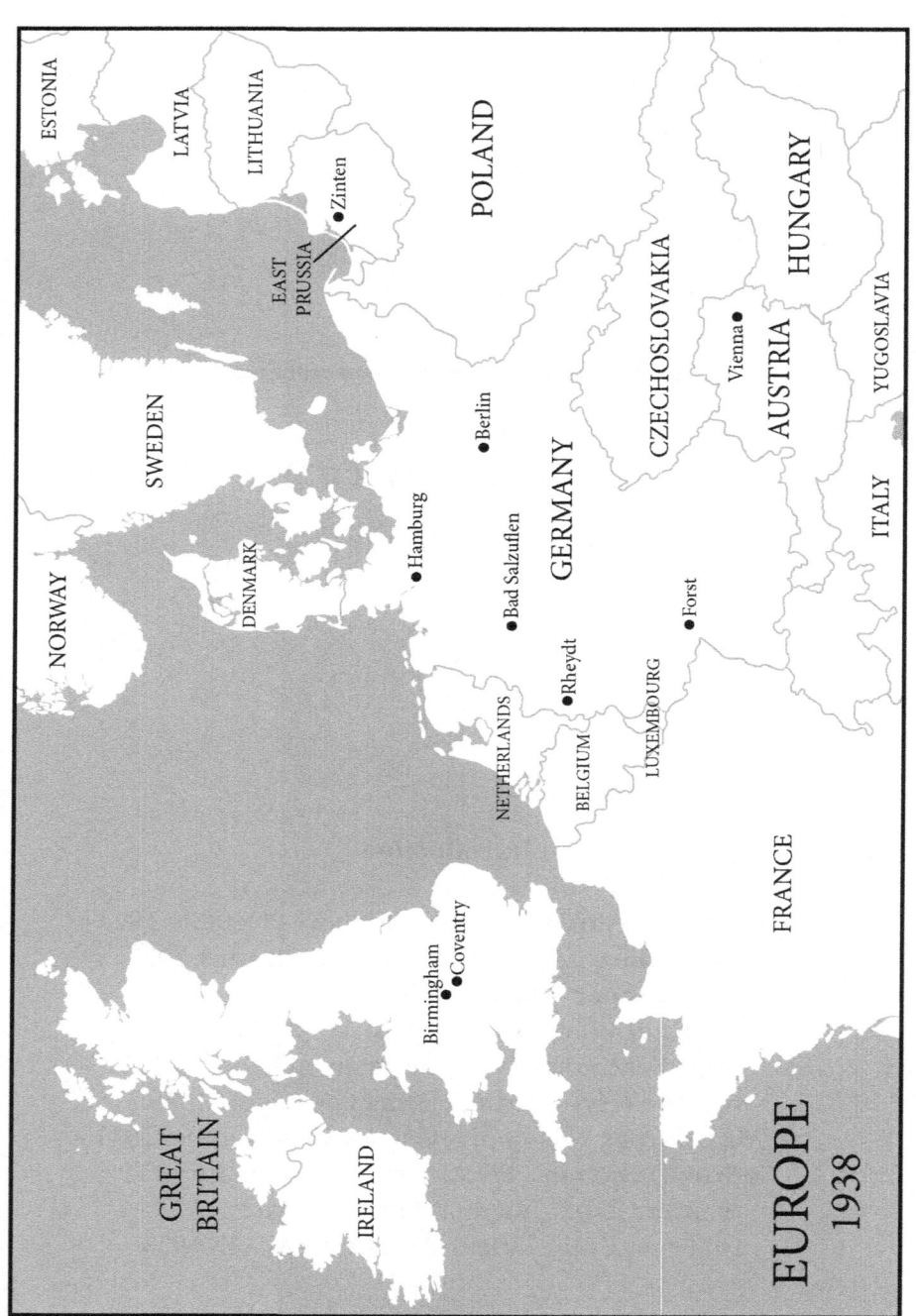

NETTY GLADSTONE

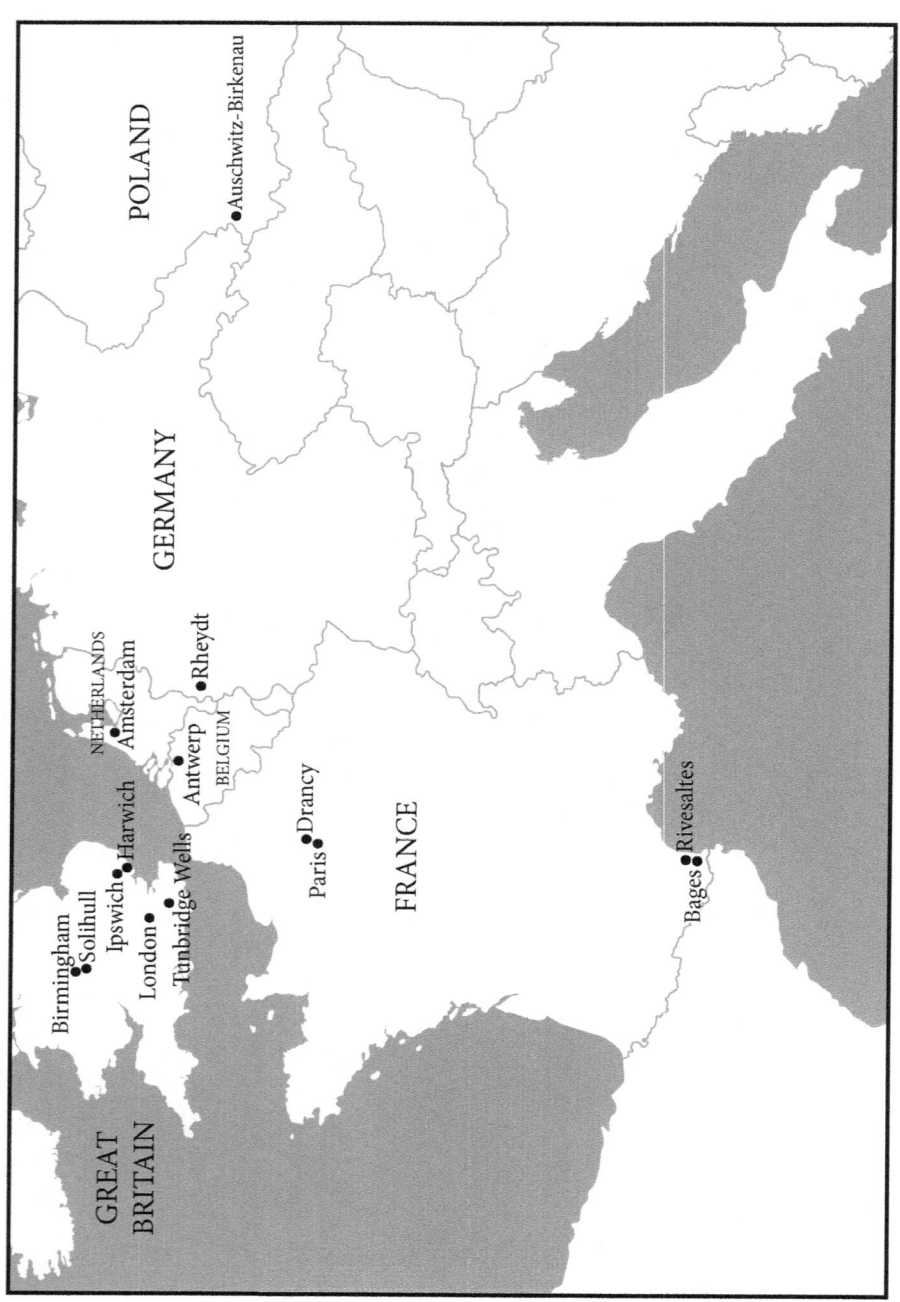

1

NETTY GLADSTONE (NÉE KUPPERMAN)

Rheydt, Germany, was the hometown of the infamous Joseph Goebbels. Born in 1897 to a pious Catholic family, and educated at a Roman Catholic school,[1] Goebbels succeeded Adolf Hitler as the propaganda minister of the Nazi party. Given the position in 1933, the year Hitler became Chancellor of Germany,[2] Goebbels spearheaded the promotion of vitriolic Nazi ideology and did so vehemently until the day he died. Goebbels is credited with the following maxim:

> If you tell a lie big enough and keep repeating it, people will eventually come to believe it. The lie can be maintained only for such time as the State can shield the people from the political, economic and/or military consequences of the lie. It thus becomes vitally important for the State to use all of its powers to repress dissent, for the truth is the mortal enemy of the lie, and thus by extension, the truth is the greatest enemy of the State.[3]

Joseph Goebbels had an inauspicious, humble start. During the First World War, he was dismissed from military service because of a clubfoot. Therefore, instead of serving his country militarily, he attended multiple universities and received his PhD in German philology from Heidelberg University.[4] From there, he attempted to become a journalist, novelist, and playwright—all of which attempts were unsuccessful.[5]

Dr. Goebbels joined the Nazi party in 1924.

That same year, on July 4, he wrote the following in his diary:

> We need a firm hand in Germany. Let's put an end to all the experiments and empty words, and start getting down to serious work. Throw out the Jews, who refuse to become real Germans. Give them a good beating too. Germany is yearning for an individual, a man—as the earth yearns for rain in the summer. Only our reserves of strength, enthusiasm and utter commitment can save us now. Can only a miracle—and nothing less—save us?[6]

In 1930, Dr. Goebbels was sentenced to six weeks in prison for instances of libel appearing in his newspaper. That year, *The New York Times* described both Goebbel's paper and the depth of the issue: "His newspaper, the Attack, [sic] is one of the most violent inciters in the whole list of radical papers. Many cases for which Herr Goebbels is now answering go back to 1928."[7]

Shortly after being appointed the propaganda minister in 1933, Goebbels orchestrated the boycott of Jewish businesses. He then became the principal organizer of burning books classified as un-German. After World War II began, Dr. Goebbels was assigned the task of using the cinema to support the war effort. One of his more well-known films was *Der ewige Jude,* or *The Eternal Jew,* produced in 1940. The film depicts Jews as parasites.[8]

As the German war effort began to fail, Goebbels turned to advocating an all-out battle to the death. Germans, he claimed in 1944, should fight the Allies until there were no Germans left to fight.[9]

Hitler's will, written shortly before his suicide in 1945, split the job of the Führer into multiple offices and gave one of those offices, chancellor of the Reich, to Joseph Goebbels.[10] Hitler committed suicide on April 30, 1945, in the Führerbunker, under the city of Berlin. Goebbels, his wife, and their six children were with him in the bunker. The day after Hitler's suicide, Goebbels ordered his six children poisoned and had himself and his wife shot.[11] Some of his last words include these: "We shall go down in history as the greatest statesmen of all time, or as the greatest criminals."[12]

Indeed, in the decades after the Holocaust, Dr. Joseph Goebbels has been marked as one of history's most foul mass-murderers.

Beginnings

Netty Kupperman was born in Rheydt on October 14, 1924, at almost exactly the same time Dr. Goebbels joined the Nazi party. In fact, on one occasion, Netty remembers seeing him: "You've heard of Dr. Goebbels? His mother lived in Rheydt . . . I saw him once . . . he came to the school to make a speech, and he was outside."[13]

Little did she know that Dr. Goebbels and the antisemitism that he so actively promoted and instilled in Germany would annihilate almost every member of her family in the ensuing years.

Suger Anber Kupperman, Netty's father, was 29 years old when Netty was born, and her mother, Zara Kupperman, was 27. Netty was an only child, and she recalls that during her childhood, her parents doted upon her.

When it was time for Netty to attend kindergarten, her parents chose to enroll her in a Catholic school. The teachers there were nuns, and surprisingly, though she was a Jew in a Christian school, Netty remembers being treated well and enjoying it. For the first few years of her life, both Netty and her parents were happy.

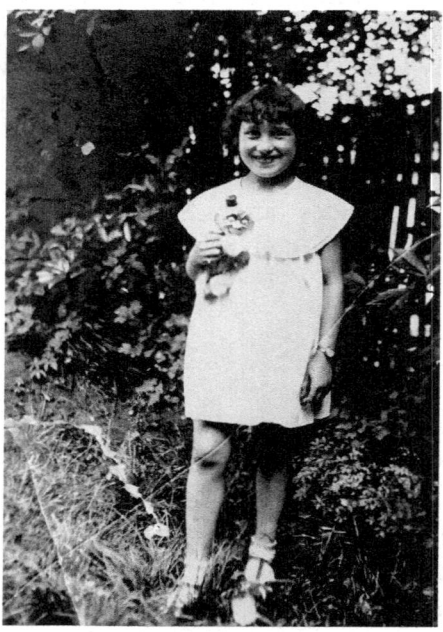

Netty before she left Germany.

But that doting spirit was soon crushed by the man who came to power just a few years following Netty's birth. Even the safety Netty enjoyed in her school would vanish. In 1933, Adolf Hitler was appointed chancellor of Germany, and everything began to change for the worse.

Though her parents sought to create a wonderful and carefree childhood for their cherished daughter, no matter what, the deteriorating situation could not be hidden: "They were bad

Netty Gladstone

times. Children know when it's bad, you know. . . . I was glad to get out of Germany."[14]

Antisemitism

Shortly after Hitler came to power, the torchlight processions began. Netty remembers German men marching along the street, in the darkness, carrying burning torches. They sang songs and chanted as they menacingly passed by her house—and the chorus of one of the songs still haunts Netty today: "Hängt die Juden, stellt die Pfaffen an die Wand," which translates to "Hang the Jews and put the priests against the walls."[15]

Netty remembers that one of these processions took place during the day, when she was visiting one of her friends. The two ventured outside to watch the march, as they had never really been able to see what went on during the processions; they had previously only heard them.

Suger and Zara Kupperman enjoying a meal with a friend and her daughter in Dusseldorf, 1937. No one in the picture survived.

Suddenly, as they were watching all the men marching by, one man broke out of the ranks and demanded to know why Netty and her friend had not saluted the flag as it passed. Everyone had saluted—except for them—and they stuck out terribly. The two children answered him in honesty: "We're Jewish."[16] How could a Jew salute the Nazi flag and all that it stood for?

In rage, the man pulled back his arm and slapped them across their faces.

From then on, Netty studiously avoided the parades.

This was just a taste, though, of the way Nazi policy would force Jews to become outsiders. Netty recalls that an incident in which she was at her music lessons, and her instructor informed her that the lessons were to be discontinued—he decided he could no longer teach Jews. Netty's family also had a Polish maid, and she wound up leaving the country to get married. The man she wanted to marry was Jewish, and the civil servant refused to perform the ceremony, saying that he could not "shake hands with an Aryan and non-Aryan."[17]

Exclusion, however, could be endured. The Jews had suffered it for centuries in Christian Europe. But exclusion was just the beginning, as illustrated by Netty's experiences at school. Even as a child, she began to be isolated by the other children, and not just isolated, but targeted for bullying:

> I didn't enjoy my school years; let's put it that way.... We had one big classroom ... and we had to have Hitler's picture on the wall. That was the law.... I couldn't play with the German children, because they were chasing me, they used to chase me. But I had one girlfriend who was Jewish; she went to the school there. She had platinum blond hair, blue eyes.... And they used to say, the German kids, the real Germans,

they used to say don't chase that one, chase the dark one.[18]

Though the prejudice only manifested itself as simple chasing in her early years, eventually the actions grew worse. Netty remembers a time that her German schoolmates approached her menacingly and surrounded her—she was terrified, not knowing what they might attempt:

> One day I came home from school, because it was walking distance, and a whole bunch of German kids came around me and started yelling at me. . . . I was so afraid, and I yelled for my father. I didn't know where my father was, but I kept on yelling, 'Papa! Papa!'[19]

And here, this poor little girl knew of no other option—she could only yell for her father and hope that somehow, though she had no idea where he was, that he would hear her and come to her rescue. It was a pitiful scene; magnified by the fact that Netty had no idea what the bullies had in store for her.

School photo from Germany. Netty is in the front row, in plaid. The girl next to her with blond hair is the Jewish girl that Netty used to play with.

But astonishingly, her father heard her cries.

For those of us who are parents, it is difficult to think of something more heart-wrenching and galvanizing than the cry of our own child. Thus, Suger Kupperman did what any father would do—he came rushing to the aid of his cherished only daughter. But he did not dispel the crowd—and his reaction to Netty's cry of distress is just another plaintive indication of the perilous Jewish situation at the time: "I don't know where he was when he heard me. He came running, and he picked me up and took me away. He could do nothing to those kids. [He could not] touch them. . . . He took me away."[20]

All her father could do to the children harassing his daughter was pick her up and whisk her away. There would be no justice and there would be no consequences for his daughter's tormentors.

Soon, however, Netty's father would not even be able to deliver her from the clutches of her pursuers—because right around the time of Netty's 14th birthday, her father was arrested, and she never saw him again.

The Polish Expulsion

In October 1938, the Polish government, in fear that a number of Jewish Polish citizens would either flee Germany and return to Poland or be expelled by the German government to Poland, declared that all Polish citizens who had lived outside Poland for five years had thus demonstrated that they no longer had a connection to the Polish state and that unless they went to the Polish consulate to have their status verified, their passports would be declared invalid. They then would lose their Polish citizenship. Without Polish citizenship, the Jews of Polish descent could not be expelled to Poland.

When the German government learned of this Polish decree, it sought to preempt Poland's measure by expelling the Polish Jews before the decree went into effect. By the end of October 1938, Germany had arrested thousands of Polish Jews and sent them to refugee camps on the Polish border. They were destitute and homeless, caught between two countries that refused to accept them.[21]

Netty's parents were Polish.

It was the middle of the night in October. There was a knock at the Kupperman household's door, and then there was confusion. The police entered and informed both Netty's father and mother that they were to get dressed, as they were both under arrest. Their daughter, however, was not; Netty learned later that this was because both of her parents had been born in Poland, but she had been born in Germany.

Upon hearing the news of her arrest, Zara Kupperman rushed into her daughter's room with a message: Netty must get up, get dressed, walk through the darkness to a friend's home, and let the friend know what had happened. Netty could not stay in the house alone. She had to go.

Hence, this 14-year-old girl was now on her own. It was the middle of the night, her parents had been taken, and she was to journey through whatever might have been lurking outside to find safety in a friend's house. It was a terrifying prospect.

But, obedient to her mother, Netty rose out of bed and began to get dressed.

Before she had finished dressing, however, her anxiety was tempered with relief: Zara had returned.

It turned out that only Suger had been arrested. Both Netty's father and mother had sent their passports to the Polish consulate, in line with the Polish government's decree. Suger's passport had been evaluated, and his status had been rejected, as was the case with most Jewish Poles. By chance, Zara's passport had not yet been returned. Because her status had yet to be declared, she was released: "My mother came back before I was even dressed. She came back and she said, 'They have just taken your father.' . . . That was the last time I saw my father."[22]

Netty's last memory of the man who had doted on her and saved her from her bullying peers is his being led away by the German police in the middle of the night.

Kristallnacht

But all this took place before *Kristallnacht,* November 9–10, 1938. So in a sense, Netty's troubles were really just beginning.

Once again, that night there came a knock on the door. This time, Netty and her mother did not answer. Because there was no answer, the police went to their neighbor's house and then asked the neighbors about Netty's family. The police had heard that the family was Jewish—was that true?

The neighbors lied—Netty's family was not Jewish, they claimed. The police must have the wrong information. As such, the night that was so terribly destructive for countless Jewish families ended relatively peacefully for Netty and her mother.

However, after two malicious knocks on the door in the space of a month, Netty could not handle the situation any longer. She could not sleep at home, and she could not concentrate; there was just too much anxiety. What was going to happen next?

Netty pleaded with her mother, and the two moved into the neighbor's house—at least the police did not have that marked as a Jewish family's home. From there, Zara determined that Netty would escape to Holland, where some of Zara's siblings lived. Thus, Zara's sister traveled to Rheydt, and she and Netty boarded a train for Holland. Netty had just lost her father, and now it was time to say goodbye to her mother. But it was also a relief to be leaving the hatred, the racism, and the terrifying unexpected visits by the police.

Netty and her aunt traveled by train to the Dutch border. But upon arrival, they encountered a serious problem. Because Netty was a German Jew, her citizenship had already been taken from her in 1935.[23] She could not simply travel to another country. Therefore, the Dutch border guards refused to let her enter Holland—they looked at her aunt, said, "You can go through," and then declared of Netty, "but she can't."[24] Netty was turned back at the border. She reboarded the train and returned home.

Zara, however, remained undeterred. If it were the case that her daughter could not enter legally, then Zara would send Netty to Holland illegally: "My mother decided that we should go to Holland because she had a brother in Holland. . . . My uncle in Amsterdam, he arranged for a smuggler to take us out of Germany."[25]

The smuggler took Netty, her cousin Sigmund, also known as Bob, who was seven, an aunt, and one of her mother's brother-in-laws. Netty remembers that her cousin had brought with him a case that contained a little toy tin tractor. As they were fleeing, he would shake the case, and the clanging of the tractor and the case caused quite a bit of ruckus, making Netty nervous, so she urged him to be quiet. Nevertheless, their little group was not sufficiently careful: "The four of us were smuggled out first. . . . But the Germans caught us. We had to walk through the woods to get into Holland, and the German patrol caught us."[26]

In the woods, the Germans brought them into a building where they were forced to remove all of their clothes. From there, they were searched for valuables. After that, they dressed again, were brought back outside, and were commanded to lie face down on the ground. At that point, however, the smuggler got up and entered the toll booth.

A few minutes later, unbelievably, he returned to the little group and told everyone to keep going. The Germans were allowing them to pass. Somehow, the smuggler had arranged for their safe passage.

Netty, her cousin Bob, and the two adults reached Holland safely. About one month later, Netty's mother came to Holland with the same smuggler—thus, mother and daughter were together once again.

Kindertransport

Because of a direct border with Germany, the Netherlands experienced a huge influx of Jewish refugees—ones who came legally as well as illegally, as with Netty and her family. In 1938 and 1939, the Dutch government decided that something needed to be done about all the Jewish refugees within its borders. In his book *Refugees from Nazi Germany in the Netherlands 1933–1940*, Robert Moore wrote these words:

> From November 1938 onwards, it was accepted . . . by the government . . . that to accommodate even the refugees who had already been admitted by the

> authorities, camps would have to be created to house at least some of the legal, as well as the illegal refugees. . . . While the conditions in any of these camps was never good, the quality did vary from one to another and the large number of refugee children involved also presented problems, many having arrived in the Netherlands without their parents. Unaccompanied children could not be kept in camps and had to be spread among many orphanages and institutions with the result that in May 1939, there were 24 institutions housing refugee children as well as eight camps for legal and four camps for illegal adult refugees.[27]

As the Dutch government began to place both the legal and illegal refugees in camps, Netty's family attempted to find another place of refuge for both her and her cousin Bob.

> My uncle knew about the train that went through Amsterdam to England . . . he knew about the children's transport, and he told my mother, 'Maybe you should put Netty on the transport with Bob.' . . . My uncle arranged for Bob and myself to get on the train. Bob had a brother, but he was too old. He was already 18, and they only took children up to 16.[28]

Lest, however, it sounds as though Netty's trip to England was well planned and organized, it should be stated that it was not—the situation simply did not allow for that. Netty's family was feeling the pressure of being sent to orphanages and camps, and so in a desperate attempt to rescue the children, the family put Netty and Bob on the earliest transport they could—one leaving the very next day.

One moment, Netty was living with her family in Amsterdam, and the next moment, she was told that she and her

Netty (on the far left) with a cousin and two uncles in Amsterdam, 1939, approximately one month before she departed for England. Netty is the only one in this photo who survived.

seven-year-old cousin were leaving for England the following day:

> The night before I had to leave, I knew . . . I didn't have a week's notice or anything like that. My uncle came and said you have to put her on the train tomorrow . . . and you're only allowed to take a small suitcase with one change of clothes . . . that was it.[29]

Despite the suddenness, it was likely that this spontaneous decision saved both Netty and Bob's lives. Germany invaded Holland on May 10, 1940, and deportations from Holland to Auschwitz began in the summer of 1942.[30]

The Journey

At the train station, Netty said goodbye to her mother for the last time. Though they had parted and been reunited when they left for Holland, this was the final parting. Zara did not follow her daughter.

Netty and Bob approached the train that would take them to the coast, where they would board a boat bound for England. The entire train was filled with children—boys were on one end of the train, and girls were on the other. Netty had just said goodbye to her family, and now she and her little cousin were split up. A number of months passed before Netty saw Bob again.

She was alone at just 14 years old.

She was going to a new country, and a new language—and unlike some of the other children, Netty did not have a sponsor family. She was going into the unknown, not even sure where she was going to live and what life held in store for her.

Netty arrived in England on July 7, 1939.

Arrival

Though Netty had escaped the terror of Nazi Germany, her first few weeks in England were quite tumultuous. After the boat had arrived in Harwich, Netty was taken to Tunbridge Wells, a holding house for Jewish refugee girls who did not yet have sponsors. Bob went to a boy's camp in Ipswich. Netty was there for only two days, yet she still recalls it being "beautiful" and remembers the matron, who was German, with affection.[31] After those two days, Netty was told that arrangements had been made for her and that she would be picked up—that is when her situation in England became considerably worse.

In Tunbridge Wells, the matron could communicate with Netty, and Netty had been surrounded by other Jewish refugees her own age. All of that was about to change. That day, a man arrived to take Netty to his house to live with his family. Though the family was willing to sponsor Netty, her experience with this family was far from pleasant:

> [He] couldn't speak a word of German; I couldn't speak a word of English. And he took me to his house . . . just outside London. Oh, I hated it. Here I go from one big loving family to this cold family; they were so cold. The house was so dark. . . . I don't know why they wanted me. I don't know if they got paid for me or not. . . . They showed me to the room, and I stayed in that room. . . . They would call me to eat, so I would go down to eat. I just couldn't stand it. . . . They didn't even try to teach me English. They just left me completely alone.[32]

When Netty had left Holland, she was given a small amount of money, just for emergencies. To her, this living situation was an emergency. Hence, without being able to speak English, she desperately tried to find a bank where she could exchange the money and then somehow use the funds to run away. However, once she actually found a bank and sought to exchange the money, the bank employees asked for her address. She gave it to them, and when she returned home, she learned that the bank had communicated with the family. Now the family knew that she had some money.

Though the family never communicated with her, this was something important enough to discuss, so they approached her with a demand. Netty could understand enough of what they were gesturing and saying to get the gist of their communication. They were not asking about her health or her well-being. Instead, they wanted to know about the money. Did she have any more?

Such was Netty's living situation until finally, after a few weeks of this, she could no longer handle more. She related:

> One day I really felt bad, and I got hysterics. And I was in my room. And I didn't know what to do; you get to a point where you go crazy. You don't know what to do anymore—because you can't understand them, and they can't understand me. I can't tell them what I want. So I started banging the floor . . . and crying of course. The next thing I knew there was somebody there to come and pick me up from the Jewish Committee.[33]

This family felt as though Netty was too much of a handful, so they notified the Jewish Committee that she was no longer welcome in their house.

The Jerred Family

After Netty was taken from this family near London, her case came to the attention of the Christadelphians. Somehow, the refugee committee notified the Christadelphians that Netty needed a home. Thus, her plight was immediately announced from the platform at Eardley and Edna Jerred's ecclesia: "That's when, at the meeting on the Sunday, they announced, 'There's a Jewish child in dire need of a home. . . . When they announced that, Eardley Jerred put up his arm and said, 'We'll take her.'"[34]

Thus, Netty was put on a train to Birmingham:

> They put me on a train with a tag by myself, and it said 'Birmingham' and my name . . . . It was a local train, and every stop it made, I would look around the compartment, and I'd ask, 'Birmingham?' and everybody said, 'No!' . . . . When we got to Birmingham, everybody yelled, 'Birmingham!'[35]

When she arrived in Birmingham, Netty disembarked from the train, stood on the platform, and found that, unlike the way in which she had been ignored by the first family, people in Birmingham were quite interested in her. She stated:

> I was on the platform, and I had a whole crowd around me. I don't think they had ever seen anybody who couldn't speak English. And then this couple came running down the stairs (you have to go down the stairs to the platform) and they said, 'Are you Netty?' I said, 'Yes!' and they introduced themselves . . . . The first stop he did, he stopped at a bookstore to buy a German English dictionary, that was really nice. And then we went for lunch, and he looked through the dictionary to see what I might like to eat, and he found

'fish,' but it's the same in German! So we had that, and then he went back to work, and she [Edna] took me to Solihull by train.

On the way to his work, he stopped off at a furniture store; he didn't have a bedroom for me. He had the room, but no furniture—they had just moved into a new house. So he told them 'I want this bedroom suite delivered this afternoon'—but he's the type of guy if he tells you to do something, you do it. He may not be big, but he would look at you and tell you that you have to

In the back, Netty is standing with Henny Spier (another Jewish refugee who came to live with Christadelphians), who is holding Peter Miles. The little girl in the front left is Molly Lawrence (née Jerred).

do this, and you do it. So they did it; they delivered it that afternoon. That was really nice.[36]

Netty immediately felt welcomed by this family. She described some of her first moments in her new home:

> When we got home, there were the two girls . . . . Molly was I think four years old . . . and Pauline was seven— and a big dog, an Airedale. And I was scared of dogs. The grandmother, Edna's mother, was there to take care of the children while [Edna] was gone [at the train station], and she pointed at the dog and she said, 'Billy, Billy,' and she looked at me and pointed, and I said, 'Billy.' And then I thought that all dogs were called Billy! They had to tell me 'It's a dog; it's not a Billy.' They were really nice.[37]

This was Netty's first English lesson, and from then on, Netty resolved never to speak German again:

> I had to learn English, and they were very good at teaching me English. Because when I got there, I made up my mind, I'm not going to speak German ever again. That was it. And I haven't. . . . So every time I needed to know something, I would point at it, and I would look at Edna, and she would tell me what it is. So gradually I learned English.[38]

For Netty, out of all the places she lived in England, and even after the war when she came to America, the Jerreds' house felt most like home:

> Oh, I was very happy. I had a really good time. I was part of the family. They made me feel really at home. And then, her mother came to live with us— Edna's mother. She thought the world of me. . . . She

Netty during the years she lived with the Jerreds.

really liked me; I loved her too. . . . And she was [also] a Christadelphian.[39]

Molly, Netty's foster sister, echoed Netty's sentiments about Netty's arrival and the relationship Netty had with Edna's mother:

Netty with Billy.

> Well she just fitted in. . . . I think everybody liked Netty. . . . My grandmother, she came to live with us because . . . it was safer with us. She was a widow, and she came. She had a room with Netty, and oh, she thought the world of her.[40]

Emphasizing the fact that Netty was family, just as the case was in many of the other stories, Netty called Eardley and Edna "Auntie" and "Uncle,"[41] and Eardley very much saw himself as her guardian, there to take care of her on behalf of her parents: "He was very strict with me because he promised my parents he would take care of me, and he took it very seriously."[42]

Hence, as Netty grew older, Eardley took it upon himself to discuss Netty's career path with her parents. Eardley ran a factory, and after hearing from her parents, he decided to take Netty with him into the factory. There she worked with a number of Christadelphians and other refugees Eardley had hired. She was taught by an architect, tool designer, stress analyst, and office worker; with them, she learned to do drafting and architectural drawing—and that was the beginning of her career as a designer. Thus Eardley made sure that his foster daughter received training that would provide her a solid foundation for later years.

Even the visitors from the refugee committee could see how well Netty was treated. The report of Netty's home for November 1941 reads, "This girl lives as one of the family in a happy and comfortable Christadelphian home where she is much loved."[43]

Netty's Family

Netty's experiences with the Jerreds were a stark contrast to what she would have experienced had she stayed in mainland Europe. Soon after Netty departed for England, Zara

Kupperman learned that Suger had been released from the camp on the Polish border and had fled to Belgium. Thus, to reunite with her husband, Zara made her way to Belgium. From there, she wrote the following letter to the Jerreds:

> Antwerp 25/8/39
>
> Dear Family Jerred.
>
> I thank you many times that you have so lovingly taken my daughter into your home. My daughter wrote to me that she has been very fortunate, and that you are so good to her and treat her like your own daughter.
>
> To me, as the mother of an only child, it is a great comfort that she is in good hands and with such nice, decent people. It was a very great pain to me to have to send my child away into the unknown, and at first she had a difficult time. I could find no rest day or night, and I prayed to God that he might protect her from all evil so far from home. God has taken pity on me and has heard me, and I now am comforted as my child writes that she is in good hands with you. May the Lord God prevent there being a war.
>
> I should be very pleased if you would be so kind as to write to me and tell me how my daughter is adapting, whether she is homesick.
>
> I send you sincere (friendly) greetings, also from my husband, although he has no acquaintance with you.
>
> Frau Kupperman[44]

Exactly one week after this letter was written, Germany invaded Poland and unleashed World War II—the war Zara Kupperman so dreaded had arrived.

Seven months later, the Kuppermans wrote another letter to the family that was caring for their only daughter. Here, they revealed that their hopes to follow Netty to England had been dashed. Unlike the first letter, which was sent to the Jerreds in German, this letter was written in English—perhaps having been first translated in Belgium:

>13 April 1940
>197 Statie Str.
>Berchem-Antwerpen
>
>Dear Mr. and Mrs. Jerred,
>
>Our daughter has written to us, that she is very happy with you, and how wonderful you are to her.
>
>She likes very much the job, what she is learning, as we understand it must be very easy to learn, especially for her as she was very good in school for painting and designs.
>
>We are very greatfull [sic] to you for everything you are doing for our dear child, it is only impossible for us to explain in full our gratitude in this letter.
>
>We hope to God that the war will soon be over, and the British will winn [sic], so that we could see our child again.
>
>We hoped till now, to go to England, but under the present circumstances, it's impossible.

The best regards to all of you, and thank you again. God will repay you for all your kindness.

Famile Kuppermann[45]

Belgium surrendered to the Nazis on May 28, 1940,[46] a month and a half after the Kuppermans had written the second letter to the Jerreds. From Belgium, Suger and Zara fled to Paris, France, where they thought they would be free from Hitler's grasp. Tragically, Belgium was simply Hitler's steppingstone to France. Thus, Paris fell to the Germans only two weeks after Belgium had, on June 14, 1940.[47] The Germans divided France into two parts—the German-occupied portion in the north and the southern puppet state known as Vichy France. With a better chance at freedom in the south, the Kuppermans fled to Vichy France. Throughout this time, Netty received letters from her parents. She stated: "And when Hitler went to France, they went to Vichy France, to the south. They used to write from there. I got letters up to 1942. That's when they were rounded up by Vichy France and sent to a concentration camp."[48]

The specific date they were arrested is unknown; however, it is known that both Suger and Zara Kupperman were imprisoned in Rivesaltes transit camp,[49] a military facility located near France's border with Spain. The first prisoners to this camp arrived on January 7, 1941, and the camp functioned as a holding center and transit location to Auschwitz-Birkenau until November 1942. Its peak population in 1941 was 8,000, approximately 3,000 of whom were children who were kept separate from their mothers.[50]

On September 4, 1942, Suger and Zara were placed on transport number four, which took them to Drancy,[51] another transit camp. Drancy was located in the northeastern suburb of Paris, which bears the same name. It was established in

August 1941 and became the major transit camp for French Jews. For nearly two years, it was staffed by French police, under the supervision of the German Security Police, and in July 1943, the Germans took direct control of the camp. Between August 1941 and August 1944, approximately 70,000 prisoners passed through Drancy; the majority of whom were sent to Auschwitz.[52]

On September 11, 1942, just eight days after their deportation from Rivesaltes, the Kuppermans were sent to Auschwitz.[53] There is no further information about them after their arrival at Auschwitz. As such, it is believed they were both murdered there.[54] When he arrived at Auschwitz, Suger Kupperman was 47, and Zara Kupperman was 45. The exact dates of their deaths are unknown. Although Netty learned of her parents' fate, she never gained any sense of closure. She stated, "I never knew [exactly] how old my parents were [when they died]."[55]

The War Years

Yet Netty remained safe—at least as safe as one could be when the country in which they are living is at war.

However, despite being with a family that cherished her and protected her, the war years were extremely difficult. After learning English, Netty began attending night school to further her education. And Eardley Jerred was constantly on call at work; throughout the war, the factory was operating 24 hours a day.

Both Netty and Molly can remember the way fuel was rationed, so visiting friends or driving anywhere was often not an option. In addition to the rationing of gasoline, fuel to heat the house was also in short supply. Molly remembers the way in which the cold affected Netty. In Molly's words:

Netty in front of a statue at the Birmingham Hall of Memory, 1940. Netty sent this picture to her parents, but it was returned to her. A censor had deemed it unacceptable, as the statue could be used to identify Netty's location.

> It was a very happy house. We were all busy, and it was a very happy house. Very cold because of course we didn't have central heating, and you couldn't get fuel. Poor Netty used to get chilblains, and the ice used to form; and if you took a glass of water to bed, you'd get ice in the morning.... We did have a coal fire for Christmas day and special days ... but you know, people were happy; they didn't want so much.[56]

But the war years were more than just hard work and inconveniences. Even though Solihull, where the Jerreds lived, was considered to be in the country, it was still on the outskirts of Birmingham, and thus, when the Blitz began, Solihull, too, was bombed. At one point, a bomb was dropped in the field right behind the Jerreds' house, and Molly recalled that Eardley had a shelter built underneath the house and that the family regularly needed to go down into the shelter to avoid being injured or killed. Netty even remembers one of Molly's cousins, Peter Miles, coming over with his family to find shelter. She stated: "During the war, he used to come over every night. They used to come and sleep in our house because we were outside Birmingham—to be safe.... We could see the fires from Birmingham and where they lived."[57]

The Christadelphians

Throughout all the years Netty lived with the Jerreds, she attended the meeting with them every Sunday, and it turned out, through Netty's intervention, that a Christadelphian family also took in Bob:

> Every Sunday ... in the Midland Institute, it was a very big hall, huge hall. They used to come from all the outlying areas. It was the center.... It was rather nice because you got to see everybody. I got to see my

cousin every week. . . . Actually when I went back to visit, I went to the meeting with them, with Molly.[58]

In addition to participating in the Sunday meetings, Netty also attended Sunday school and remembers doing the daily readings with the Jerreds: "I went to Sunday school; I did that . . . it was nice; I liked it . . . [the people] were all nice. . . . [The Jerreds] read every night. They gave me a Bible."[59]

Netty kept that Bible until the 1960s, when she met a man at work who told her that he had never read the Old Testament. Wanting to help him, she lent it to him but never received it back. In 1961, over 20 years after she had come to live with the Jerreds, she mentioned in their correspondence that she had lent her Bible to a coworker and no longer had one—and the Jerreds sent her another. This one was even nicer than the first was; it was printed at Cambridge University Press and bound in leather with gold-leaf pages. In the front was written a brief note: "To Ronnie and Netty, with love from Eardley & Edna, Peter & Molly, David & Pauline. Psalm 119. v 1-8."[60]

The verses mentioned in the note all concern the blessings that come upon those who follow the divine commandments and statutes—and the Jerreds never wanted Netty to forget those blessings.

Nevertheless, although she took part in their Christadelphian functions and even read the Bible with them, when Netty was asked whether she ever felt any pressure to become a Christadelphian, she responded immediately with these words: "No, never. They never pushed me, because they used to say to me, 'We are Jews by adoption . . . . So I figured, if this is Jews by adoption, I'm already a Jew . . . why should I be a Jew by adoption?"[61]

*Top: Netty's Bible, given to her by the Jerreds in 1961.
Bottom: The inscription in the front of Netty's Bible.*

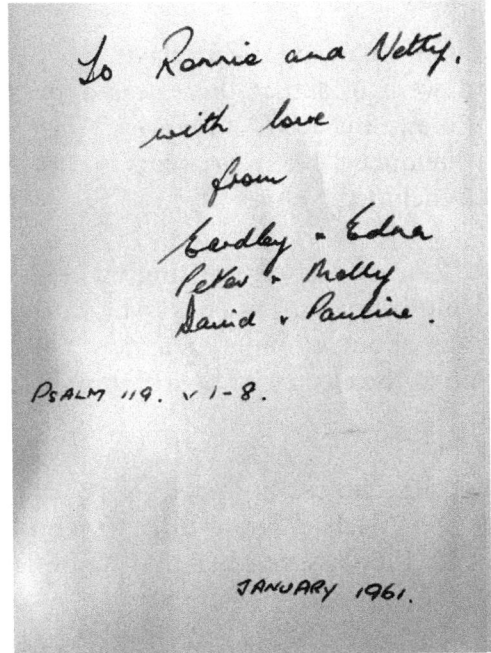

The United States

After the war, Netty continued to live with the Jerreds and, after leaving Eardley's factory, continued to work in drafting and design, taking a position with the Midland Electricity Board. Though she did not enjoy her position at all, she continued to work there until she came to the United States.

Netty came to the United States in 1950. She was nervous about the prospect of moving, but her parents had been good friends with a couple, the Thons, who lived in New York. In fact, this couple had gotten Netty's parents an affidavit to come to America. They were unfortunately never able to use the affidavit. But because the Thons had approached Suger Kupperman's cousin in the United States (who was not friendly with Suger) and offered to pay the fee for the affidavit and support the Kuppermans, the cousin had agreed to help secure the affidavit.

Nevertheless, after obtaining the affidavit, her parents went to get a visa and were told that there was a five-year waiting period for Poles. Because, however, they had placed themselves in the queue, Netty's parents had received a quota number, which included Netty.

For years, the Thons had been writing to her, urging her to leave England and come to New York to be with them. Though she was nervous about coming to a new place, Netty, not enjoying her job at the electricity board, thought that a change might be good.

Before making the choice, however, Netty approached the Jerreds about her decision—wanting to know what they thought about it. They assured her that if she left, she could always return to them—she was family.

"So they said, 'Well go and try it, you can always come back to us.' So I had that feeling that I could go back. I still feel that way; if I had gone back, they would have taken me. Because I felt I was one of them."[62]

Consequently, Netty decided that she would go to the United States for one year. But when she attempted to get her visa, she was told that there was a one-year waiting period for Germans, so her plans would be foiled. But thinking quickly, Netty responded: "Oh no, the Germans never recognized me as a German. But I have a Polish quota number my parents had, and I was on that number: there were three of us."[63]

Amazingly, when the number was checked, the State Department agents were able to find it, and they granted her a visa.

When Netty came to the United States, she first lived with her father's cousin. She was not happy there, however, and eventually came came to live with the Thons. While she was there, the Thons gave her one of the last letters her parents ever wrote. Written from Bages, France, in May 1942, just four months before they were sent to Auschwitz, the letter focused on their two primary concerns: their only daughter and escaping Nazi-dominated Europe.

> Bages 12.5.1942
>
> Dear Thon family,
> We have received your kind letter. You cannot imagine how happy we were. The same day we also received a letter from Netty. We had not heard from Netty for six months.
>
> I have done everything that you wrote. . . . [The letter goes on to describe extra steps required for the

Kuppermans to acquire tickets out of Europe to New York]. Herr Thon, we beg you to do this immediately. It is possible that we shall soon get the visa ...We know that you have already gone to a lot of trouble for us, and we would like to see the day when we can thank you. Trayber [another family friend who was also in Europe] has written to us that he has telegraphed to you that you should engage a lawyer in order to expedite matters. That would be better...

How are you all—I hope well. Why did you not write to us for so long? Our Netty has written us a good letter. She says that she has received 12 shillings increase. She earns 37 shillings a week; she says that is a lot at her age and that later on she will earn a lot of money.

How are . . . Hany and Heinz? I cannot say much about us. We await an answer from you soon. Many greetings and kisses for you all.

Kuppermann[64]

Conclusion

Eventually, Netty met her husband, Ronald Gladstone, and chose to continue living in the United States. She went on to become an engineer and now makes her home in Los Angeles.

Much changed on the day Eardley Jerred sat in the Christadelphian ecclesia in Birmingham and raised his hand after hearing the announcement about a desperate Jewish refugee. Bonds were formed and relationships created that have remained strong throughout the many decades that have passed.

NETTY GLADSTONE

Top: Netty and the Jerreds together again in England, 1984. From left to right: Eardley Jerred, Ronald Gladstone, Tim Lawrence, Netty Gladstone, Molly Lawrence (née Jerred), Edna Jerred, Sara Tibbs, and Peter Lawrence.

Bottom:: Netty, on another visit back to England, 2009. With Sara Tibbs (Molly Lawrence's [née Jerred's] daughter) and her husband Adam Tibbs.

Netty and Molly have never lost contact. They speak often to one another by phone and see each other as sisters. But this relationship extends beyond just their generation. Molly's children and grandchildren know of Netty—and they have visited her in California.

When Netty came to live with the Jerreds, it was during the most distressing time of her life. Yet she was loved and respected as a daughter. And, for Netty, it was that caring treatment, which contrasted so greatly with the way she was treated in her first residence in England, that made all the difference. The Jerreds helped her with the language, supported her with her work, and trusted her. Even though she is now in her 90s, she has not forgotten the way the Jerreds embraced her. If Netty could say one final thing to Uncle Eardley and Auntie Edna, "I would . . . thank them for saving my life, being good to me, and treating me like one of their own."[65]

A Christadelphian family chose to act upon their faith, and in doing so, a Jewish refugee who was facing almost certain death, found that she had become *part of the family.*

---

[1] "Joseph Goebbels," *Jewish Virtual Library,* accessed April 28, 2017, http://www.jewishvirtuallibrary.org/jsource/Holocaust/goebbels.html.

[2] "Joseph Goebbels" *History.com,* accessed April 28, 2017, http://www.history.com/topics/world-war-ii/joseph-goebbels.

[3] "Joseph Goebbels: On the 'Big Lie,'" *Jewish Virtual Library,* accessed April 28, 2017, http://www.jewishvirtuallibrary.org/jsource/Holocaust/goebbelslie.html.

[4] "Joseph Goebbels" *History.com,* accessed April 28, 2017, http://www.history.com/topics/world-war-ii/joseph-goebbels.

[5] Ibid.

[6] "The Man Behind Hitler," *PBS,org,* accessed April 28, 2017, http://www.pbs.org/wgbh//amex/goebbels/filmmore/pt.html.

[7] "Reich Fascist Convicted," *The New York Times* (New York, NY), September 2, 1930.

[8] "Joseph Goebbels" *History.com,* accessed April 28, 2017, http://www.history.com/topics/world-war-ii/joseph-goebbels.

[9] Ibid.

[10] Greg Bradsher, *Hitler's Final Words* (Washington D. C.: Prologue Magazine, 2015), 20.

[11] "Joseph Goebbels," *Jewish Virtual Library,* accessed April 28, 2017, http://www.jewishvirtuallibrary.org/jsource/Holocaust/goebbels.html.

[12] Joseph Goebbels, quoted in Ibid.

[13] Netty Gladstone in discussion with the author, April 15, 2016.

[14] Ibid.

[15] Ibid.

[16] Ibid.

[17] Ibid.

[18] Ibid.

[19] Ibid.

[20] Ibid.

[21] For more information on this declaration by the Polish government and the Polish expulsion, see Charles Ohlenberg's biography in *Part of the Family - Volume 1*, 73–74.

[22] Netty Gladstone in discussion with the author, April 15, 2016.

[23] "The Nuremberg Race Laws," *United States Holocaust Memorial Museum,* accessed April 28, 2017, https://www.ushmm.org/outreach/en/article.php?ModuleId=10007695.

[24] Netty Gladstone in discussion with the author, April 15, 2016.

[25] Ibid.

[26] Ibid.

[27] Robert Moore, *Refugees from Nazi Germany in the Netherlands 1933-1940* (Dordrecht: Martinus Nijhoff, 1986), 90.

[28] Netty Gladstone in discussion with the author, April 15, 2016.

[29] Ibid.

[30] "The Netherlands," *United States Holocaust Museum and Memorial,* accessed April 28, 2017, https://www.ushmm.org/wlc/en/article.php?ModuleId=10005436.

[31] Netty Gladstone in discussion with the author, April 15, 2016.

[32] Ibid.

33 Ibid.

34 Ibid.

35 Ibid.

36 Ibid.

37 Ibid.

38 Ibid.

39 Ibid.

40 Molly Lawrence in discussion with the author, April 27, 2016.

41 Netty Gladstone in discussion with the author, April 15, 2016.

42 Ibid.

43 World Jewish Relief case files for Netty Kupperman, "Report of Home" for November 1941.

44 Zara Kupperman, letter to the Jerreds, August 25, 1939. Translated by Graham Jackman. Copy of translation in possession of the author.

45 Zara Kupperman, letter to the Jerreds, April 13, 1940. Copy of translation in possession of the author.

46 "1940: Belgium Surrenders Unconditionally," *History.com*, accessed April 28, 2017, http://www.history.com/this-day-in-history/belgium-surrenders-unconditionally.

47 "German Invasion of Western Europe, May 1940," *United States Holocaust Memorial Museum*, accessed April 28, 2017, https://www.ushmm.org/wlc/en/article.php?ModuleId=10005181.

48 Netty Gladstone in discussion with the author, April 15, 2016.

49 Document from the International Tracing Service regarding Zara Kupperman, March 27, 2008. Copy in possession of the author.

Document from the International Tracing Service regarding Suger Kupperman, March, 27, 2008. Copy in possession of the author.

50 "Nazi Transit Camps: Rivesaltes," *Jewish Virtual Library*, accessed April 28, 2017, http://www.jewishvirtuallibrary.org/jsource/Holocaust/Rivesaltes.html.

51 Document from the International Tracing Service regarding Zara Kupperman, March 27, 2008. Copy in possession of the author.

Document from the International Tracing Service regarding Suger Kupperman, March 27, 2008. Copy in possession of the author.

52 "Drancy," *United States Holocaust Memorial Museum*, accessed April 28, 2017, https://www.ushmm.org/wlc/en/article.php?ModuleId=10005215.

[53] For more information about this extermination camp, see the glossary and also Charles Ohlenberg's biography in *Part of the Family - Volume 1*, 81.

[54] Document from the International Tracing Service regarding Zara Kupperman, March 27, 2008. Copy in possession of the author.

Document from the International Tracing Service regarding Suger Kupperman, March, 27, 2008. Copy in possession of the author.

[55] Netty Gladstone in discussion with the author, April 15, 2016.

[56] Molly Lawrence in discussion with the author, April 27, 2016.

[57] Netty Gladstone, in discussion with the author, April 15, 2016.

[58] Ibid.

[59] Ibid.

[60] Note in the front of Netty Gladstone's Bible. In possession of Netty Gladstone.

[61] Netty Gladstone in discussion with the author, April 15, 2016.

[62] Ibid.

[63] Ibid.

[64] Zara and Suger Kupperman, letter to the Thons, May 12, 1942. Translated by Graham Jackman. Copy of translation in possession of the author.

[65] Ibid.

RUDI HART

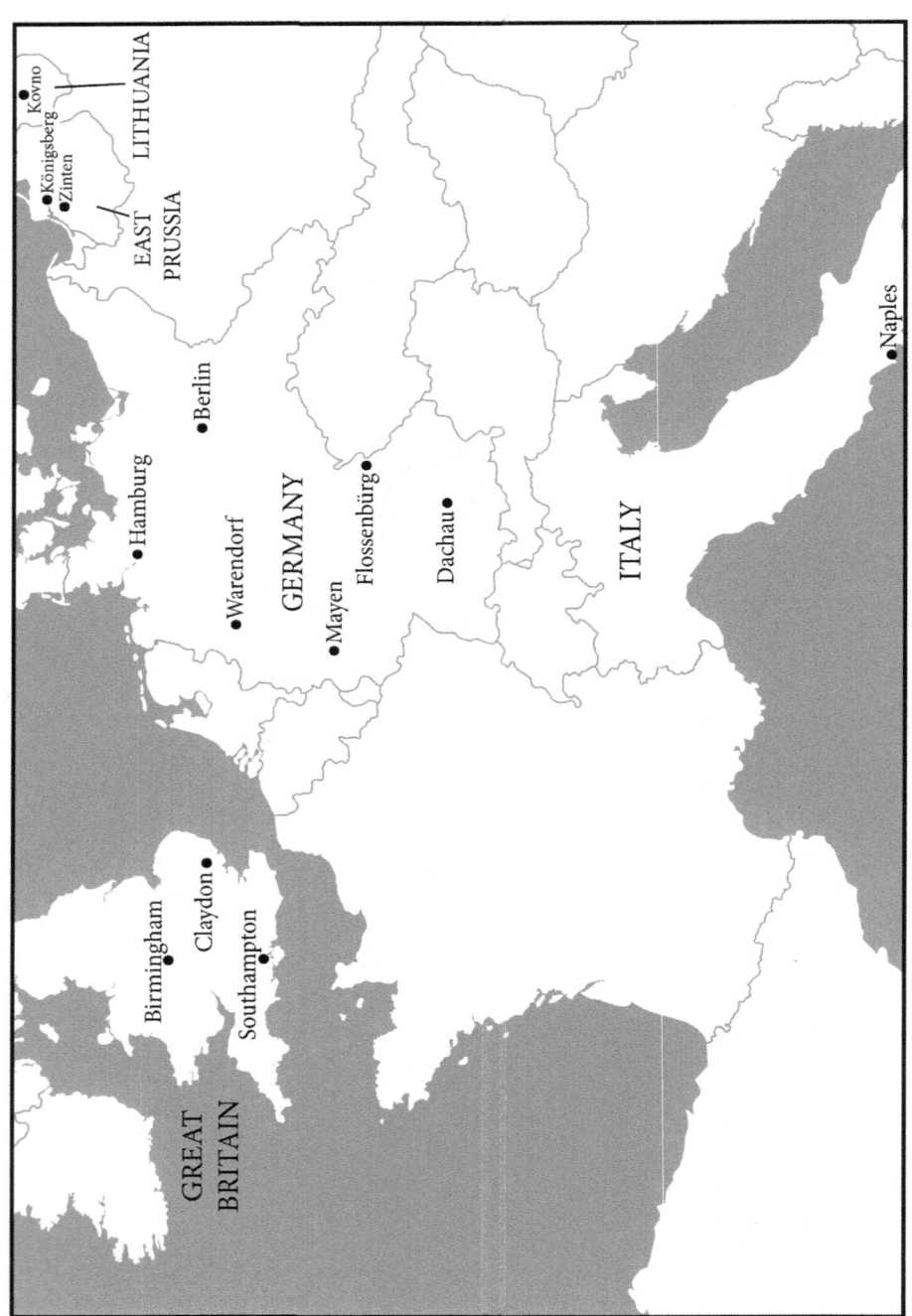

2

RUDI HART

As a result of the Treaty of Versailles, East Prussia was separated from the rest of Germany by the Polish Corridor—a strip of land, 20 to 70 miles wide, which gave Poland access to the Baltic Sea. The population of the corridor was primarily Polish, the territory itself was historically Polish, and the Germans were given free access to cross the corridor to travel between the German mainland and East Prussia. Nevertheless, it seems that this stipulation of the treaty caused more German anger than any other.[1] William Shirer, in *The Rise and Fall of the Third Reich*, wrote:

> Even more than France, Poland was the hated and despised enemy in the minds of the Germans. To them the most heinous crime of the Versailles peacemakers had been to separate East Prussia from the Reich by the Polish Corridor, to detach Danzig and to give to the Poles the province of Posen and part of Silesia, which, though predominantly Polish in population, had been German territory since the days of the partition of Poland. No German statesmen during the Republic had been willing to regard the Polish acquisitions as permanent.[2]

Thus, when Nazi Germany invaded Poland on September 1, 1939, starting World War II, they did so under the pretext of retaking the territory of the Polish Corridor and reuniting East Prussia with the remainder of Germany.[3]

Nevertheless, after the war, the demographics of the Polish Corridor and East Prussia changed dramatically. Many Germans fled the area, and those who did not were expelled by the victors. The territory was then divided between Poland and the Soviet Union.[4] The German city names were changed to reflect the change of ownership: Königsberg, the capital of East Prussia, became Kaliningrad, Nordenburg became Krylovo, and Insterburg became Chernyakhovsk.

Rudi Hart (née Hertz) was born in Zinten, East Prussia, on December 25, 1925. Today, this town is part of Russia and has been renamed Kornevo, although it is largely in ruins, as it was heavily bombed at the end of World War II and never rebuilt.

In the 1920s, Zinten was a small town only a few miles southeast of the Baltic Sea. It was approximately 20 miles southwest of Königsberg, which was the nearest city.

The Jewish population of Zinten was relatively new at the time of Rudi's birth, with the first Jew being allowed to settle in the town in 1810. Just seven years later, 1817, the Jewish community had grown significantly, so that it numbered 70 individuals,[5] which was approximately four percent of the town's 1,500 inhabitants.[6] In 1869, the Jewish community consecrated a synagogue.

Nevertheless, this growth did not continue. By 1925, the year of Rudi's birth, the Jewish community had slowly dwindled until it was composed of only 43 members. This decrease persisted so that in 1933, only 32 Jews remained in the village. Five years later, in 1937, the community sold the synagogue. At that point, there were only four Jewish families still living in Zinten.[7]

Rudi's family was one of those four.

Two years later, Rudi's mother and younger brother were the only member of his immediate family still in Zinten—all the others either had been arrested or had fled.

Beginnings

Rudi's father was Paul Hertz (b. July 28, 1893)[8] and was originally from Warendorf, a town in western Germany. His mother was Paula Hertz (b. August 14, 1893), whose maiden name was Lichtenstein, and who was originally from Mayen, another town in western Germany.[9] At some point, both Paul and Paula must have made the trek across the Polish Corridor, as their children were all born in Zinten.

Paul Hertz, 1935.

Paul and Paula Hertz.

Rudi was preceded by an older brother, Leo, who was born in 1920. Four and a half years after Rudi's birth, on May 5, 1930, the family had another son, whom Paul and Paula named Kurt.[10]

The weather in Zinten was quite similar to the weather that both Paul and Paula had experienced in western Germany. The warm season lasted from the end of May until the beginning of September, with temperatures beginning to drop to the freezing point around November. Only at the beginning of February would the temperatures rise above freezing.[11]

Nonetheless, it was not Zinten's freezing weather specifically that colored Rudi's memories of his childhood. Despite that snow could be piled up more than 10 feet outside, Rudi remembered the warmth of his childhood home. He remembered the tiled stove that radiated heat. He remembered the double glazing on the house that helped keep the cold outside and the heat from the stove inside. And no doubt the warmth that he remembered was not just physical warmth, but also was the warmth of a family whose members loved one another—with a love that was powerfully evidenced in the ensuing years.

Paula, Rudi, Leo, and Paul Hertz.

Paul Hertz was a cattle dealer. At times, Rudi was allowed to accompany his father on his excursions from farm to farm in the local area. On those excursions, Rudi and his father would ride together on a horse-drawn wagon, and they would wrap themselves up in animal furs to stay warm.

Paula Hertz was a homemaker—caring both for the home itself and for the animals and the children who lived there.

Rudi, like so many of the children who were whisked away from their childhood on the Kindertransport, described his family in fairly idyllic terms: "My father, Paul, was a cattle-dealer, Paula, my mother, a typical Jewish mum. They were prosperous in a way, good family people."[12]

Changes

Because East Prussia was part of Germany, life for Rudi would have begun to change almost immediately after Adolf Hitler came to power in 1933. Perhaps the first large change in Rudi's life—or the first extremely noticeable one for him—might have been the closing of the synagogue in 1937. It was just one year before Rudi was to turn 13 and celebrate his *bar mitzvah*.

The next year, 1938, brought *Kristallnacht* upon the family. Perhaps in response to *Kristallnacht,* Paul and Paula decided to make the heart-wrenching decision to send their children away to safety. That year, Leo, approximately 18 years old, was able to get the proper papers to immigrate to Buenos Aires, Argentina, where he lived for the remainder of the war and a number of years afterward.

After Leo's departure to Argentina, the situation for the Hertz family deteriorated rapidly. They were already separated from one member—by thousands and thousands of miles—and the separation would occur with two other members that year. On

Top: Rudi and Kurt Hertz (the two boys), with Paula (directly behind Kurt) and some friends, March 1939.
Bottom: Rudi's passport, June 1939.

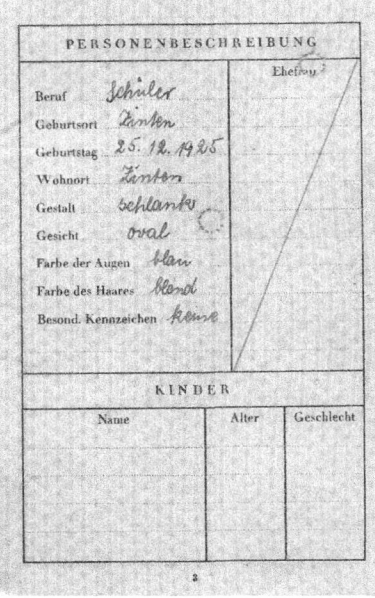

May 17, 1939, Paul Hertz was arrested for a crime he never committed. He was then sent to Alleinstein penitentiary.

One month later, with his father still in prison, Rudi Hertz stood at the train station in Königsberg. Just like Leo, a place of refuge for him had been found outside of Germany. But, unlike Leo, Rudi was not going to Argentina. He was not even going to the Americas. Instead, Rudi had been given a place on the Kindertransport.

Rudi was going to Great Britain.

The Kindertransport

It was June 27, 1939. The beginning of the bloodiest conflict in human history was just two months away.

In Königsberg, it was likely a pleasant day. The weather had steadily been growing warmer, as the summer had just begun. Rudi was holding a small suitcase. It contained some clothes, a few books, and a couple of photographs. Aside from the letters that he would receive over the course of the next two years, this pitiful collection was all that he would have to remind him of who he was and where he had come from. Rudi kept this suitcase, this reminder of who he was, for the next 50 years of his life—until the years and the use had taken their toll and it fell apart in his hands.

That day, when Rudi said goodbye to his mother and his brother, he fully intended to reunite with them after a time. Rudi stated:

"The pathos was that the parents and the children genuinely believed they'd meet again. . . . The enormity of what we now know as the Holocaust didn't cross our minds."[13]

With his limited knowledge of what was happening in Germany, Rudi simply thought that he was going on a little trip.

> Once I heard [my father] tell my mother that, if war broke out, we'd all be put against a wall and shot, but it passed over my head. . . . My elder brother, Leo, had already left Germany and ended up in the Argentine, so I think I reckoned that Germany wasn't a good place for Jews to be for a while. . . . I'd had holidays before. I had a little suitcase and perhaps, looking back, I felt it was rather an adventure.[14]

And so, in "good spirits," Rudi said goodbye to his mother and his little brother. His mother's final words were for him "to be good" and "to behave."[15]

They had no idea of the horror into which the world would descend: "We parted at the station. Our thoughts then were no different from the thoughts of British parents and their children parting for evacuation."[16]

From Königsberg, Rudi rode the train to Hamburg. In Hamburg, Rudi boarded the *SS Washington,* which brought him out of Germany, out of his homeland, and into the unknown.

He arrived in Southampton, England, on June 30, 1939. He was 13 years old. For those three days, Rudi behaved like a typical kid his age: "I was [traveling] for about three days, running up and down corridors, exploring like all kids. There was no hardship."[17]

At least, there was no hardship until they realized that this separation was permanent.

Perhaps Rudi's playful attitude at the time was also due in part to his having made a friend at the train station: "I met Heinz on Koeningsberg station. We've been friends ever since. We were both thrilled to board SS *Washington* for the three-day voyage to Britain. . . . We were pretty distinctive in our plus-four suits, in those days Sabbath best for young German lads. . . . We thought that because British pennies were large, they must be worth a lot, and we'd sneak into the first-class passenger lounges for a glimpse of the champagne glasses and the thick carpet."[18]

Paula Hertz was now without a husband and without two of her sons. Kurt was the only one still at home—and despite her love for him and her desire for his safety, the prospect of sending a child who had recently turned nine to a foreign country seemed more dangerous than the alternative. But, just as Rudi had left the country a year after Leo had, it was thought that Kurt could come after he had grown a little more as well. Rudi stated: "There was still my little brother, Kurt, at home, and we expected him to follow me later on."[19]

Thus, Paula and her baby boy remained in Zinten—not knowing that the opportunity for Kurt to leave on the Kindertransport would disappear in less than two months.

England

After arriving in Southampton, Rudi was taken by coach to Claydon, a city just north of Ipswich, where he lived for the next few months. In Claydon, he was brought to a boy's home called Barham House (see Ben Weiss's biography in this volume for more information about Barham House). Peter Hart, Rudi's son, described Rudi's time at Barham House:

> He was with 10 other Jewish boys and they worked in the fields picking fruit, sugar beet and digging trenches

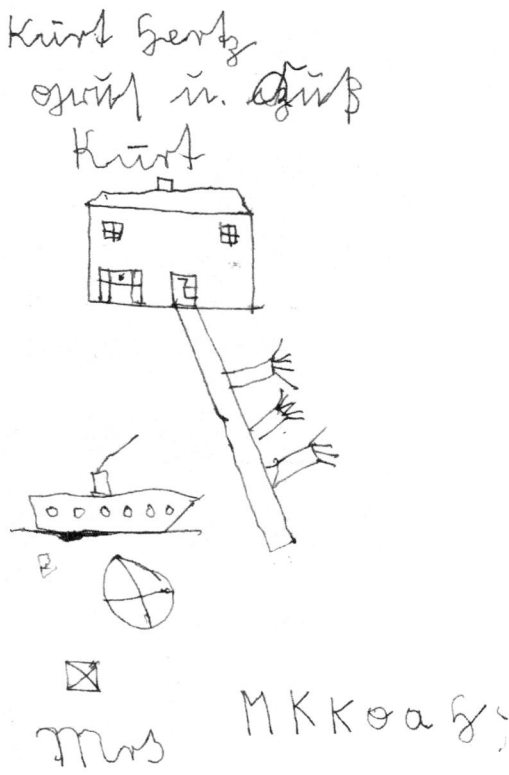

A drawing that Kurt sent to Rudi on July 23, 1939.

for shelters. Rudi was colder here than he had ever been before in his life and says that the boys used to crowd around one fire fighting for the warmest spot. He found everything confusing but most especially the food.[20]

Even as an adult, Rudi would not consider eating treacle pudding—his palate had still not fully acclimated to British food.

Rudi Hertz in Claydon, March 30, 1940.

After nearly two months of living in Barham House, Rudi wrote the following letter to his brother. It was written in German, as Rudi was living in a country where the primary language was English, and Leo was living in a country where the primary language was Spanish. Within the letter is an idea that would continue to echo throughout all of Rudi's letters—the hope that their family would once again be brought together:

Claydon, 17.9.39
Dear Leo!

Today I want to write to you again. Hopefully you are healthy, unlike myself. The day before yesterday we had a lot of excitement, [*unreadable text*], and I totally forgot to congratulate you. I wish you all the best, and maybe God will bring all of us together again. Dear Leo, there are also children from East Prussia here. Yesterday, we played a game of soccer and we won 4:0. Dear Leo, have you received any more mail from Mama, and what did she write? What kind of work are you doing now? Write to me with the details. The weather is very beautiful here. It will be very hot where you are. Next week is Yom Kippur, and I wish you a pleasant fast. So for today, be in good spirits.

Love and Kisses,

from your dear Brother,

Rudi[21]

It is a letter filled with the mundane: they played a game of soccer and won; the weather is beautiful in Claydon, and it is hot in Buenos Aires. Yet the letter is peppered with reserved emotion: maybe God will bring us together again; have you received any more mail from Mama, and what did she write? It is as though by this point, he could barely dare to hope.

Rudi lived in Claydon for 11 months, until the middle of 1940. By this time, the British government had determined that the refugee boys no longer live so close to the east coast—so Rudi had to move further inland.

This move brought Rudi to Birmingham, and to a hostel named Elpis Lodge.

Elpis Lodge

Rudi was part of the first group of boys to come to the hostel—when describing the lives of the first 16 boys to come to the hostel, E. W. Newman, the hostel's treasurer, wrote the following:

> In placing the boys in the trades they are now learning, Dr. Hirsch (the Warden) has been at pains to find out their natural aptitudes, and has taken into account their family history. Some of the Viennese families, for instance, have been tailors for generations, and one boy's grandfather is a tailor's cutter of considerable repute in Vienna. The father of the boy who is doing wood-work is a turner of chessmen. The boy learning upholstery hopes some day to join his brother, who is an upholsterer in the Argentine.[22]

Elpis Lodge was quite unlike Barham House. At the latter, Rudi attended school, picked fruit, and dug trenches. At Elpis Lodge, he focused on learning a trade. Hence, at 14 years old, continuing to follow in the footsteps of his older brother, Rudi became an upholsterer.

Here is how Rudi described the time:

> I came directly from a large refugee camp at Claydon near Norwich, which housed between four and five hundred boys in army barracks. The atmosphere at the hostel was a great improvement on the impersonality of the camp. I settled down quite quickly in my new home, and to the happy uneventful life there. There were rules and regulations, but on the whole it was quite easy-going and informal. We boys mixed well, and the same age groups were kept together in the dormitories. Sometimes there were interchanges and

> visits between the hostels, particularly Wheeley's Road, which was quite near. Whenever there was a special occasion in the Community, we went to the Communal Hall at Singers Hill to join in, but although Dr. Cohen solemnly warned us to behave ourselves, as we were now part of the Birmingham Jewish Community, there was not much social contact between the local Jewish population and the refugee boys. As a result I made few friends within the Community. At the age of fourteen we were found work, and as I was interested in furniture making, I served an apprenticeship.[23]

Kitty Hart-Moxon (née Felix), herself an Auschwitz survivor and Rudi's former wife, also described this time and described Rudi's time in Claydon and Birmingham:

> Like myself, he found the Jewish community less than helpful, but was looked after in a camp near Ipswich and then brought to Birmingham under the auspices of the Christadelphians. They were very kind to the children in their keeping, and never made the slightest attempt to sway any of them towards their own religious beliefs.[24]

However, both she and Rudi underscore the difficulty the Jewish community in Birmingham had to face. Overtaxed with trying to care for the great influx of Jewish refugees and shocked at the news of what was happening to the Jews in the Third Reich and how to respond to it, the Jewish community found itself in an extremely trying situation—consequently, some refugees felt as though their fellow Jews simply did not care about them.

Many of the boys at Elpis Lodge were in that vulnerable position—their care came from a non-Jewish group. Despite

Rudi Hertz in Birmingham, early 1940s.

the boys' vulnerability, the Christadelphians adhered to their position that they would not specifically seek out conversions. And so Elpis Lodge remained a hostel in which the Jewish boys continued to be taught about their Jewish heritage. In one of his letters, Rudi wrote about the arrival of Passover and the matzos he would have.[25] In another, he wrote of his weekly routine: "On Saturdays, I do not need to work. In the morning, I go to the synagogue and, in the afternoon, I go to the cinema and, on Sundays, I write my letters."[26] Once again, in a separate letter to *The Christadelphian*, E. W. Newman wrote about the classes provided for the boys—including a class on Jewish history taught by Dr. Hirsch:

> Evening classes in English, English literature and history are held at the Hostel under the direction of a qualified teacher, and every effort is made to encourage each boy to speak fluent English. In addition, some of the boys are learning shorthand, bro. L. G. Sargent having devoted himself to the task of teaching this subject. Also, Dr. Hirsch himself regularly instructs the boys in Old Testament history, and the subsequent history of the Jews.[27]

With the schedule of classes and the boys' apprenticeships, there were many ways to stay busy at Elpis Lodge. At one point, on Mondays, Rudi took carpentry lessons from 1:30–9:30. On Wednesdays, the boys at the hostel had gymnastics. Elpis Lodge also had a garden, and Rudi expressed his excitement about working in the garden in one of his letters to Leo.[28] There was not only a garden but also a ping-pong table, and Rudi found that through practice, he was able to grow quite adept at the sport.[29]

Throughout his years at Elpis Lodge, Rudi continued to write to Leo—both because he wanted to hear from Leo, and also because Leo lived in a neutral country, meaning that Paul, after being released from prison, and Paula could write full-length letters to Leo, and Leo could forward them to Rudi—in contrast to the 25-word Red Cross messages that Rudi could send to Germany. Thus Rudi wrote to Leo, to his parents via Leo, and to his parents via the Red Cross.

Hence the very month that he arrived at Elpis Lodge, Rudi wrote the following to Leo:

>ELPIS LODGE
>117 GOUGH RD.
>EDGBASTON
>BIRMINGHAM 15.
>Birmingham 18.5.1940

Dear Leo!

I will write to you again today. Hopefully, you are in good health, and so am I. Dear Leo, why don't you write to me? I am waiting for news [from you] every day, but to no avail. Dear Leo, I am writing to you every week and you too should write every week. What is uncle Siegmund doing? And how is he keeping? Dear Leo, are you still in the settlement, or are you now working as an upholsterer? Upholstery is my profession now, and I like the work very much. I have been working [as an upholsterer] for the last two weeks. Today, the weather here is very good, and it seems to be very hot where you are. Have you heard something from our dear mother? And how is she doing? It has been a long time since I last heard from her. How is uncle Felix Kaufmann doing, is he in good health? Convey him my greetings.

Dear Leo, I have received a mail from Selma Elias, and is she healthy. She greets you warmly. Dear Leo, I am now speaking English pretty well; I am able to communicate now. Dear Leo, on June 30th it will be a year since I came to England, and it is one year since I left home. And we have to get used to it.

Dear Leo, stay healthy and write soon. Otherwise, there is no news. So, this is it for today.

Heartfelt greetings and kisses from your

Brother

Rudi[30]

Really, these letters, written by a boy who was not yet 14 and had been separated from his family, his homeland, his culture, and his language for almost a year, speak for themselves. Truly, he was treated well in Elpis Lodge, but he yearned for home and for his family. How is uncle Siegmund? How is uncle Felix? And most of all, how is "our dear mother?" because he had not heard from her in "a long time."

And so the letters continued—a desperate attempt to keep up the communication and keep the family ties active. Two months later, he wrote the following to Leo:

Birmingham, 28.7.40

ELPIS LODGE
117 GOUGH RD.
EDGBASTON
BIRMINGHAM 15.

Dear Leo,

Today you are hearing from me again. I hope you are healthy, a blessing for me. I did not write to you last week because I have been waiting for a response from you. Hopefully, I will hear something from you this week.

How is the Siegmund family and Felix Kaufmann? Give them my regards. Dear Leo, today is dear Papa's birthday, and he is turning 47 years old.

May God grant that he remains healthy. The same goes for mommy and little Kurt.

Dear Leo, how is the weather there? Dear Leo, yesterday I was at the cinema, and the film was very good. Selma Elias and Otto send their greetings. Dear Leo, enclose a letter for Otto and Selma Elias sometime. Dear Leo, write Felix Kaufmann and ask him to write to me. Hope to hear from you soon. I will write to you again next week.

Otherwise, nothing else to speak of. So for today, consider yourself warmly greeted and kissed by your

Brother

Rudi.[31]

The next month, Rudi wrote again to Leo after having received a letter from him. But he had still heard nothing from their dear mother.

Birmingham 25.8.1940

ELPIS LODGE
117 GOUGH RD.
EDGBASTON
BIRMINGHAM 15.

Dear Leo,
Yesterday I received a letter from you, of July 17th, and from it I understand that you are well.

Rudi Hertz (second row, far right, next to the woman in white) at Elpis Lodge, early 1940s.

I am keeping well, thanks God, which, I hope, will be the case with you too. Dear Leo, hopefully, I will be coming to you soon; I would be very happy. Dear Leo, it has been such a long time since I received a letter from our dear mother. I was so happy that you had received a mail from our dear mother, and especially that you all were in good health. Dear Leo, how does our dear mother look in the picture, and dear little Kurt will soon be taller than me. I will enquire about Gerda Katz's address. Dear Leo, I do not know Gerda at all. How is Felix Kaufmann doing? Write to him; he would like to write to me sometimes. Convey my regard[s] to family Gumbert and to all the other acquaintances. I will write to you more next time. So, this is it for today, heartfelt greetings and kisses

from your Brother

Rudi.[32]

Though Leo had now been separated from the family for two years, Rudi was still clinging to the hope that all this would simply prove to be an extended trip apart from one another.

But as the months continued to pass, the terrifying reality became harder and harder to deny. This was not just temporary. This could be for life.

ELPIS LODGE
117 GOUGH RD.
EDGBASTON
BIRMINGHAM 15.

18.5.1941

Dear Leo!

Today, like always, you should hear from me again. Hopefully you are in good health. Dear Leo, have you heard again anything from our beloved parents, and how are they doing. On May 5th little Kurt reached the age of 11, hopefully he is doing well. I am full of worries about our beloved parents and little Kurt. I wish they were already out of Germany. Nobody knows how much longer it will take. At my workplace I now work overtime: I work from 8 o'clock in the morning to 6:30 p.m., as we have lots to do. In the evenings I am tired. For a long time I did not hear from Otto and Selma. Hopefully they are healthy. Dear Leo, how does aunt Selma feel in Argentine? She can thank God that she is already out. Hopefully, Aunt Selma will sometime write to me about everything. Dear Leo, I go often to the cinema, and the movies are very good. How are the movies in your place? I can communicate quite well with the people. On June 30th I will be one

Aunt Selma Kaufmann, on the far left, at the beach with her husband, Alex, along with a young Paul and Paula Hertz.

year in England. The time goes by very fast. What else is new? How are families Gumbert and Loewenstein doing? Send them my regards. Sincere regards to Aunt Selma and Felix. So far for today, sincere regards and kisses

from your

Brother

Rudi[33]

Rudi's thoughts were for his family—and as news of Germany and the treatment of the Jews in Germany and the occupied territories reached England, it must have terrified him. That very year, Hitler had given a speech at the Berlin Sports Palace, and in it he made his vision for the Jews perfectly clear:

Finally this year will help to assure the basis for understanding between the peoples, and thereby, for their reconciliation. I do not want to miss pointing out what I pointed out on 3rd of September [1940] in the German Reichstag, that if Jewry were to plunge the world into war, the role of Jewry would be finished in Europe. They may laugh about it today, as they laughed before about my prophecies. The coming months and years will prove that I prophesied rightly in this case too. But we can see already how our racial peoples which are today still hostile to us will one day recognise the greater inner enemy, and that they too will then enter with us into a great common front. The front of Aryan mankind against Jewish-International exploitation and destruction of nations.[34]

Hitler blamed the Jews for the start of the war. And he continued making his ominous threat: "The role of Jewry [will] be finished in Europe."

The BBC had recorded the speech.[35] Messages like this would have certainly reached Rudi's ears. And he could do nothing to change the situation—all he could do was, as often as possible, think of his beloved family members and attempt to contact them.

Thus, his letter to Leo from May 1941 reads as one big question mark about family, interspersed with small talk: "I now work overtime," and "What else is new?" Ultimately, no matter what he did, there was a nagging terror that would not allow his mind any peace: "I am full of worries about our beloved parents and little Kurt. I wish they were already out of Germany."

As such, once a month, Rudi went to the Birmingham Town Hall to ask the Red Cross to attempt to deliver a letter to his parents—and then to return a response. The letters were just 25 words, and Rudi's were written in all capital letters, perhaps for clarity.

Only two of Rudi's Red Cross letters remain today. The first was written on July 22, 1941, just two months after his letter to Leo describing his anxiety over his family's circumstances. It's truncated German—likely for the sake of saving words—reads as follows, and it is interesting to consider what he includes in his limited space and what he does not:

LIEBE ELTERN BIN GESUND. HABE GUTE ARBEIT. LEO LAESST GRUESSEN. GRATULIERE EUCH ZUM GEBURSTAG. HOFFENTLICH SEID IHR GESUN KUESSE RUDI.

This translates to: "Dear parents I am healthy. I have good work. Leo leaves greetings. I congratulate you on your birthday. I hope you are well. Kisses Rudi."[36]

There is nothing about his circumstances, nothing about his profession, and nothing about England. It is simply the thoughts of a boy with a single message to convey: that he loves his parents and is thinking of them. And, in condensing these thoughts, Rudi fit them into only 20 words.

The letter took an incredibly long time to go through the censorship and approval process. The English authorities approved it on September 16, 1941. Its German approval is marked as November 19, 1941. And then its return to England, with a short message from Rudi's parents—both Paul, who had been released from prison, and Paula—is stamped December 2, 1941, in bold red letters.

Nevertheless, it appears as though his parents' return letter was further delayed for a number of months afterward, because in a letter dated *September 1942,* Rudi wrote to Leo *about this letter* and the subsequent response received from their parents as though their response was *current news:*

Elpis Lodge
117 Gough Rd.
Edgbaston
Birmingham 15.

20.9.1942

Dear Leo,

Today as always you are to hear from me again. I received your letter and gathered from it that you are well. I can report the same thing about myself. Dear Leo, I received the latest letter from our dear parents last week. They are well, thank God, and they send greetings to you. You wrote that I should send one of their letters to you. Unfortunately, I cannot send you one because I write the answer on the same letter (paper). I am always glad to hear from them. I hope we will all see each other again soon. I congratulated Daddy, Mummy and little Kurt on their birthdays. Let us hope that we shall soon be able to celebrate their birthdays together…

So for today many greetings and kisses

from your brother

Rudi[37]

The process of writing 25-or-fewer-word letters back and forth with his parents took one year and two months.

And in that year and two months, the fate of the Jews in mainland Europe continued to look increasingly bleak. On December 16, 1941, a terrifying speech had been given by Hans Frank, the head of the General Government for the occupied territories of Poland. In his speech, he made clear his views of what should happen to the Jews:

> One way or another—I will tell you quite openly—we must finish off the Jews. The Fuehrer put it into words once: Should united Jewry again succeed in setting off a world war, then the blood sacrifice shall not be made only by the people driven into war, but then the Jews of Europe will have met their end. I know that there is criticism of many of the measures now applied to the Jews in the Reich. There are always deliberate attempts to speak again and again of cruelty, harshness, etc; this emerges from the reports on the popular mood. I appeal to you: before I now continue speaking, first agree with me on a formula: We will have pity, on principle, only for the German people, and for nobody else in the world. The others had no pity for us either. As an old National-Socialist I must also say that if the pack of Jews (*Judensippschaft*) were to survive the war in Europe while we sacrifice the best of our blood for the preservation of Europe, then this war would still be only a partial success. I will therefore, on principle, approach Jewish affairs in the expectation that the Jews will disappear. They must go.[38]

While Hans Frank was head of a large swath of territory in the former nation of Poland, and Rudi's parents lived in East Prussia, many of the Jews from Germany were being deported to Poland. In fact, Rudi's September 1942 letter to Leo included the following foreboding words about a mutual friend's parents: "Otto had post from dear granny. She is now quite alone as Otto's parents have been sent to Poland. I am very sorry for dear Otto."[39]

Otto's parents had been deported to Poland.

In October 1942, just one month after Rudi received his parents' Red Cross letter, Anne Frank recorded the following in her diary:

> Today I have nothing but dismal and depressing news to report. Our many Jewish friends and acquaintances are being taken away in droves . . . We assume that most of them are being murdered. The English radio says they're being gassed. Perhaps that's the quickest way to die.[40]

The news was horrifying. The Germans sought to eliminate the Jews, and they were accomplishing this by cold-blooded murder.

Sometime after this last letter to Leo, Rudi went again to the Birmingham Town Hall to see whether he had received any mail from his parents.

There was a Red Cross letter waiting for him.

He picked it up, unfolded it, and noticed something odd about it. It was certainly the same message that he had sent to his parents, months prior, in January 1942. The message and the handwriting were what he had penned to send to his mother and father:

LIEBE ELTERN. BIN GESUND. WIE GEHT ES EUCH. HÖRE ÖFTERS VON LEO. GRATULIERE KURT. ARBEIT GEFALLT ALS POLSTERER. GRUSSE OMA. OTTO GESUND. GRUSS KUSS RUDI.

> **RED CROSS MESSAGE BUREAU**
> No. 651
> TOWN HALL, BIRMINGHAM.

WAR ORGANISATION OF THE BRITISH RED CROSS AND ORDER OF ST. JOHN

To:
Comité International
de la Croix Rouge
Genève

Foreign Relations Department

PASSED
P 156

ENQUIRER
Fragesteller

Name: HERTZ
Christian name / Vorname: RUDOLF
Address:

Relationship of Enquirer to Addressee: SON
Wie ist Fragesteller mit Empfänger verwandt?

The Enquirer desires news of the Addressee and asks that the following message should be transmitted to him.

LIEBE ELTERN. BIN GESUND WIE GEHT ES EUCH. HÖRE ÖFTERS VON LEO. GRATULIERE KURT ARBEIT GEFÄLLT ALS POLSTERER. GRÜSSE OMA OTTO GESUND. GRUSS KUSS RUDI.

Date: 6.1.42.

ADDRESSEE
Empfänger

Name: HERTZ
Christian name / Vorname: PAUL
Address: KOENIGSBERG (PR)
SCHNURLINGSTRASSE 32 A
No 32 GERMANY

3 FEV. 1942

The Addressee's reply to be written overleaf. (Not more than 25 words)
Empfänger schreibe Antwort auf Rückseite. (Höchstzahl 25 worte)

Rudi's second Red Cross letter to his parents. The back of the letter, where his parents had formerly written a response, is blank.

This translates to: "Dear parents. I'm healthy. How are you? I hear more often from Leo. I congratulate Kurt. I am working as an upholsterer. I greet Grandma. Otto is healthy. Regards kiss Rudi."[41]

But, it was this sameness that was the problem. There was no response to his message. The backside, where Paul and Paula would have written their 25 words to him was utterly blank.

What did that mean? Why had the letter been returned to him without any response?

Rudi's Family

Rudi was worried. But never, in all of his worst fears, did he imagine that a blank, returned letter was a sign that the Holocaust had descended upon his family: "Even then, the truth didn't cross my mind. I had heard that Jewish people were being sent to the East to be resettled. I never guessed the truth at that stage, that my people were being eliminated in the Holocaust. I believed that, once the war was over, we'd all meet up again."[42]

After having been arrested on May 17, 1939, it appears as though Paul Hertz was eventually released—Rudi's Red Cross letters were to his *parents,* and specifically addressed to his father. Nevertheless, at some point, Paul was imprisoned again, but this time in a ghetto.[43]

The Kovno ghetto was located in the Lithuanian city of Kaunas. Split into two sections, known as the "small" and "large" ghetto, the Kovno ghetto was created in the summer of 1941. It was plagued with overcrowding. Each person was allotted less than 10 square feet of living space.

After just a few months, the Germans decided to destroy the "small" ghetto, leading to the murder of most of its inhabitants. Just a few weeks later, at the end of October 1941, the Germans shot 9,200 Jews in a single day—an event that came to be known as the "Great Action."

A number of the Jews in Kovno worked as forced laborers for the German military—in doing so, they hoped that the Germans would see them as productive and would spare their lives.

Nevertheless, when the SS took over the ghetto in the fall of 1943, they converted it into the Kauen concentration camp. In July 1944, the camp was evacuated, and most of the prisoners were sent to either Dachau or Stutthof.[44]

Paul Hertz was one of those sent to Dachau,[45] in Germany, on a journey of approximately 900 miles.

He was imprisoned in Dachau for six months. Then, on January 7, 1945, he was moved to Flossenbürg,[46] a concentration camp in eastern Germany, near the old border between Germany and Czechoslovakia. It was at that point that a number of Jews were being transported to Flossenbürg—as the eastern and western fronts moved closer and closer to Germany. Up until this point, Flossenbürg had held over 4,000 inmates. The winter and spring of 1945 saw the population of the main camp spike to 14,500, with a total of 53,000 in Flossenbürg and its surrounding subcamps.[47]

Exactly one month after being taken to Flossenbürg, on February 7, 1945, Paul Hertz was murdered in Leitmeritz, one of Flossenbürg's subcamps.[48] It was just two months before Flossenbürg was liberated.[49] Paul was 51.

Paula and Kurt have an entirely different—and much shorter—story.

In 1942, they were deported on an *Osttransport*, or east transport[50]—a euphemism that today is notoriously recognized as meaning "transport to the killing centers and mass murder."[51]

The location of their deportation is not known. Nor is the exact date within 1942. But, it is known that they never returned. Consequently, it appears that they never read Rudi's second Red Cross letter—written to them at the beginning of 1942—and held up through the machinations of censorship and the inner workings of the Red Cross. Hence the reason for the letter's return.

Rudi's 20 words, congratulating them on their birthdays, were the last few things he would ever get to say to his mother and his brother.

According to *Das Bundesarchiv*, the German Federal Archive, Paula Hertz has been "officially declared dead."[52] Paula turned 49 in 1942, and Kurt turned 12. Or perhaps they did not live long enough to do so.

Conclusion

Rudi continued to live in Elpis Lodge until after he turned 18 in 1943. After that, he kept working as an upholsterer and eventually opened his own upholstery business in Birmingham. When the war ended, Rudi changed his last name, just as so many other German refugees who no longer wanted a German last name. Thus, Rudi Hertz became Rudi Hart.

Rudi Hart in the late 1940s.

Twenty years later, in 1963, Rudi arrived in Naples, Italy. He had an important matter that required him to travel the nearly 1,500 miles from Birmingham to the coast of Italy: Leo was emigrating with his family from Argentina to Israel, and their ship was docking for a time in Naples.

This was the first time that the brothers had seen each other—or had seen *any* member of their immediate family since 1939. Rudi was now almost 40, and Leo was approaching 45.

On a ship in the waters of Italy, the two brothers embraced and wept upon each other.

Though so much had been broken in their lives, not everything had been lost.

Top: Rudi Hart and Kitty Felix at their wedding, March 1949.
Bottom: Leo and Rosel Hertz with Rudi Hart, in Birmingham in the 1970s.

Rudi Hart

Top: Rudi Hart in front of his upholstery shop (note the sign in the window). Bottom: Rudi in Birmingham with his two sons, Peter Hart (on the left) and David Hart (on the right), 2009.

Top: Moira Hart, Peter's wife, holding Rudi's birthday cake on his 85th birthday, December 2010.
Bottom: Rudi Hart with four of his grandchildren, October 2012. From left to right: Simon, Michael, Jonathan, and Daniel.

Rudi Hart

[1] "Polish Corridor," *Encyclopedia Britannica Online,* accessed May 30, 2017, https://www.britannica.com/place/Polish-Corridor.

[2] William Shirer, *The Rise and Fall of the Third Reich* (New York: Simon and Schuster, 1960), 212.

[3] "Polish Corridor," *Encyclopedia Britannica Online,* accessed May 30, 2017, https://www.britannica.com/place/Polish-Corridor.

[4] "East Prussia," *Encyclopedia Britannica Online,* accessed May 30, 2017, https://www.britannica.com/place/East-Prussia.

[5] "Zinten," in *The Encyclopedia of Jewish Life Before and During the Holocaust,* eds. Shmuel Spector and Geoffrey Wigoder (Jerusalem: Yad Vashem, 2001), 1512.

[6] "Zinten," in *The London General Gazetteer, or Geographical Dictionary, Volume III* (London: William Baynes and Son, 1825), 671.

[7] "Zinten," in *The Encyclopedia of Jewish Life Before and During the Holocaust,* eds. Shmuel Spector and Geoffrey Wigoder (Jerusalem: Yad Vashem, 2001), 1512.

[8] "Gedenkbuch - Opfer Der Verfolgung Der Juden Unter Der Nationalsozialistischen Gewaltherrschaft in Deutschland 1933-1945," *Das Bundesarchiv,* accessed June 5, 2017, https://www.bundesarchiv.de/gedenkbuch/en861241.

[9] "Gedenkbuch - Opfer Der Verfolgung Der Juden Unter Der Nationalsozialistischen Gewaltherrschaft in Deutschland 1933-1945," *Das Bundesarchiv,* accessed June 5, 2017, https://www.bundesarchiv.de/gedenkbuch/en861242.

[10] "Gedenkbuch - Opfer Der Verfolgung Der Juden Unter Der Nationalsozialistischen Gewaltherrschaft in Deutschland 1933-1945," Das Bundesarchiv, accessed June 5, 2017, https://www.bundesarchiv.de/gedenkbuch/en861212.

[11] "Average Weather in Kaliningrad Russia," Weather Spark, accessed June 5, 2017, https://weatherspark.com/y/86511/Average-Weather-in-Kaliningrad-Russia.

"Average Weather in Warendorf Germany," Weather Spark, accessed June 5, 2017, https://weatherspark.com/y/58173/Average-Weather-in-Warendorf-Germany.

"Average Weather in Mayen Germany," Weather Spark, accessed June 5, 2017, https://weatherspark.com/y/57723/Average-Weather-in-Mayen-Germany.

[12] Rudi Hart, quoted in Maureen Messent, "Saved from Hell," Birmingham Mail (Birmingham, UK), May 8, 2000.

[13] Ibid.

[14] Ibid.

[15] Ibid.

[16] Ibid.

[17] Ibid.

[18] Ibid.

[19] Ibid.

[20] Peter Hart, "Rudi Hart (Hertz)" (presentation, Rudi Hart's Second Bar Mitzvah, Birmingham, UK, January 2009).

[21] Rudi Hertz, letter to Leo Hertz, September 17, 1939. Translated by staff at translated.net. Copy of letter and translation in possession of the author.

[22] E. W. Newman quoted in "Birmingham Refugee Boys' Hostel," The Christadelphian, July 1940, 334.

[23] Rudi Hart, quoted in Zoë Josephs, Survivors: Jewish Refugees in Birmingham (West Midlands: The Birmingham Jewish History Research Group, 1988), 80.

[24] Kitty Hart, Return to Auschwitz (New York: Atheneum, 1982), 21.

[25] Rudi Hertz, letter to Leo Hertz, March 16, 1942. Translated by staff at translated.net. Copy of letter and translation in possession of the author.

[26] Rudi Hertz, letter to Leo Hertz, September 8, 1943. Translated by staff at translated.net. Copy of letter and translation in possession of the author.

[27] E. W. Newman, "Elpis Lodge: Six Months' Work Reviewed," The Christadelphian, January 1941, 39.

[28] Letter from Rudi Hertz to Leo Hertz, March 16, 1942. Translated by staff at translated.net. Copy of letter and translation in possession of the author.

[29] Letter from Rudi Hertz to Leo Hertz, August 4, 1942. Translation by Graham Jackman. Copy of letter and translation in possession of the author.

[30] Rudi Hertz, letter to Leo Hertz, May 18, 1940. Translated by staff at translated.net. Copy of letter and translation in possession of the author.

[31] Rudi Hertz, letter to Leo Hertz, July 28, 1940. Translated by staff at translated.net. Copy of letter and translation in possession of the author.

[32] Rudi Hertz, letter to Leo Hertz, August 25, 1940. Translated by staff at translated.net. Copy of letter and translation in possession of the author.

[33] Rudi Hertz, letter to Leo Hertz, May 18, 1941. Translated by staff at translated.net. Copy of letter and translation in possession of the author.

[34] "Adolf Hitler: Speech at the Berlin Sports Palace," Jewish Virtual Library, January 30, 1941, http://www.jewishvirtuallibrary.org/hitler-speech-at-the-berlin-sports-palace-january-30-1941.

[35] Ibid.

[36] Rudi Hertz, letter to Paul Hertz, July 22, 1941. Translation by the author. Copy of letter and translation in possession of the author.

[37] Rudi Hertz, letter to Leo Hertz, September 20, 1942. Translated by Graham Jackman. Copy of letter and translation in possession of the author.

[38] Hans Frank, "We Must Finish with the Jews," in The Jew in the Modern World, ed. Paul Mendes-Flohr and Jehuda Reinharz (Oxford: Oxford University Press, 2011), 750.

[39] Rudi Hertz, letter to Leo Hertz, September 20, 1942. Translated by Graham Jackman. Copy of letter and translation in possession of the author.

[40] Anne Frank, The Diary of a Young Girl (Seattle: Kindle, 2015), entry for October 9, 1942.

[41] Rudi Hertz, letter to Paul Hertz, January 6, 1942. Translation by the author. Copy of letter and translation in possession of the author.

[42] Rudi Hart, quoted in Maureen Messent, "Saved from Hell," Birmingham Mail (Birmingham, UK), May 8, 2000.

[43] "Gedenkbuch - Opfer Der Verfolgung Der Juden Unter Der Nationalsozialistischen Gewaltherrschaft in Deutschland 1933-1945," Das Bundesarchiv, accessed June 6, 2017, https://www.bundesarchiv.de/gedenkbuch/en861241.

[44] "Kovno," United States Holocaust Memorial Museum, accessed June 6, 2017, https://www.ushmm.org/wlc/en/article.php?ModuleId=10005174.

[45] "Gedenkbuch - Opfer Der Verfolgung Der Juden Unter Der Nationalsozialistischen Gewaltherrschaft in Deutschland 1933-1945," Das Bundesarchiv, accessed June 6, 2017, https://www.bundesarchiv.de/gedenkbuch/en861241.

[46] Ibid.

[47] "Flossenbürg," United States Holocaust Memorial Museum, accessed June 6, 2017, https://www.ushmm.org/wlc/en/article.php?ModuleId=10005537.

[48] "Gedenkbuch - Opfer Der Verfolgung Der Juden Unter Der Nationalsozialistischen Gewaltherrschaft in Deutschland 1933-1945," Das Bundesarchiv, accessed June 6, 2017, https://www.bundesarchiv.de/gedenkbuch/en861241.

[49] "Flossenbürg," United States Holocaust Memorial Museum, accessed June 6, 2017, https://www.ushmm.org/wlc/en/article.php?ModuleId=10005537.

[50] "Gedenkbuch - Opfer Der Verfolgung Der Juden Unter Der Nationalsozialistischen Gewaltherrschaft in Deutschland 1933-1945," Das Bundesarchiv, accessed June 6, 2017, https://www.bundesarchiv.de/gedenkbuch/en861242.

"Gedenkbuch - Opfer Der Verfolgung Der Juden Unter Der Nationalsozialistischen Gewaltherrschaft in Deutschland 1933-1945," Das Bundesarchiv, accessed June 6, 2017, https://www.bundesarchiv.de/gedenkbuch/en861212.

[51] "Deportations to Killing Centers," United States Holocaust Memorial Museum, accessed June 7, 2017, https://www.ushmm.org/wlc/en/article.php?ModuleId=10005372.

[52] Ibid.

SUSAN CLAPPER

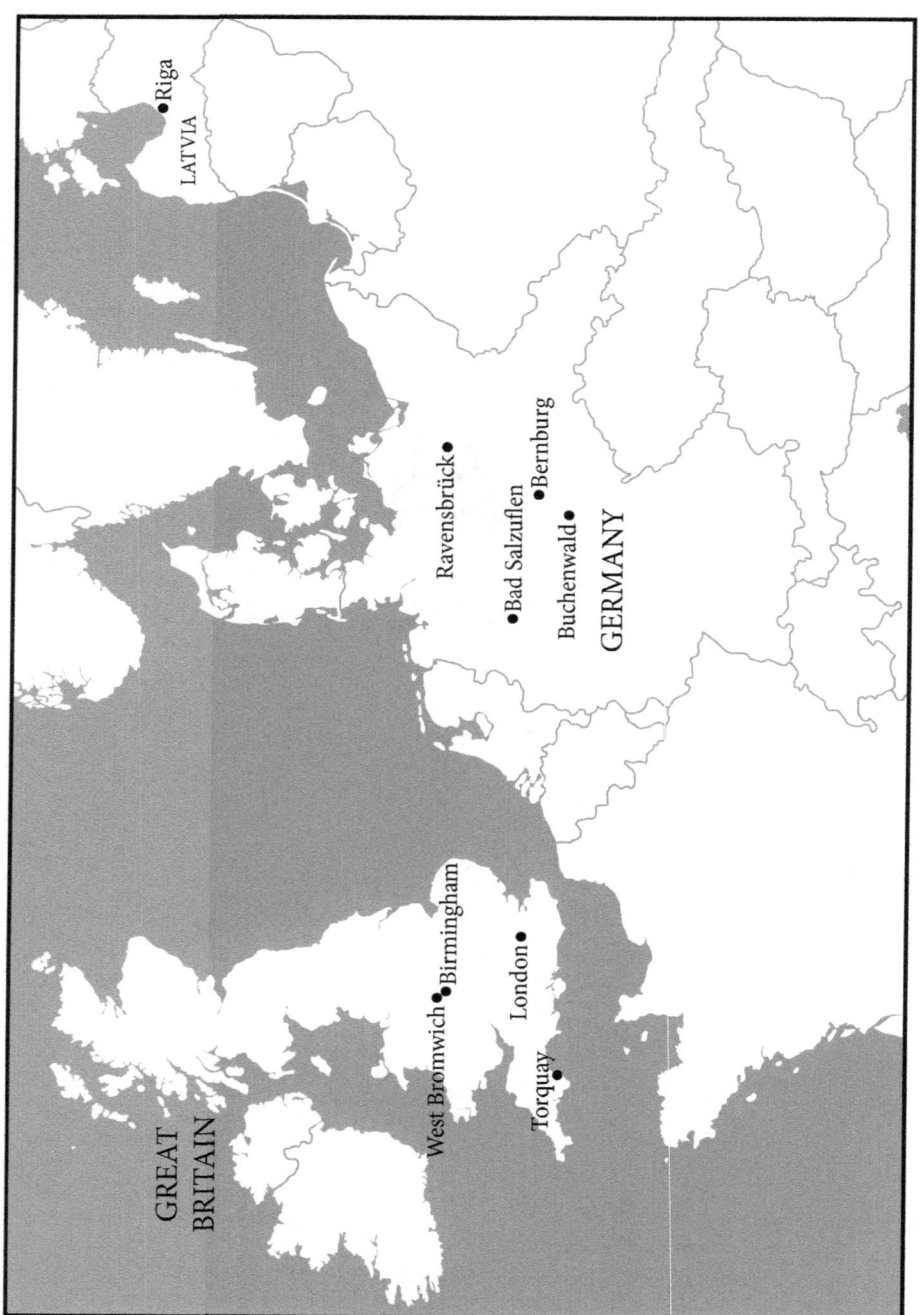

3

Susan Clapper (née Eichmann)

Between 1925 and 1929, the influence of the Nazi party in Germany waned. Hitler had been released early from prison in December 1924, but despite the fame that resulted from his attempted coup and later his book, *Mein Kampf*, he was banned from speaking publicly between 1925 and 1926 by a number of German states.[1]

During the early 1920s, when Germany was fraught with hyperinflation, the radical views of the Nazi party gained much support. However, as Germany began to receive more loans from the United States to pay its reparations, and as life in Germany began to improve, Hitler and his influence began to decrease. In his quintessential work on Nazi Germany, William Shirer described this period:

> The years from 1925 until the coming of the depression in 1929 were lean years for Adolf Hitler and the Nazi movement. . . .The climate of material prosperity and of a feeling of relaxation which settled over Germany in those years was not propitious for his purposes. . . . Between 1924 and 1930 German borrowing amounted to some seven billion dollars and most of it came from American investors, who gave little thought to how the Germans might make eventual repayment. The Germans gave even less thought to it.[2]

As the money flowed into Germany, it seemed like the

financial chaos of the early 1920s was gone, never to return. Things were good in Germany, with the economy picking up, and with the unemployment rate dropping far below what it had been in previous years.

Why think of Adolf Hitler and his radical views at the time? There was no need. Thus, Hitler's influence over Germany gradually diminished. Again, William Shirer wrote of this diminished authority:

> One scarcely heard of Hitler or the Nazis except as butts of jokes—usually in connection with the Beer Hall Putsch, as it came to be known. In the elections of May 20, 1928, the Nazi Party polled only 810,000 votes out of a total of thirty-one million cast and had but a dozen of the Reichstag's 491 members.[3]

But Hitler was most definitely not a joke. On February 14, 1926, Hitler convened the Bamberg conference, which worked to confirm his absolute leadership over the National Socialists.[4] For the next few years, as undisputed Führer of the Nazi party, Hitler waited, believing that the American funding upon which Germany depended would eventually cease. With his leadership secured and with his anti-Weimar policies clearly known, Hitler simply had to wait until everything came crashing down. William Shirer wrote:

> He was confident that the good times would not last. So far as Germany was concerned, he said, they depended not on her own strength but on that of others—of America above all, from whose swollen coffers loans were pouring in to make and keep Germany prosperous.[5]

Thus, Adolf Hitler waited, along with those who followed him—looking for the eventual collapse of the Germany economy and the time the nation would again be ready to look to him for direction. But for the rest of the world, the Nazi movement was simply a thing of the past. On January 24, 1926, the *New York Times* described the National Socialists as: "A movement which might have inflamed all Germany [which] remains in the minds and hearts of a few who cherish it against better days to come."[6]

At that point, the Nazi party only seemed to capture "the minds and hearts of a few."

Beginnings

Susanne Eichmann was born on June 12, 1926, in Bad Salzuflen, Germany. Her father, Hans Eichmann, was in his early 30s, and her mother, Gertrud Eichmann, was in her early 20s. Susanne grew up with Ursula Meyer, née Eichmann, her first cousin, whose story is detailed in Volume 1 of this series. Susanne's father, Hans, worked as a farmer and cattle dealer and eventually worked in this business together with Bruno Eichmann, his younger brother and Ursula's father. Her mother, Gertrud, was a homemaker. Susanne was an only child.

In describing her family, Susanne used the words "quiet," "reserved," and "extremely kind"[7] to characterize her father. Her mother was "very vivacious" and "very kind."[8] Growing up, Susanne idolized her mother and wanted to be just like her.

Susanne's family was observant and celebrated the holidays together. Bad Salzuflen had a small synagogue and small Jewish community—but Susanne and her family participated in the activities there. They attended the synagogue, and Susanne went to Hebrew lessons once a week.

The Eichmann family was immediately affected by Hitler's rise to power in 1933. Susanne's grandfather was part owner of a mattress factory in Bad Salzuflen, having two or three other German partners in the business. As soon as Hitler came to

Susanne, Gertrud, and Hans Eichmann.

power, her grandfather's partners threw him out. Furious over what had happened, and expecting that he could have some type of legal recourse, her grandfather contacted his lawyer the next day—and was told "I'm very sorry, under these political circumstances, there is nothing I can do to help you."[9] Sadly, a similar type of thing would happen to her father. In 1937, Hans was forced to close his business—not because the law required it at that point, but because the attitude toward Jews in Germany had caused his business to become unprofitable. The family lost the farm and moved into the city. It was at that point that he began working with Bruno.

Though her parents attempted to shield her from the antisemitism, Susanne still had her experiences. She recalled that even as a child she felt different from the other children—because many of the German children refused to play with her. There were, however, exceptions. One little girl, Annelise Funk, sat down next to Susanne—and Susanne warned her that she was sitting next to a Jew: "I am Jewish, and if you don't want to sit by me, it is all right." Annelise went home, asked her father what to do, and was told that if Susanne was anything like her father Hans, then Annelise should feel honored to sit next to her. Mostly, though, Susanne only spent time with the other Jewish children, including her cousin Ursula.

For the most part, though she was excluded by many of the girls, Susanne felt as though the girls at the school were at least nicer to her than the non-Jewish boys were to the Jewish boys. She remembered one boy who was constantly targeted by some of his peers.

At one point, however, she remembered a rock being thrown at her, along with the age-old condemnation: "You Jews, you killed Jesus."[10] It apparently did not matter that Susanne was only a little child and had absolutely nothing to do with Jesus.

Susanne's son, Michael Clapper, described some of the further antisemitism that his mother experienced:

> She was apparently one of very few Jews in her school, and the family suffered increasingly antisemitic acts as she grew up. I asked about what form this took and she responded that initially she would come home to antisemitic slogans daubed on their house. Then their windows were regularly smashed and their cat had its throat slit and its body dumped outside the front door.

But the worst was yet to come.

Kristallnacht

The Eichmanns lived in the city, having lost their farm. They had a flat upstairs, and an elderly widow and her daughter lived downstairs. On *Kristallnacht*, Susanne and her parents were all together in their apartment. Then the windows downstairs were smashed. Later, Susanne's grandmother sent one of Susanne's cousins to their flat with a warning: Jewish men were being rounded up, and Hans's brother had already been taken—Hans needed to go into hiding.

But Hans refused.

Upon hearing the warning, he stated that he was not going to leave his house or his routine. He had done nothing wrong, so why should he hide?

That morning, the "quiet," "reserved," and "extremely kind"[11] Hans Eichmann went to work.

And astonishingly, after work, he returned home.

But that night, they came for him. Susanne remembered the scene—the Nazis had prepared for the arrests and had brought in additional police officers to work alongside the local police—in case any of the local ones had a difficult time arresting people whom they knew or with whom they had become friendly. When the police came to arrest Hans, two of them came—one local policeman and one whom Susanne did not know. As they took him, the local policeman began to cry.

Apparently Hans Eichmann had quite a reputation—which had served Susanne well in the incident with Annelise but, tragically, had not changed the situation when Hans was taken away from his wife and daughter and transported to Buchenwald.

Buchenwald was one of the largest concentration camps constructed within the old German borders (1937; before the annexation of Austria and occupation of the *Sudetenland* in Czechoslovakia) and was located about five miles northwest of Weimar in east-central Germany. As a result of the roundups at *Kristallnacht*, approximately 10,000 Jewish men were brought to the camp and detained. Their treatment upon arrival was so poor that 255 of them died shortly thereafter.[12]

Susanne was 12 when her father was taken.

After a few weeks, on December 12, 1938,[13] Hans Eichmann was released, along with a number of the other men who had been taken. He returned home in the middle of the night—and Susanne recalled that he was a completely different man. All of his hair had been shaved, and he had experienced a taste of the terror that was to come upon the Jewish people.

After these experiences, Hans and Gertrud agreed that for Susanne's sake, they needed to find a way for their only child to escape the evils that had fallen upon their family and to leave both them and Germany.

The Kindertransport

In 1938 and 1939, in response to *Kristallnacht,* Britain agreed to allow an unspecified number of children to flee Germany for the United Kingdom. Most of these children were Jewish, and after the last transport came from Germany before war was declared between Germany and Great Britain, the number of children who had been brought over the sea came to approximately 10,000.

Susanne was one of them.

At that time, one of Susanne's relatives was already living in England—and he happened to hear about an unmarried woman who was looking for a girl about Susanne's age. She did not want a child, but she also did not want a teenager. This relative put Susanne's name forth to this woman, Hilda Hayes, Susanne's family sent a picture, and Hilda then agreed to house Susanne. Hilda was a Christadelphian.

On the day Susanne left Germany, she was allowed to have one parent accompany her to the train station. Hans was given that honor. It was August 2, 1939—one month later, Great Britain declared war on Germany, and all Kindertransports out of Germany ceased.

As Susanne approached the train, she felt as though she were on a big adventure. She had just turned 13 years old, she was just beginning to yearn for independence, and now she was off to a new country, to new friends, and to freedom.

Susanne and Hans Eichmann stood in front of the train together—and Hans passed his "little girl" over to the man on

Top and bottom: Photographs of the suitcase that accompanied Susanne from Germany to England.

the train. As Susanne boarded the train, embarking on her great adventure, the man on the train told her to say goodbye to her father. And that is when reality set in. From that point on, Susanne realized that she was not simply going on some glorious journey—she was leaving everything she knew, including her parents, and she might not ever return.

As it turned out, when Susanne waved goodbye, this was the last glimpse she would ever have of her father.

For about six hours, Susanne sat on the train as it chugged toward Holland. When the transport reached Holland, sometime in the evening, Susanne was greeted by people offering her food and sweets.

At 8 p.m., she boarded a boat bound for England.

Susanne Eichmann did not know what awaited her in England. She could not speak English. She had never met the people with whom she would be living, but she assumed that they must be good people to be willing to take a child whom they had never met into their home. She understood why she was leaving her family—but she did not realize how desperate the situation truly was. Nor, apparently, did many others. When England first agreed to allow these unaccompanied children to flee for safety within the United Kingdom, it was simply thought that after a few years, when the situation in Germany and Austria changed, the children would be sent home.[14]

Susanne would not be sent home, because at the end of the war, for her, there would be no home return to. Susanne stated, "I never saw my parents again."[15]

Susanne's Family

Hans and Gertrud Eichmann continued to live in Bad Salzuflen, without their daughter, for another two years or so. In 1941, however, the two of them were separated.

That year, Gertrud was taken and deported to Ravensbrück concentration camp.

Ravensbrück was a camp dedicated nearly exclusively to women—and it was the largest concentration camp for women in the Reich. In comparison to the camps that held both men and women, it had the second largest population, with only Auschwitz-Birkenau being larger. Construction on Ravensbrück began in November 1938, and by the end of 1942, the camp had a female population of almost 10,000. In January of 1945, the population had grown to 50,000 (a few of whom were males).

At Ravensbrück, the SS held periodic "selections," in which they took the prisoners who were considered too weak or sickly to work and murdered them. At first, these prisoners were simply shot. Then, in 1942, the SS instead took the prisoners and sent them to Bernburg Euthanasia Center, a site with gas chambers that had previously been used to murder those with disabilities.[16]

Gertrud Eichmann was one of those who was chosen in a "selection." On April 3, 1942, she was murdered at Bernburg.[17] She was 39 years old.

The same year that Gertrud was sent to Ravensbrück, 1941, Hans Eichmann was deported to the Riga ghetto.

Riga had been the capital of independent Latvia, with a population of approximately 40,000 Jews. The ghetto was created in October 1941 with about 30,000 of these Jews. In late November and early December, 26,000 of these people were taken into the Rumbula Forest and shot.[18] Just days after these mass killings, on December 13, 1941, Hans, along with Bruno and Ilse Eichmann, Susanne's aunt and uncle, arrived in Riga.[19]

The ghetto was divided into multiple sections—one section became the "Latvian" ghetto, where the few remaining Latvian Jews were kept. After the initial mass murders, a "German" ghetto was created, where the prisoners from Germany and Austria, such as Hans, were taken. Many of those in the German ghetto shared the same fate as that of the initially imprisoned Latvian Jews. They were taken into the forest and murdered.[20]

Hans Eichmann was murdered in Riga. He was in his late 40s.[21]

Life in England

Hilda Hayes met Susanne Eichmann at Liverpool Street Station in London. Hilda brought with her a little English-German dictionary, a book Susanne became so used to seeing that she dubbed it the "little red book," so she could look up words and communicate with Susanne. That night, Hilda and Susanne stayed in London, and the next day, Susanne had an experience that was forever imprinted on her mind:

> The next day, she took me outside of Buckingham Palace to see the changing of the guard . . . and we went to one of the parks afterwards, opposite Buckingham Palace, and there was a notice up: 'Keep off the grass,' and I tried to read it, and from that moment, my love of England had grown, and nothing ever, ever changed

Susanne Eichmann, while living in England.

it. Because in Germany, it would have read, 'Jews not allowed.' In England it said, 'keep off the grass....'[22]

Though she was in a different country and with a woman whom she had never met, Susanne realized that she was free. Michael Clapper, Susanne's son, wrote of Susanne's appreciation for this freedom:

> The Queen, and particularly the Queen Mother, were such an enormous comfort to my mother throughout

her life, even though she had never met any of them. They represented an institution that didn't condemn her for what she was, but in fact welcomed her and of course saved her life.[23]

Eventually, Hilda and Susanne made their way to West Bromwich, a city just outside of Birmingham, where Hilda lived with her brother and his wife, Walter and Ethel Hayes, who were also both Christadelphians. Hilda was a nurse, and she worked at the local school clinic in West Bromwich. And though Hilda was officially Susanne's guardian, Hilda, Walter, and Ethel helped raise and take care of Susanne, with Ethel watching over Susanne when Hilda was at work.

Susanne loved her life in England—although it was difficult. Just a few weeks after she arrived, war was declared on Germany, and she was a German Jew. Everything was rationed. At the same time, though Hilda was good to her, she also found the relationship difficult at times: "She was quite

From left to right: Walter Hayes, Hilda Hayes, Susanne Eichmann, and Ethel Hayes in the garden in West Bromwich.

kind to me in many ways. Because she saved my life, after all. But she was very strict, very severe."[24] They had very little money, and Susanne was required to do chores, one of which was scrubbing the stone floors, early in the morning, before going to school.

Life in England was further complicated by Susanne's aunt Kate Katz, who had fled to England with her husband, Karl. Kate and Hilda had a difficult time getting along with one another—Susanne stated that both were possessive of her but described Aunt Kate as "a difficult person," stating that in the entire family, it was only Gertrud who had been able to get along with Kate. This difficulty and possessiveness was no doubt compounded by the fact that Karl and Kate had no children of their own, and living near Susanne, felt the need to watch over her and make sure that she was well attended to.

While living with Hilda, Susanne went only once to a synagogue—Hilda took her there for Yom Kippur. Nevertheless, when Susanne went there, she felt ashamed—not because of something that she did but because of what the others were doing. In the synagogue, people were eating, reading letters, and "treating it like a social club."[25] Coming from an Orthodox family, Susanne was not pleased and resolved not to go to a synagogue again in England.

Instead, Susanne attended the Christadelphian meetings with Hilda and Hilda's family. Eventually, Susanne chose to join the Christadelphians and was baptized on December 4, 1941, when she was just 15 years old—an age younger than that typically chosen by young people to be baptized.[26] Perhaps Susanne was one of the rare cases of children who were taken in by the Christadelphians who felt pressured to convert— decades later, in an interview for the USC Shoah Foundation, Susanne described Hilda's desire to house an adolescent refugee, rather than a child or a teenager. She stated that Hilda wanted someone she could "still influence a little in her way of life."[27] It was understandable that Hilda, as an unmarried woman, would want someone like this, but perhaps these words hinted at the pressure Susanne felt to become a Christadelphian. Underlining this point, within the next eight years, Susanne returned to Judaism, and would remain a practicing Jew for the rest of her life.

Around the time of her baptism, Susanne left school and started working in an office. However, she was determined to continue her studies, so she enrolled in a night school and, after work, rode the bus to class.

On top of all the difficulties in England and the change in religion, that same year, 1941, Susanne received a message from her grandmother, who was still alive and in Germany. The message stated that her mother was dead and that her father had gone missing.

Susanne had to process all of this and carry on at the tender age of 15.

After the War

In 1945, Hilda Hayes married Wilfred Wakefield, another Christadelphian. At that point, Susanne was 19 and chose to move out of her foster mother's house. She lived in "digs" and supported herself—all the while attending night school.

During this time, Susanne attempted to discover her father's fate—she knew that her mother was dead, but she filled out form after form, trying to learn her father's whereabouts. Walter Hayes, Hilda's brother, was, according to Susanne, the only one willing to help in this endeavor. These efforts, unfortunately, proved unfruitful, and Susanne only found out what had happened to Hans when she lived in South Africa, many years later.

Two years later, in 1947, Susanne, along with her cousin Ursula, chose to move south to Rhodesia, now Zimbabwe, where they had an aunt who had fled Europe and had established herself in Salisbury, Rhodesia. The two of them made their way into the mainland of Europe and then took a boat down to Africa, where they met with their aunt, who became like a second mother to Susanne.

Eventually, after living for a few months in Rhodesia, Ursula moved to South Africa while Susanne stayed in Rhodesia and married Max Clapper, a Jewish man whose family had also fled Germany and who had purchased a farm in Rhodesia. Max was the principal of the Hebrew school in Salisbury. The two of them were married in 1949, and by this point, sometime

Photo of Hilda's 100th birthday at the Bethesda Christadelphian Care Home in Torquay. Front row from left to right is Walter Hayes, Hilda Wakefield (née Hayes) and Susan Clapper.

between leaving England in 1947 and her marriage,[28] Susanne chose to leave the Christadelphians and return to Judaism. She stated that she has always been very proud that she was Jewish.

In 1952, Susanne and Max moved to Durban, South Africa, where Max taught Hebrew. This pleasant life, however, would only last for a few years.

Unfortunately, tragedy struck again, when Max Clapper died suddenly in 1960. Susanne had three children—Paul, Michael, and Trudy, and now she had to raise them on her own. She stated in retrospect that the war years and her time in England—living so frugally—had proved good training ground for learning how to keep herself and her family afloat financially all on her own.

Conclusion

On March 12, 2001 in Durban, South Africa, Susan Clapper, as she was then known, passed away. Her story will not be forgotten.

Michael Clapper beautifully summarized some of his mother's experiences:

> It is impossible to imagine the suffering an only child felt when, at an early age, she was put on a boat by her parents who were subsequently murdered . . . to an unfamiliar country to face an uncertain future. She came from a small village (Schotmar, Bad Salzuflen) and must have been baffled by her "crime," which was to have been born a Jew.[29]

Susan never returned to Germany. She felt as though she could not face it—so many horrible things happened there that she could not bring herself to go back. Michael wrote: "She could never return to Germany, nor could she even speak German. I think she found it too painful. I recall when any relatives wrote or spoke to her in German, she responded in English only."[30]

On the other hand, despite the difficulties Susan had faced in England, she loved the country tremendously and certainly felt grateful for what Hilda Wakefield had done for her. She and Hilda had developed a relationship, so much so that when Susan first began considering moving to Rhodesia, Susan's aunt felt bad that Hilda would be left without Susan—so Susan's aunt wrote to Hilda and offered her a place to live as well!

The two continued to keep their relationship intact, even for decades after the war. On Hilda's 100th birthday, Susan traveled north from South Africa, to Torquay in the United Kingdom, to celebrate with Hilda. Walter and Ethel also traveled to visit Susan while she was living in South Africa.

Nevertheless, though she continued this relationship with her Christadelphian foster mother, her Judaism was an integral part of who she was. Susan raised all of her children in an Orthodox Jewish home, sent them to a Jewish school, had them taught Hebrew, and gave each of them a bar or bat mitzvah. Their family celebrated the Jewish holidays together. For Susan, her Judaism and heritage was one of the most important things in life.

Michael Clapper, in writing about his mother's experiences, echoed her sentiments—though she was grateful to the Christadelphians, she was proud of her heritage, and that was the absolute most important thing to her. He wrote: "I am extremely grateful for the Christadelphians in taking in my mother. I feel that family is more important than anything. I thank G-d for the Christadelphians, but I feel proud to be Jewish."[31]

This pride in her heritage was something that Susan never lost, but at the same time, she could not forget the kindness shown to her by a small Christian community, the Christadelphians, in offering her safety when the world was crashing down around her.

---

[1] Detlef Mühlberger, *Hitler's Voice: The Völkischer Beobachter 1920-1923* (Bern: Peter Lang, 2004), 110.

[2] William Shirer, *The Rise and Fall of the Third Reich* (New York: Simon and Schuster, 1960), 117.

[3] Ibid., 118.

[4] Joseph Nyomarkay, *Charisma and Factionalism in the Nazi Party* (Minneapolis: University of Minnesota Press, 1967), 82.

[5] William Shirer, *The Rise and Fall of the Third Reich* (New York: Simon and Schuster, 1960), 117.

[6] Dorothy Thompson, "As to Werfel," *The New York Times* (New York, NY), January 24, 1926.

[7] Susan Clapper, *USC Shoah Foundation Institute Testimony of Susan Clapper*, USC Shoah Foundation Interview, November 23, 1995.

[8] Ibid.

[9] Ibid.

[10] Ibid.

[11] Ibid.

[12] "Buchenwald," *United States Holocaust Memorial Museum*, accessed April 27, 2017, http://www.ushmm.org/wlc/en/article.php?ModuleId=10005198.

[13] "Gedenkbuch - Opfer Der Verfolgung Der Juden Unter Der Nationalsozialistischen Gewaltherrschaft in Deutschland 1933-1945," *Das Bundesarchiv*, accessed April 27, 2017, http://www.bundesarchiv.de/gedenkbuch/de854544.

[14] Judith Tydor Baumel-Schwartz, *Never Look Back: The Jewish Refugee Children in Great Britain, 1938-1945* (West Lafayette: Purdue University Press, 2012), 2.

[15] Susan Clapper, *USC Shoah Foundation Institute Testimony of Susan Clapper*, USC Shoah Foundation Interview, November 23, 1995.

[16] "Ravensbrück," *United States Holocaust Memorial Museum*, accessed April 27, 2017, https://www.ushmm.org/wlc/en/article.php?ModuleId=10005199.

[17] "Gedenkbuch - Opfer Der Verfolgung Der Juden Unter Der Nationalsozialistischen Gewaltherrschaft in Deutschland 1933-1945," *Das Bundesarchiv*, accessed April 27, 2017, http://www.bundesarchiv.de/gedenkbuch/de854556.

[18] "Riga," *United States Holocaust Memorial Museum*, accessed April 27, 2017, http://www.ushmm.org/wlc/en/article.php?ModuleId=10005463.

[19] "Gedenkbuch - Opfer Der Verfolgung Der Juden Unter Der Nationalsozialistischen Gewaltherrschaft in Deutschland 1933-1945," *Das Bundesarchiv*, accessed April 27, 2017, http://www.bundesarchiv.de/gedenkbuch/de854552.

"Gedenkbuch - Opfer Der Verfolgung Der Juden Unter Der Nationalsozialistischen Gewaltherrschaft in Deutschland 1933-1945," *Das Bundesarchiv*, accessed April 27, 2017, http://www.bundesarchiv.de/gedenkbuch/de854559.

[20] "Riga," *United States Holocaust Memorial Museum*, accessed April 27, 2017, http://www.ushmm.org/wlc/en/article.php?ModuleId=10005463.

[21] "Gedenkbuch - Opfer Der Verfolgung Der Juden Unter Der Nationalsozialistischen Gewaltherrschaft in Deutschland 1933-1945," *Das Bundesarchiv*, accessed April 27, 2017, http://www.bundesarchiv.de/gedenkbuch/de854544.

[22] Susan Clapper, *USC Shoah Foundation Institute Testimony of Susan Clapper*, USC Shoah Foundation Interview, November 23, 1995.

[23] Michael Clapper, e-mail message to author, March 19, 2016.

[24] Susan Clapper, *USC Shoah Foundation Institute Testimony of Susan Clapper*, USC Shoah Foundation Interview, November 23, 1995.

[25] Ibid.

[26] Paul Ensell, recording brother of West Bromwich Christadelphian ecclesia to the author, March 13, 2016.

[27] Susan Clapper, *USC Shoah Foundation Institute Testimony of Susan Clapper*, USC Shoah Foundation Interview, November 23, 1995.

[28] W. H. Hayes, "Intelligence," *The Christadelphian*, July 1947, 124.

[29] Michael Clapper, e-mail message to author, March 9, 2016.

[30] Michael Clapper, e-mail message to author, March 10, 2016.

[31] Michael Clapper, e-mail message to author, March 21, 2016.

RUDI WEIL

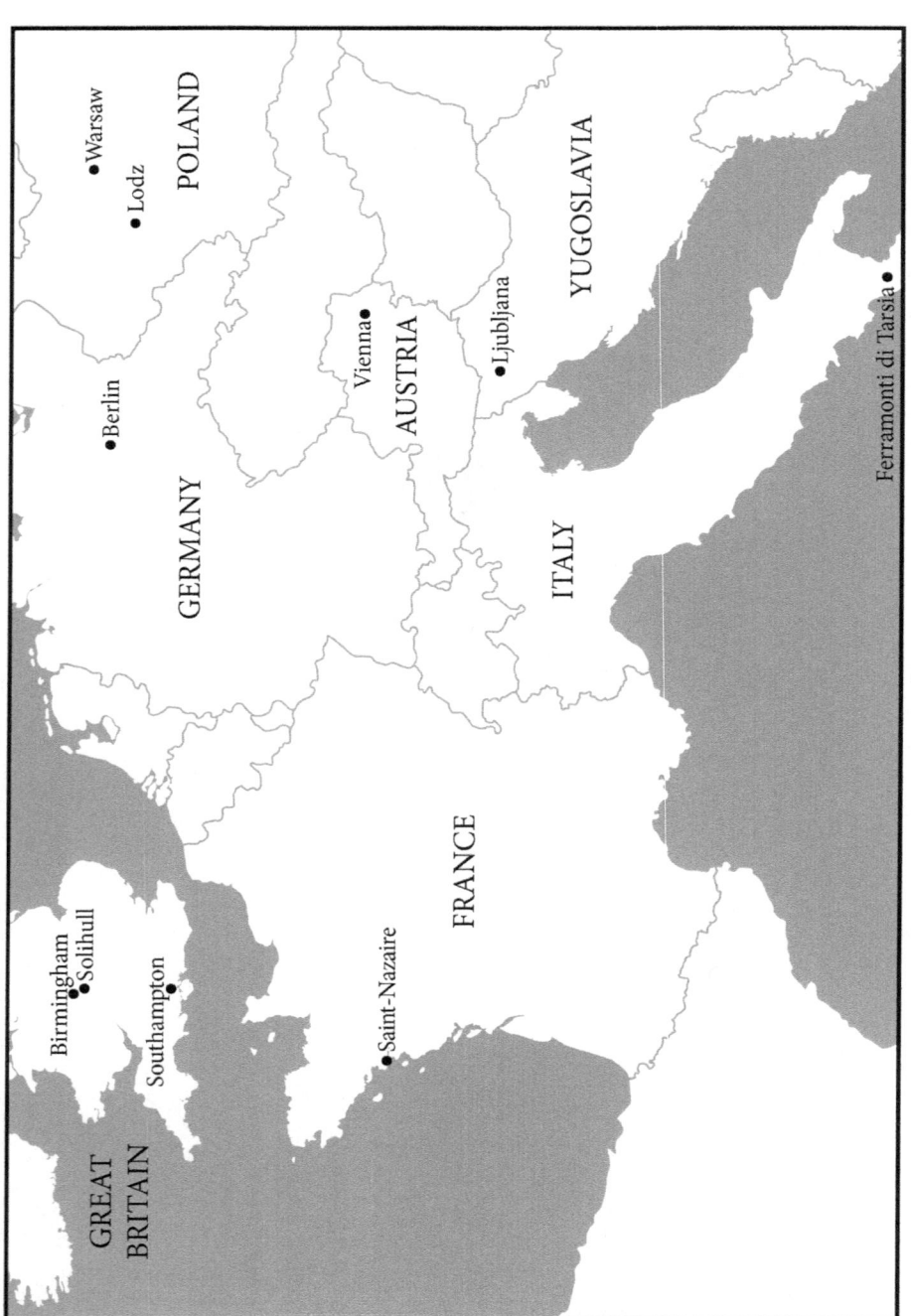

4

Rudi Weil

In April 1938, *The Christadelphian* magazine, quoting from the latest *Jewish Year Book*, noted the Jewish population of specific cities and nations of the world. New York had a Jewish population of 1.5 million. This was only slightly smaller than the entirety of Russia and Ukraine, which had 1.8 million—the highest number within the list. Vienna, the capital of Austria, had the third largest number mentioned in this list—but the difference between its Jewish population and that of New York was fairly massive. Vienna, as reported, had 300,000 Jews.[1]

Nonetheless, 300,000 was quite a large number. It was more than twice the number of Jews reported in Berlin (which had 142,000). It was 50 percent more than the Jewish population listed in the *Year Book* for the entire region of Palestine. Although this number could be contested—more modern sources record that Vienna had a Jewish population closer to 200,000,[2] it was still one of the largest Jewish populations of any European city. The only cities with more Jews were to be found in Poland—Warsaw had 352,000 Jews in 1931,[3] and Lodz had 233,000 before World War II began.[4]

The same month in which that article was published in *The Christadelphian*, Rudi Weil was born in Vienna—increasing the Jewish population there by one. In just 10 years, however, almost every synagogue in Vienna would be destroyed. In less than 20 years, two-thirds of that population would be expelled from the city, and over 65,000 people would be murdered in the camps.[5]

At the same time, in 1928, no one could have predicted precisely what was to come. The year was one in which the Nazis seemed relatively unimportant—Hitler's popularity, which had hinged on a dislike of the democratic Weimar government, had slowly been dropping. The German economy had been piecing itself back together, and for the first time since the Great War, unemployment had dropped below one million.[6] William Shirer wrote, "The lower middle classes, all the millions of shopkeepers and small-salaried folk on whom Hitler had to draw for his mass support, shared in the general prosperity."[7]

And thus, since its initial publication in 1925, the sales of *Mein Kampf* had been dropping steadily. In its first year of publication, the book sold 9,473 copies. In 1928, it sold only 3,015—less than one-third the number it had sold only three years prior.[8] Moreover, German elections were held in 1928— a year in which, as reported in Susan Clapper's chapter, the Nazis received a pitiful 810,000 votes out of the 31 million cast.[9] Laurence Rees, the well-known British historian, described the fortunes of the Nazi party at that time:

> Hitler—largely because he seemed no longer to be a threat—had seen his speaking ban gradually lifted across Germany, starting with Saxony in January 1927, then Bavaria in March 1927 and finally Prussia in September 1928. However, even though Hitler could speak openly, and even though Nazi membership stood at around 100,000 in 1928, there seemed little objective chance of a breakthrough for the party. The lowest point was the election of May 1928 when the Nazis polled just 2.6 per cent of the vote. More than 97 per

cent of the German electorate still rejected Adolf Hitler and his policies.[10]

And that was in Germany.

The same held true in Austria. Bruce Pauley, in his essay on the Austrian Nazi party before 1938 wrote the following:

> After reaching a early peak around August 1923, the Austrian Nazi party entered a long period of decline and stagnation that did not end until 1930. The Party's fate in these years and beyond was closely tied to that of its brother party in Germany.[11]

At the same time, the Austrian Nazi party had its own troubles. Not only did it suffer with the German party after the failed Beer Hall Putsch, but also, from 1925 to 1926, it was plagued with internal conflict over who should be considered its leader—Adolf Hitler, who led the German Nazis, or Karl Schultz,[12] who advocated a specifically Austrian brand of Nazism and an independent Austria. By 1928, these two Nazi parties were extremely small in Austria, with the former boasting less than 5,000 members and the latter only 6,300.[13]

Thus, for the hundreds of thousands of Jews who lived in Vienna in 1928—three of whom made up the Weil family—the Nazis would not have presented much of a concern. They undeniably held antisemitic views, but so did so many other Austrian political parties.[14]

In fact, life was good. Vienna was a cultured city and had been the capital of the Habsburg dynasty for centuries. The Jewish community there was well studied and well integrated—and a number of prominent Jewish names are connected in some way to the city. It was at the University of Vienna that Theodor Herzl, the father of Zionism, studied.[15] It was in Vienna that

that Sigmund Freud, the father of psychoanalysis, did much of his work.[16] And it was from Vienna that composers such as Gustav Mahler and Arnold Schoenberg hailed.[17]

With such a large Jewish population, Vienna was also home to a number of synagogues. There were two main temples—the Vienna Synagogue and the Leopoldstädter Tempel (both of which were built in the 1800s)—and another 40 smaller synagogues located throughout the city. In 1895, the first-ever Jewish museum was founded.[18]

The Jewish population in Vienna flourished. From the mid-1800s when it numbered approximately 6,000 to 1900 when it numbered approximately 150,000 and to 1928 when it was multiple hundreds of thousands, the Viennese Jewish community was vibrant and thriving.

Within 10 years, all that would change. Freud and Schoenberg, both alive during the 1930s, were forced to flee the Nazis. Freud left Austria for Great Britain.[19] Schoenberg took flight to the United States.[20]

And every synagogue save one was destroyed.

Early Life

The Weil family witnessed the destruction of this community, and indeed suffered through it. But for the time being, with the birth of their one and only child, the couple was happy.

Rudi Weil was born on April 24, 1928. His father's name was Hugo, and Hugo (b. February 17, 1887) had recently turned 41. Aranka Weil, his mother (b. August 18, 1898), was about to turn 30. Rudi lived with both of his parents until August 1939—at which point he was forced to flee the country.

But for 11 years, Rudi lived with his parents in Vienna.

Vienna is a huge city, and since 1850, it has been divided into 23 districts—with the first district being the medieval core of the city, the Innere Stadt, and the other districts numbering and radiating from this central one.[21] Oftentimes, rather than saying the name of the district, many simply refer to the districts by their numbers. Thus, Rudi's address was Durergasse 23, Vienna VI, Austria—up until 1938 and the *Anschluss*, when "Austria" became "Germany." The "VI" in his address stood for the sixth district, Mariahilf, part of the city's inner suburbs and close to the downtown. It is a small district—only about 500 yards wide for much of its length, but filled with shops.[22] Mariahilfer Strasse, a major commercial street, runs along the northern end of the district.

The main synagogue of Mariahilf was located at Schmalzhofgasse 3 and was only half a mile from the Weils' home. It was an 11-minute walk. The synagogue itself was a large and beautiful building. It had space for 322 men and 236 women along with a platform for the choir and an organ. Its architecture was neo-gothic, specifically chosen as an imitation of many of the churches of Vienna—with the intention of showing reconciliation between Judaism and Christianity. The synagogue was built in 1883 and 1884. It stood for less than 50 years.[23]

Hugo Weil was a businessman who, according to Fay Weil, Rudi's wife, owned a coverall factory.[24] His parents, Rudolf and Hermine Weil, were also both residents of Vienna. Rudolf passed away in 1925,[25] but Hermine lived for another 11 years, passing away in 1936.[26] Most likely she lived with Hugo, who was her only child, from the time of her husband's death until her own. With the Jewish custom of naming children after deceased relatives,[27] it is almost certain that Hugo named Rudi after Rudolf, and thus, for much of Rudi's life growing up, his

Rudi and Aranka Weil.

grandparents played a part—due to his grandmother's physical presence and his own name.

During these years, Rudi found great enjoyment in playing the piano—which he excelled at—and taken all together, his childhood was a happy time.[28]

Much of that began to change, however, shortly before Rudi turned 10.

Anschluss

The *Anschluss* was the German annexation of Austria—much of whose population was ethnically German and thus supported the union.[29] On March 12, 1938, German troops marched into Austria and proclaimed it part of the German Reich. On that day, persecution was unleashed upon the Jews and anyone who opposed the Nazis. The United States Holocaust Memorial Museum describes this violence:

> Widespread antisemitic actions and political violence followed quickly on the heels of the *Anschluss*. Austria's leading politicians were imprisoned, and anyone opposing the Nazi rule was subject to arrest, torture, and death. Jews particularly were attacked and humiliated on the streets. The Gestapo, along with Austrian Nazis and sympathizers, looted Jewish belongings, seized Jewish businesses, and arrested those who refused to surrender their property. Furthermore, anti-Jewish legislation was in place almost immediately, forcing Jews from their positions, and essentially expelling them from the country's economic, social, and cultural life.[30]

This was the beginning. For Hugo, a Jewish business owner, life would have been significantly harder, as it is likely that his business was targeted. For Rudi, who attended public school in Vienna, life was no longer that of a carefree 10-year-old. He was forced to sit in the back of the room, with his arms folded for hours—to keep him from following along with the class.[31] Eventually, many Jewish students were removed from public school entirely and forced to attend a separate institution with other Jewish children.[32]

Kristallnacht

Only seven months later, on November 9–10, *Kristallnacht* occurred—completely shattering the life Rudi had once known. Fay Weil recalls Rudi's telling her of the destruction of his father's factory: "They burned it down completely."[33] And it didn't stop there. The angry mobs also broke into the Weil home and smashed Rudi's piano.[34]

The synagogue had the same fate as Hugo's factory. On the morning of November 10, the 89th SS division targeted Schmalzhofgasse 3 for destruction—yet, according to the notes of Obersturmfuehrer Riegler, who commanded the 89th division, when they arrived at the synagogue, it was already in flames. Apparently the synagogue's Viennese neighbors decided to set it on fire before the SS arrived—to seize the opportunity to plunder the synagogue's lavish interior completely unimpeded. That night, the synagogue's rabbi, Dr. Jakob Drobinsky, committed suicide.[35]

It was most likely at this point Hugo and Aranka realized that escape from Austria—both for themselves and for their only son—was essential to survival. Thus all three set out to escape.

England

Horace and Lily Ford were a young couple. In fact, at this point, only Lily had been baptized as a Christadelphian, and that had occurred fairly recently. Her baptism took place in July 1938.[36] Horace Ford was not baptized until April 1940, about seven months after Rudi's arrival.[37] Thus, for the majority of Rudi's time with the Fords, both Horace and Lily were Christadelphians, but not at the very beginning.

Horace and Lily lived in Birmingham, England, in an area now no longer part of the city of Birmingham, and instead called Solihull. At the time, they had no children, but their home was about to be filled with childish energy because Rudi was just 11 years old. In February 1944, while Rudi was still living with them, they had their own son, Stephen.

It is not known how the Weil family came into contact with the Ford family—most likely through a refugee committee in Vienna that worked with the Christadelphian refugee committee in Rugby that was headed by Alan Overton. The contact and the agreement was made just in time. On August 23, 1939, just a little over a week before Germany invaded Poland, and thus began World War II, Aranka Weil wrote the following letter to Mrs. Ford:

> Vienna, August 23rd, 1939
>
> Aranka Weil,
> Durergasse 23.
> Vienna VI
> Germany (Ostmark)
>
> Mrs. Ford
> 60 Shalford Road,
> Near Clay Lane,
> South Yardley,
> Birmingham.
>
> Dear Madam,

I was so glad to hear by the intervention of Mrs. Phillips, that you are so benevolent to care for my son and I am glad now to inform you that I and my son will arrive there in about a fortnight. Rudi, my little sunny boy is jumping for happiness to come there, he is so lovely and diligent, Madam, that you will have pleasure with him. Excuse me, dear Madam, that it is only today that I am writing you, I had to pass so many troubles that I could not do it earlier. Please accept my best thanks for blessings for your kindness.

Hoping to be very soon there, I beg to remain with best thanks,
Yours very obliged.
Aranka Weil[38]

On August 23, Rudi was due to arrive in Birmingham "in about a fortnight," or around *September 6*. But war was declared on Germany by Britain on *September 3*. Factoring in a few days for travel, it would seem most likely that Rudi left Germany for England just as England was declaring war on Germany. Though immigration from Germany to England was still possible during wartime,[39] it would appear as though at this particular time, for some,[40] the borders were shut down. For the 250 children on the September 1, 1939, Kindertransport organized by Nicholas Winton, the man who brought 669 Czech children to safety in Great Britain, their journey to the United Kingdom never began. With the German invasion of Poland, the borders were closed, and their train never left. As far as is known, *all* 250 children were deported to the camps, where they were murdered.[41]

Surely the timing of Rudy's flight would have made an already tense journey even more suspenseful. Would his immigration suddenly be stopped? Would he be forced to turn around? The door was open to freedom—and everything looked as though it was going to work—but suddenly, with war declared, it would have appeared as though the door could slam shut at any time.

However, perhaps making the journey a little less nerve-wracking, it appears as though Rudi's trip from Germany to England was not part of the Kindertransport—where the children traveled unaccompanied. Instead, in their attempts to secure an escape for all three of their family members, both Rudi *and* Aranka were able to find respite in England. They traveled together: "I am glad now to inform you that I and my son will arrive there in about a fortnight." They did not live together—it was extraordinary enough that a

```
Aranka Weil,                                    Vienna, August 23rd, 1939.
    ViennaVI.
Dürergasse 23.
Germany ( Ostmark )


            Mrs. Ford,
            60 Shelford Road,
            Near Clay Lane,
            South Yardley,
            Birmingham.

            Dear Madam,
                    I was so glad to hear by the intervention of
            Mrs. Phillips, that you are so benevolent to care for my
            son and I am glad now to inform you that I and my son
            will arrive there in about a fortnight. Rudi, my little
            sunny boy is jumping for happiness to come there, he is
            so lovely and diligent, Madam, that you will have pleasure
            with him. Excuse me, dear Madam, that it is only today
            that I am writing you, I had to pass so many troubles
            that I could not do it earlier. Please accept my best
            thanks and blessings for your kindness.
                    Hoping to be very soon there, I beg to remain
            with best thanks,
                                        Yours very obliged.
                                          Aranka Weil
                                        Aranka Weil,
```

Aranka's letter to Mrs. Ford, shortly before she and Rudi left Germany.

home was found for Rudi and that Aranka was able to find employment as a domestic. This was a typical situation—the children who came to Great Britain as refugees did not live with their parents; the only work permitted to the parents (and work was essential to survive) was that of a live-in servant. Often the employer was not prepared to take both the employee *and* any of his or her children.[42] Thus Aranka lived and worked for one family while Rudi lived with the Fords. Aranka's address was likely 62 Shirley Road,[43] whereas the Fords lived at 60 Shalferd Road. The two homes were only 1.4 miles apart—so fortunately, although they lived apart, they were not *far* apart, and one of the pictures from this period shows that they at least were able to see one another.

Thus, Aranka and Rudi narrowly escaped Germany.

Hugo, however, had a completely different experience.

Hugo's Journey

Although Aranka was able to secure work in England, the same was not true for Hugo. As his wife and his only child departed the mainland, war was unleashed by Germany. Hugo did do all that he could to escape, but it seemed that escape was simply impossible.

Though the Weils lived in Vienna, it appears as though Hugo somehow made his way from Vienna to Saint-Nazaire—a town on the western sea coast of France and perhaps the closest that he could get himself to the United Kingdom at the time. It was a journey of 1,000 miles—in which Hugo crossed nearly the entire breadth of Austria, Germany, and France.

This is where Hugo found himself in June 1940, and at that time, he wrote a postcard to his wife, which was curiously sent to the *Fords' home*:

St. Nazaire
5th June.

My dear Aranka,

I hope you have received my letter of 28th (or 29th) May.

I am very well, my health is better than ever before. You see I am in a very nice region.

I have here a very good [word is unclear] and I am happy to tell you that I am very content with my situation. You can write to me to the address I have communicated to you in my letter or to [word is unclear], but the mail is very long.

A lot of kisses to you and Rudy[44]
Your Hu[45]

At this point, it had been 10 months since Hugo had seen either Aranka or Rudi, and Rudi had recently turned 12. Furthermore, the German invasion of France had begun just one month earlier, on May 10, 1940. Hugo's postcard was written in the midst of this invasion. Less than three weeks later, on June 22, France signed an armistice with Germany. Under the terms of the armistice, Germany occupied the northern and western portion of France, whereas the southern and eastern portions remained unoccupied but governed by the collaborationist Vichy regime.[46] Saint-Nazaire was in the German-occupied portion of France.

It is likely because of this invasion and takeover that Hugo fled France.

The front of the postcard that Hugo sent from St. Nazaire, 1940.

Hugo's next known location is Ljubljana, in present day Slovenia (but at that time part of the Kingdom of Yugoslavia).[47] From Saint-Nazaire, it was again a journey of over 1,000 miles—and a journey that brought him within 40 miles of the southern Austrian border. He was again close to where he had started.

It is unknown why Hugo chose to go to Ljubljana, especially after having initially fled so far west. But at the time, a number of Jewish refugees were attempting to flee southeast to Palestine via any country that appeared to offer a safe route,[48] so it is possible that Hugo was attempting to find a way to get to the Holy Land. Or perhaps Hugo simply chose the Yugoslavian city because Yugoslavia was not yet controlled by the Axis powers. Regardless of why he chose Ljubljana, it was here that Hugo found himself when the city came under Italy's control in April 1941.[49]

During this Italian occupation, the Jews in Ljubljana were deported. Gregor Kranjc, in his essay on "Jews, Slovenes, and the Memory of the Holocaust," described the situation as follows:

> In the fall of 1941, most of the established Jewish families in Ljubljana . . . were deported to camps in northern Italy. In the same period, 134 Jewish refugees from various countries in Eastern Europe and Yugoslavia were deported from Ljubljana to the concentration camp in Ferramonti di Tarsia in southern Italy.[50]

Hugo evaded capture for another few months—but he was arrested in 1942. On May 15, 1942, he too was deported to southern Italy and interned in the Ferramonti di Tarsia concentration camp.[51]

Out of the 15 concentration camps set up by Mussolini, Ferramonti was the largest—from its establishment in 1940 to its close in 1943, the camp held 3,800 Jews.[52] Susan Zucotti describes the situation:

> Jewish men and women were held for weeks in filthy city prisons before being marched in handcuffs to the trains that carried them to such wretched camps as Ferramonti Tarsia in the province of Cosenza, and Campagna in the province of Salerno. There they lived in flimsy huts without electricity, heat, or running water until they could construct better facilities for themselves. Food was scarce, medicine almost nonexistent, and malaria and typhus endemic. And the population of internees continued to swell.[53]

Moreover,

Life in Ferramonti di Tarsia.

Rudi Weil

Top: Life in Ferramonti di Tarsia.
Bottom: Hugo's postcard from Ferramonti di Tarsia, 1943.

> Scarcities and deprivation at Ferramonti were indeed grave, for internees, except for a small daily bread ration, were not fed free of charge. Instead, they were given small subsidies with which to buy food, clothing, and medicine wherever they could. By mid-1942, when a cooked meal prepared in a camp kitchen cost 6 or 7 lire, men at Ferramonti received 8 lire a day, women 4, and children 3. . . . Most families were obliged to buy their own food from local peasants and prepare their scanty meals themselves. Often there was nothing to buy.[54]

Yet, the situation for the Jews in Ferramonti was different from what might be initially imagined for those in a concentration camp during World War II. Although the internees suffered extreme deprivation, the camp was not as brutal as those in Germany or German-occupied Poland. Yad Vashem's Shoah Resource Center explains as follows:

> Ferramonti was never a concentration camp like those that the Nazis ran: the relationship between the prisoners and camp staff was rather peaceful, the prisoners were not tortured or executed, and they were allowed to receive packages of food, visit sick relatives and participate in cultural activities.[55]

In fact, four weddings actually took place at the camp.[56] And, when describing Hugo's experience in Ferramonti, Fay Weil related, "Rudi's father was in a concentration camp in Italy and was treated very well"[57]—in which she likely meant that he was treated well compared with how he would have been in other camps. Gregor Kranjc, again writing about the Jews of Ljubljana, stated, "By virtue of their deportation to Italy, a larger number of these Jews would survive the Holocaust."[58]

Such was the case for Hugo Weil. Though he was 55 years old when he entered an Axis-controlled concentration camp, he was able to endure the conditions of the camp until its closing in September 1943. During that time, one year after his arrival in Ferramonti, in May 1943, Hugo wrote a postcard from Ferramonti to Horace and Lily Ford. Hugo had not seen his wife and his child for three and a half years, nor had he heard from them in a long while:

Ferramonti 29 V 43

Dear Mr. Ford and Mrs. Ford!

I am the father of Rudi and I use the opportunity to beg you to accept my best thanks for all the good you have done him and his mother. Our good God may pay you all love. I am very anxious because I have not had any letter for so long time from my dear family, and therefore I beg you to have the goodness to answer me why they have not written to me. Please let me know truly and exactly if they are both in good health.

With many thanks in advance, I hope to receive best information and remain
Yours very faithfully
Hugo Weil[59]

It is not known whether Hugo received a response. But indeed, his wife and his son *were* still alive—and one day would see him again.

The British liberated Ferramonti on September 14, 1943.[60]

At that point, Hugo was a Jewish refugee in Italy. He remained there for another 11 months, and then, in August 1944, he became part of a special program undertaken by the United

States. In the only attempt that the United States made to create a camp for refugees on American soil during the Holocaust, 982 refugees from Europe were brought to Fort Ontario in New York. Hugo Weil was one of them—but he was still not free. And many more years would pass before he would set eyes on his wife and his son.

Though he was brought to the United States, life in Fort Ontario was again the life of an internee. David Wyman, in his history of the United States and the Holocaust, describes the conditions there:

> The camp was located on the shore of Lake Ontario, thirty-five miles northwest of Syracuse. Conditions were livable, but not conductive to healthy family life; and three-fourths of the refugees belonged to family units. Meals were eaten in mess halls. Families lived in barracks buildings that had been partitioned into small apartments. The apartments had only the barest

Ariel view of Fort Ontario, showing the barracks that would become the refugees' living quarters, 1943.

Refugees having their paperwork checked at Fort Ontario, 1944.

furnishings and lacked individual bathroom facilities. More important, the thin walls allowed almost no privacy. Friction among neighbors was chronic.

Soon after the shelter opened, Army intelligence officials screened the refugees for security purposes. After that, they were allowed to leave the camp and go into the town of Oswego for up to six hours at a time, bur they had to be back by midnight. No one could travel beyond Oswego, except for essential hospitalization. Nor could anyone take employment outside the camp. Visitors could come into the shelter, but not even close relatives could stay overnight.

When the refugees agreed to come to Fort Ontario, it was conveyed to them that they would be repatriated at the end of the war. At the same time, it was also required that they *stay within the fort* the entire time they lived in the United

States. However, this stipulation was not expressed to them until sometime after they arrived.[61] Again, David Wyman writes:

> Through the last months of 1944, the misunderstanding about confinement to Fort Ontario led to increasing resentment within the camp. By January 1945, that factor, combined with several others, had depressed morale to the point where one suicide had occurred and many internees were near mental breakdown.

The refugees continued to live at Fort Ontario, even after the war ended. In December 1945, President Truman opened the United States immigration quotas to the Fort Ontario refugees, calling it "inhumane and wasteful" to force them to return to Europe. The refugees were able to stay in the United States.[62]

From this point on, Hugo Weil settled and stayed in Philadelphia, Pennsylvania. He had survived the Holocaust.

In the meantime, Aranka and Rudi were still living in England—and Hugo would not see his wife or his son until February 1948.

Life with the Fords

When Rudi lived with the Fords, he became part of the family. The Fords had no children, so he was treated as their son. Fay recalled, "They took care of him very, very well."[63] At one point, the bond between the three of them was such that the possibility of Rudi's being adopted by the Fords was raised. But Rudi still had his own family, so this was never considered seriously. In another example of their strong connection, Rudi told Fay about how he, Horace, and Lily, and eventually Stephen after 1944, would huddle under the stone slab in the pantry when the air raid sirens went off—and they would stay there, together, as a family, comforted by one another's presence.

And just as with so many of the children who lived with Christadelphian families, Rudi attended the ecclesial meetings with the Fords. Sunday school, however, actually came to him—with a number of local children coming to the Fords' home on Sundays for "a very active Sunday school."[64]

At some point, perhaps after the end of the war, it became possible for Rudi to again join his mother. By 1948, when they left England for the United States, they had both been living at 62 Shirley Road.[65]

Aranka Weil holding Stephen Ford.

Back row from left to right: Rudi Weil and Horace Ford. Middle row from left to right: Stephen Ford, held by Aranka Weil, and Lily Ford.

After the War

On February 4, 1948, Aranka and Rudi Weil boarded the Queen Elizabeth in Southampton. They were bound for New York. Aranka was now 49, and Rudi was 19—and about to turn 20 in April. Hugo had missed all but three months of his son's life as a teenager. Thirteen days later, Hugo would have his 61st birthday. The last time he had seen either his wife or his son, Hugo had been in his early 50s.

The joyful meeting likely took place that February. From there, the reunited Weil family settled in Philadelphia. And that November, Aranka and Rudi wrote to the Fords. Although they now lived in different countries and the opportunity existed for the families to forget one another, they remained in contact:

> 14/11/48
>
> 6116 North Broad St.
> Philadelphia 41/Pa
> U.S.A.
>
> My dear All.
> Many thanks for your letters, I can't tell you how glad I was with them.
>
> I am sorry that I could not write earlier but I am sure you can understand it, I have so much work to do, but we are thinking a lot about you all.
>
> We have arrived in Philadelphia very good. The journey was lovely, not very stormy but everybody was ill the first two days of course Rudi and I too. The food was very fine and plenty on the boat. . . . I am glad the traveling is over and I am at last at home. Everything

was going in <u>perfect order</u> [emphasis in original] my luggage has also arrived very safe.

Of course my husband had met us in New York, you can imagine our excitement.

Our home here is very nice, the flat is small very bright and very warm. My husband, his relation and the friends have done all the best with the furniture and the other things so I have a real lovely home. I can't believe after so many years from nothing and from the Shirley Rd to get in such [a] home.

I hope that I can hear from you very soon and that everything in the family is allright.

Hugo, Rudi, and Aranka Weil, reunited in Philadelphia.

You can not worry about the reg. letter for Rudi. It was very good that you have opened this letter. Of course you wont send the money. Please buy my sweetheart [Stephen] to his birthday something. Any way our very hearty congratulation to his birthday.

Well my dear All I will now close this letter, God bless you all and thousand thanks for everything.

Give my love to all.
Always your very loving

Aranka & Rudi
xxxxxxxxxx

Many thanks for your love to my family and kind regards
Hugo Weil[66]

As the years went by, things changed. Hugo passed away in November 1950, just two years after being reunited with his wife and son, and was buried in the Montefiore cemetery in Philadelphia. Nine years later, in 1959, Aranka passed away and was buried in the same cemetery. Hugo was 63 years old and Aranka was 60.[67]

And Rudi also made a change—marrying an American named Fay Miller on September 2, 1962.

Nevertheless, though life changed, the connection between Rudi and the Fords remained. In 1965, approximately 20 years after he had lived with them, Rudi wrote the following letter to the Fords:

Dear Lily, Horace, and Stephen: 1/4/65

Sorry for the delay but as you know I am the world's worst letter writer. We have received your card from sunny Spain and thank you very much for it. We had intended to send you a merry Christmas and happy new year card but the picture we intended to enclose did not come back in time. So we wish you all a belated merry Christmas and a very happy new year, and hope that this letter finds you in the best of good health and in high spirits.

We have a new Polaroid camera have you heard of that. This camera makes black & white pictures in 10 seconds and colour in 1 minute.

The only problem is that it takes 1 1/2 months to get copies made as you can see.

There is nothing new here, life here is very hectic.

Again we wish the very best of everything to all of you. We also hope to hear from you soon if that's not asking too much. (I should talk)

Love
Rudi and Fay.[68]

Conclusion

Though Rudi and Horace and Lily eventually lost contact, Rudi did not forget what the two had done for him and how he had been treated as part of their family. Throughout his marriage to Fay, he related stories to her and conveyed the love that he felt for the Fords.

In 2003, Rudi passed away suddenly.

Fay and Rudi Weil.

Though she had never met the Fords herself, Fay did not forget the stories—nor did Stephen Ford, Horace and Lily's son, forget the young man who had been part of his family.

Though the contact dissipated, the memories, the letters, and the pictures were not erased. And through the research for this project, that bond that had slowly broken down over the years was brought back together. For the first time in decades, on May 31, 2016, the Ford family and the Weil family spoke on the phone. Now the two families are again in regular contact.

In 1939, Hugo and Aranka Weil were desperately searching for a family to sponsor their 11-year-old boy to flee to safety from the Nazis. The family had experienced the terrors of the *Anschluss* and *Kristallnacht*. And that sponsor—that family that would give of themselves without having ever met them—was found in the Fords, Christadelphians who believed in the promises to Abraham, and because of their beliefs in that promise, were going to do everything they could to bring a terrified Jewish boy out of Hitler's Third Reich.

---

[1] C. A. Ladson, "The Jews and Zionism," *The Christadelphian*, April 1938, 177.

[2] "Vienna," *United States Holocaust Memorial Museum*, accessed March 22, 2017, https://www.ushmm.org/wlc/en/article.php?ModuleId=10005452.

3 "Warsaw," *YIVO Institute for Jewish Research*, accessed March 22, 2017, http://www.yivoencyclopedia.org/article.aspx/Warsaw.

4 "Virtual Jewish World: Lodz, Poland," *Jewish Virtual Library*, accessed March 22, 2017, http://www.jewishvirtuallibrary.org/lodz-poland-jewish-history-tour.

5 Phyllis Steinberg, "Vienna Welcomes Jews to Its Community," *Jewish Journal*, October 10, 2014, http://boston.forward.com/articles/185696/vienna-welcomes-jews-to-its-community/.

6 William Shirer, *The Rise and Fall of the Third Reich* (New York: Simon and Schuster, 1960), 117.

7 Ibid.

8 Ibid, 80-81.

9 Ibid, 118.

10 Laurence Rees, *Hitler's Charisma: Leading Millions into the Abyss* (New York: Vintage Books, 2014), 54.

11 Bruce Pauley, "The Austrian Nazi Party before 1938," in *Conquering the Past: Austrian Nazism Yesterday and Today*, ed. F. Parkinson (Detroit: Wayne State University Press, 1989), 37.

12 Ibid.

13 Daniel Siemens, *The Making of a Nazi Hero: The Murder and Myth of Horst Wessel*, trans. David Burnett (London: I. B. Tauris, 2013), 45.

14 Ibid, 36.

15 "Vienna," *United States Holocaust Memorial Museum*, accessed March 22, 2017, https://www.ushmm.org/wlc/en/article.php?ModuleId=10005452.

[16] "Virtual Jewish World: Vienna, Austria," *Jewish Virtual Library,* accessed March 22, 2017, http://www.jewishvirtuallibrary.org/vienna-austria-jewish-history-tour.

[17] Ibid.

[18] Ibid.

[19] Mary Elizabeth Brown, "Laura Fermi (1907–1977): Illustrious Immigrants," in *The Making of Modern Immigration: An Encyclopedia of People and Ideas,* ed. Patrick J. Hayes (Santa Barbara: ABC-CLIO, 2012), 223.

[20] Sabine Feisst, *Schoenberg's New World: The American Years* (Oxford: Oxford University Press, 2011), lxi.

[21] Sarah Woods, *National Geographic Traveler: Vienna* (Washington, D. C.: National Geographic, 2012), v.

[22] Ibid, 200.

[23] "Schmalzhofgasse 3 (Synagogue association) - 6th district Mariahilf / Neubau," *Synagogue Memorial "Beit Ashkenaz,"* accessed March 23, 2017, http://www.austriansynagogues.com/index.php/archive?sid=119:schmalzhofgasse-3-synagogue-association-6th-district-mariahilf-neubau.

24 Fay Weil in discussion with the author, May 26, 2016.

25 "Rudolf Weil," *Geni,* accessed March 23, 2017, https://www.geni.com/people/Rudolf-Weil/6000000010722093906.

26 "Hermine Weil," *Geni,* accessed March 23, 2017, https://www.geni.com/people/Hermine-Weil/6000000010722407518?through=6000000010722093906.

27 "The Laws of Jewish Names," *Chabad.org,* accessed March 23, 2017, http://www.chabad.org/library/article_cdo/aid/1158837/jewish/The-Laws-of-Jewish-Names.htm

28 Stephen Ford, e-mail message to author, November 2, 2016.

29 "Anschluss," *United States Holocaust Memorial Museum,* accessed March 23, 2017, https://www.ushmm.org/research/research-in-collections/search-the-collections/bibliography/anschluss.

30 Ibid.

31 Stephen Ford, e-mail message to author, November 2, 2016.

32 Albert Lichtblau, "Austria," in *The Greater German Reich and the Jews: Nazi Persecution Policies in the Annexed Territories 1935–1945,* ed. Wolf Gruner and Jörg Osterloh, trans. Bernard Heise (New York: Berghahn, 2015), 54.

33 Fay Weil in discussion with the author, May 26, 2016.

34 Ibid.

35 "Schmalzhofgasse 3 (Synagogue association) - 6th district Mariahilf / Neubau," Synagogue Memorial "Beit Ashkenaz," accessed March 23, 2017, http://www.austriansynagogues.com/index.php/archive?sid=119:schmalzhofgasse-3-synagogue-association-6th-district-mariahilf-neubau.

36 L. G. Hathaway, "Intelligence," *The Christadelphian*, September 1938, 424.

37 L. G. Hathaway, "Intelligence," *The Christadelphian*, June 1940, 288.

38 Aranka Weil, letter to Lily Ford, August 23, 1939. Copy of letter in possession of the author.

39 Hagit Lavsky, *The Creation of the German-Jewish Diaspora: Interwar German-Jewish Immigration to Palestine, the USA, and England,* (Berlin and Jerusalem: De Gruyter and Magnes, 2017) 76-77.

40 There was a Kindertransport able to leave Germany on September 1, 1939, so the borders were not closed to *everyone*. "Kindertransport, 1938–1940," *United States Holocaust Memorial Museum,* accessed March 23, 2017, https://www.ushmm.org/wlc/en/article.php?ModuleId=10005260.

41 Muriel Emmanuel and Vera Gissing, *Nicholas Winton and the Rescued Generation,* (London: Vallentine Mitchell, 2002), 125.

42 Ruth Barnett, "Therapeutic Aspects of Working Through the Trauma of the Kindertransport Experience," in *The Kindertransport to Britain 1938/1939: New Perspectives,* ed. Andrea Hammel and Bea Lewkowicz (Amsterdam: Rodopi, 2012) 162.

43 Her address in 1948, according to the ship manifest when she left England for New York. Ship manifest of the *RMS Queen Elizabeth,* departing Southampton for New York, February 4, 1948.

44 All other documentation spells "Rudi" with an "i," so this instance appears to be an outlier.

45 Hugo Weil, letter to the Aranka Weil, June 5, 1940. Copy of letter in possession of the author.

46 "France," *United States Holocaust Memorial Museum,* accessed March 24, 2017, https://www.ushmm.org/wlc/en/article.php?ModuleId=10005429.

47 Simona Celiberti, archivist at Ferrimonti Memorial Museum, e-mail message to author, March 20, 2017.

48 Ibid, March 22, 2017.

49 "Yugoslavia," *United States Holocaust Memorial Museum,* accessed March 24, 2017, https://www.ushmm.org/wlc/en/article.php?ModuleId=10007886.

50 Gregor Joseph Kranjc, "On the Periphery - Jews, Slovenes, and the Memory of the Holocaust," in *Bringing the Dark Past to Light: The Reception of the Holocaust in Postcommunist Europe,* ed. John-Paul Himka and Joanna Beata Michlic (Lincoln: University of Nebraska Press, 2013), 599.

[51] "Ebrei stranieri internati in Italia durante il periodo bellico," *Anna Pizzuti,* accessed March 24, 2017, http://www.annapizzuti.it/database/ricerca.php?a=view&recid=8840.

[52] "Ferramonti di Tarsia," *Yad Vashem,* accessed March 24, 2017, http://www.yadvashem.org/odot_pdf/Microsoft%20Word%20-%205847.pdf.

[53] Susan Zucotti, *Under His Very Windows* (New Haven: Yale University Press, 2000), 83.

[54] Ibid, 87.

[55] "Ferramonti di Tarsia," *Yad Vashem,* accessed March 24, 2017, http://www.yadvashem.org/odot_pdf/Microsoft%20Word%20-%205847.pdf.

[56] Ibid.

[57] Fay Weil's caretaker, e-mail message on behalf of Fay Weil to the author, May 26, 2016.

[58] Gregor Joseph Kranjc, "On the Periphery - Jews, Slovenes, and the Memory of the Holocaust," in *Bringing the Dark Past to Light: The Reception of the Holocaust in Postcommunist Europe,* ed. John-Paul Himka and Joanna Beata Michlic (Lincoln: University of Nebraska Press, 2013), 599.

[59] Hugo Weil, letter to the Fords, May 29, 1943. Copy of letter in possession of the author.

[60] "Life in Ferramonti," *Italy and the Holocaust Foundation,* accessed March 24, 2017, http://www.italyandtheholocaust.org/places-life-in-Life-In-Ferramonti-2.aspx.

[61] David Wyman, *The Abandonment of the Jews* (New York: Pantheon, 1984), 269.

[62] Ibid, 274.

[63] Fay Weil in discussion with the author, May 26, 2016.

[64] Stephen Ford, e-mail message to author, March 27, 2017.

[65] Ship manifest of the *RMS Queen Elizabeth,* departing Southampton for New York, February 4, 1948.

[66] The Weil Family, letter to the Fords, November 14, 1948. Copy of letter in possession of the author.

[67] "Search Burial Records," *Montefiore Cemetery Co.,* accessed April 28, 2017, http://www.montefiore.us/search.asp?pname=W.

[68] Rudi and Fay Weil, letter to the Fords, January 4, 1965. Copy of letter in possession of the author.

INGE BEACHAM

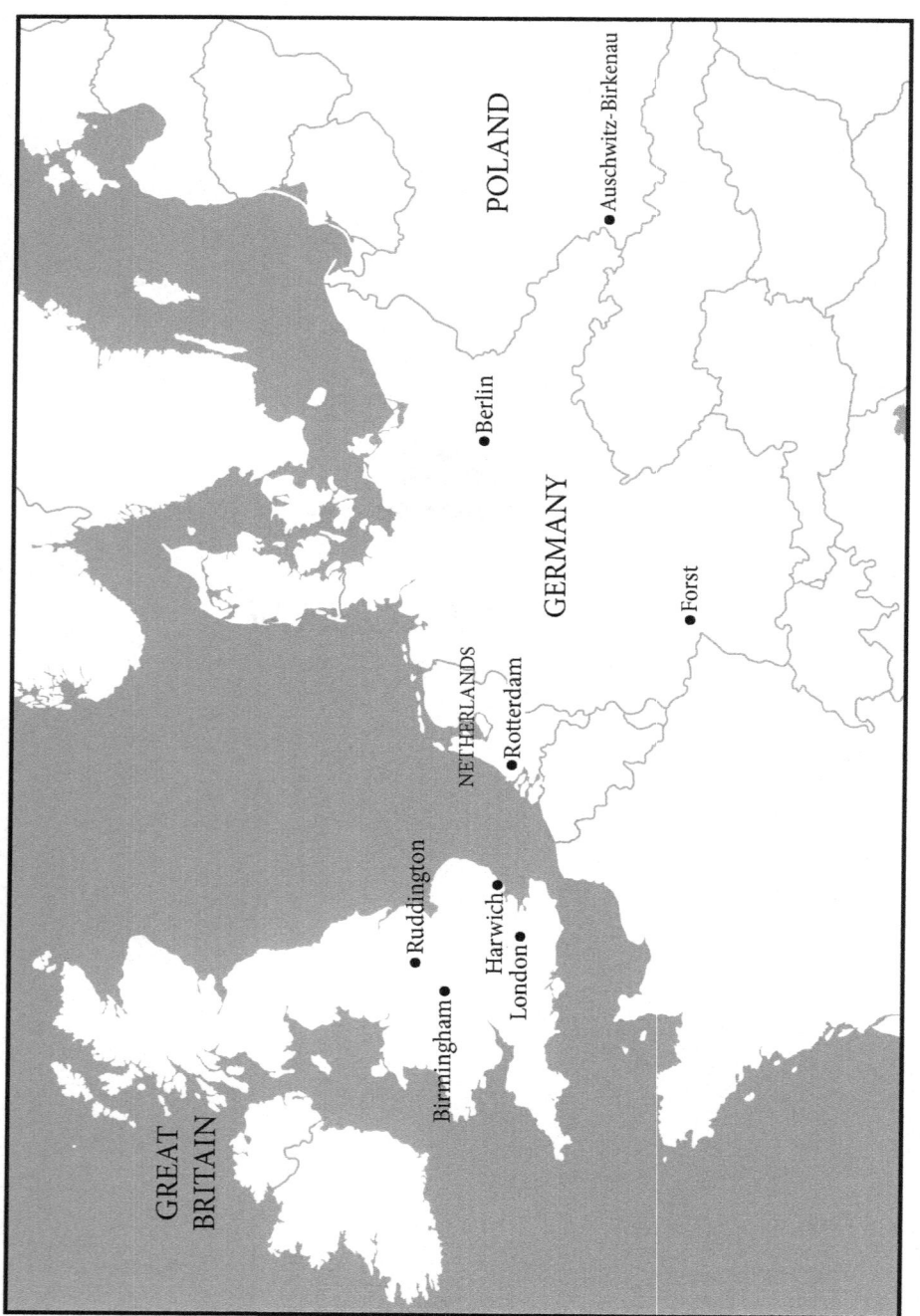

5

INGE BEACHAM (NÉE LEVY)

Adolf Hitler became chancellor of Germany on January 30, 1933.[1] From that point, until Inge and Rita Levy fled Germany for England in 1939, the Nazi Party's antisemitism pervaded Germany. On April 1, 1933, just months after Hitler had assumed power, the Nazis staged an economic boycott against the Jews in Germany. Storm troopers stood outside Jewish-owned businesses—many retail stores, department stores, doctors' offices, and law offices were targeted. The Nazis held signs with phrases such as "Don't Buy from Jews" and "The Jews Are Our Misfortune." Yellow and black stars of David were painted across doors and windows along with antisemitic slogans.[2]

This was the first nationwide government-sponsored action against the Jews. Just days afterward, on April 7, the government again took action, forbidding Jews from holding civil service positions and excluding Jewish lawyers from the bar association. On April 25, the "Law against Overcrowding in Schools and Universities" limited the number of Jewish students who could attend public schools. Three months later, on July 14, naturalized Jews lost their citizenship. Then, in October 1933, Jews were banned from holding any editorial positions.[3]

Beginnings

At that point, Ingebourg Levy, who was born on October 19, 1928 in Forst, Germany, a city approximately two hours southeast of Berlin, had just turned five. None of the laws, nor the boycott of 1933 directly affected her. In fact, her childhood in Germany was relatively normal. She had two loving parents and one sister, Rita, born in January 1932, and she attended synagogue with her family. The early days of her youth were good ones: "I had a very happy childhood, you know, a very relaxed childhood in a loving family. . . . We had a fairly large house with a large ground."[4]

Even in school, though Inge experienced bits and pieces of antisemitism, unlike other Jewish students, she did not experience any type of antisemitic violence: "And I think there began to be difficult things at school and things like that, but

Inge in the garden at home in Germany.

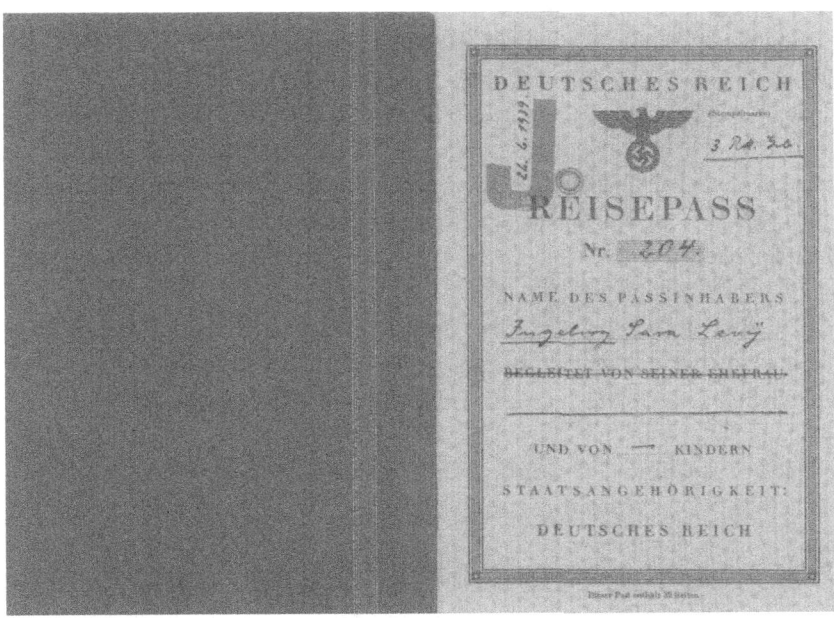

Top: the first page of Inge's passport. Note that it is stamped with a large "J" and that her middle name is recorded as "Sara."
Bottom: Inside pages of Inge's passport.

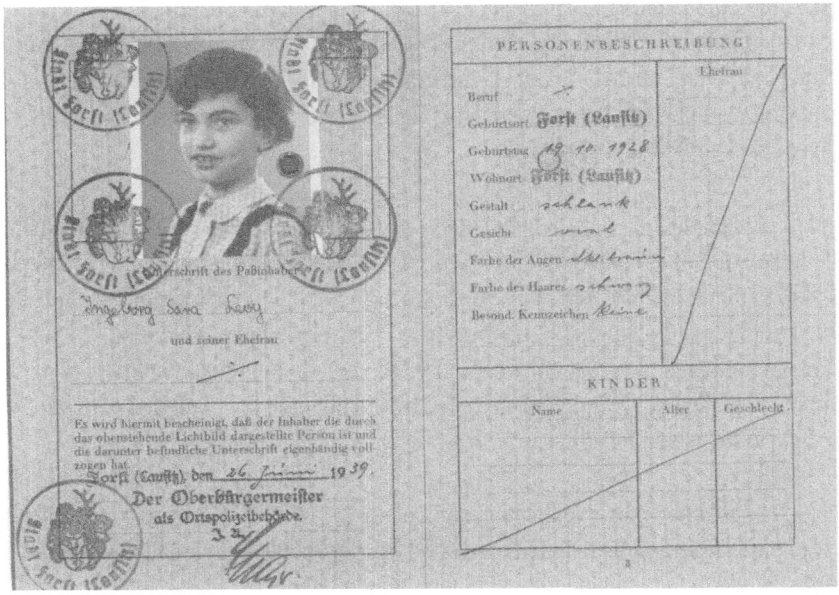

never anything major that I felt."[5]

And any of the antisemitism that was directed toward her was always from the children, never from the teachers. Thus, for Inge Levy, growing up only a few miles away from Berlin in the 1930s, despite the political environment, life was happy and peaceful.

But, less than six years later, Inge would find herself living in a new country, without her parents, without her old home, and without any of the friends she had made in Germany.

Hitler's policies, though they did not at first affect her, left their terrible, indelible mark.

Kristallnacht

As the years passed, things became increasingly frightening—and this fraught and uncertain environment caused Inge's uncle, her father's brother, to flee to Palestine in 1938. For some reason, the Nazis were looking for him, and because he had evaded them, they changed course and arrested Inge's father, Gerhard Levy, sending him to a civil prison in 1938. Inge never saw him again.

On August 17, 1938, the government issued a law that all German Jews with first names of "non-Jewish" origin were to add the name "Israel" for males and "Sara" for females to their names.[6] Inge's name thus became "Ingebourg Sara Levy." Two months later on October 5, 1938, all Jews were required to have the letter "J" stamped on their passports—without it, the passports were invalid.[7]

Kristallnacht occurred on November 9–10, 1938. Inge and Rita were at home when it unfolded. Inge was 10 years old and Rita was 6.

Suddenly, in the middle of the night, their front door was broken down, and chaos ensued. Furniture was ruined, decorations were smashed on the ground, and the linens were strewn everywhere. Not knowing what was taking place or how it would end, Inge decided to flee—she mounted her bicycle and rode through the night to the house of a family friend, Dr. Hesse, who was also the family's general practitioner. That night, Inge was reunited with her mother and her sister, and the three sought to escape by traveling to Berlin: "The Germans broke all the windows, and there was glass everywhere, you know. They came to my home and really knocked it about. And my mother and my sister and I went to Berlin on the train that night."[8]

Gerhard and Mary Levy owned a department store in Forst, along with another store outside the city. After *Kristallnacht*, the government took over the business. The Levy family was now without a father, without a business, and without a home.

Though she had avoided any major antisemitic incidents for some time, the events of 1938 meant that Inge's childhood could and would no longer be carefree.

The Kindertransport

In Berlin, Inge, Rita, and Mary stayed with friends, and Mary attempted to make life as normal as possible for her two daughters. Inge was sent to a special Jewish school because on November 15, 1938, all Jewish children were expelled from public school.[9] The school was called the Leonore Goldschmidt School and was known to its attendants as an "oasis" where the children were taught English in preparation for immigration to England or the United States.[10] The school was founded in 1935 by Dr. Leonore Goldschmidt, only to be closed by the Nazis in 1939. Dr. Goldschmidt worked tirelessly and valiantly to secure possibilities of immigration for her pupils. This work is what enabled Inge and her sister, Rita, to escape to England.

They said goodbye to their mother in Berlin, and as with so many of these stories, that goodbye was the last time they would ever see her. Her bravery—the bravery that inspired her to put her two children on a train, knowing she would likely never see them again—is something that is still poignant for Inge, even so many decades later.

Inge's final glimpse of her mother was when she was 10 years old.

Inge's Family

Inge has never wanted to research her parents' fate. The memories are painful, and she is not interested in knowing the details. However, here is what she does know:

Gerhard Levy was sent to prison and was eventually transferred from that prison to a work camp. When he was released from prison, "He came out in ill health."[11] In the 1940s, Gerhard Levy passed away. That is all that Inge knows.

Rita conducted her own research and learned that Mary Levy had been sent to Auschwitz-Birkenau. Rita then passed that information on to Inge.[12]

Inge Levy was orphaned when she was a teenager.

The Journey

The journey from Germany to England began with a train ride from Berlin to Rotterdam in Holland. From there, Inge and Rita took a boat to Harwich, England, and eventually another

Roland and Kate Day.

train to London. In London, the sisters were met by a Christadelphian, whom Inge referred to as "Brother White."[13] He had received free passes from the railway, so he was designated to meet the sisters at the station.

It was July 26, 1939, just a little over one month before Britain declared war on Germany.

The Christadelphians

Brother White took the girls to their respective families—unfortunately, they were not going to be able to live together. Inge was to live with Roland and Kate Day, and Rita was to live with the Hoverds—but both families lived in the Birmingham area, and both were Christadelphians, so the girls were able to see each other somewhat regularly. The Days did not have a car, and although the Hoverds did, only Mr. Hoverd could drive, and he was at work during the day. However, Inge and Rita were able to take the bus to visit one another.

Roland and Kate Day already had a family of seven when Inge came to live with them—they had five daughters: Nancy, Minnie, Winnie, Louie, and Margaret. Inge became their sixth daughter, calling Kate and Roland "Mum and Dad Day."[14] Despite that Inge had attended the Leonore Goldschmidt school, where many of the pupils were taught English, she had not been enrolled for very long, so she did not know English when she arrived in England. The Day family helped her learn: "We didn't speak any English so had to start leaning it quickly . . . . Dad Day bought me a dictionary which I treasured. So much that I cried one day when I spilt tea on it."[15]

Inge attended the Christadelphian meetings with the Day family, although she stated that she was given the choice about whether she would go to Sunday school—and she chose to go. That said, when asked if she ever felt any pressure to become a Christadelphian, Inge responded, "No, definitely not."[16]

Irene Jeroome, one of Inge's Christadelphian friends, and Inge in the late 1940s.

Inge had quite positive experiences attending the Birmingham Christadelphian ecclesia. She recalled that there were a number of other Jewish refugees who lived in the area and attended the meetings—some of whom have been mentioned in another volume or previous chapters. She remembered Ursula Eichmann (*Part of the Family - Volume 1*, story 3), Susanne Eichmann (volume 2, story 3), and Netty Kupperman (volume 2, story 1). She remembered that when she went to the meeting, she was treated quite well—in fact, one Christadelphian sister, wanting to help the children who had come over as refugees, actually threw a party for all of them. At the time, Inge did not really appreciate it, but she now looks back on the gesture with gratitude. The Christadelphians cared for her and wanted to help her: "The meeting of course, they were all over me, I was special. That's how they treated me, you know.... Yes, they tended to make a fuss of us all."[17]

One thing, however, that intrigued Inge was the Christadelphians' beliefs. With the Christadelphian emphasis on the Hebrew Bible and the Jewish roots of Christianity, Inge often heard about Abraham, Isaac, and Jacob at Sunday school and at the Christadelphian meetings:

> I did go to the synagogue when I was young and learnt about Abraham, Isaac, and Jacob. And because [the Christadelphians] . . . accepted the Old Testament . . . Abraham, Isaac, and Jacob were very prominent . . . . I felt quite at home."[18]

Nevertheless, all of the Christian Bible was foreign to her—and so, at one point, while her mother was still in Berlin, Inge wrote to her mother about the Christadelphians and their beliefs:

I kept contact with our mother in Germany asking her about what the Christadelphians believe. Of course, as Jews we knew all about Abraham Isaac and Jacob. She said if the Christadelphians had been good enough to take us in, their beliefs must be good enough.[19]

Life during the War

Though Inge was part of a family and treated well at the Christadelphian meetings, life in England and during the war was particularly difficult. After living with the Days for only a little over one month, war broke out, and Inge was evacuated to the country, as many children were at the time. For four months, Inge lived in Ruddington, a small village in Nottinghamshire. It was during that time that she turned 11—the tenth year of her life had perhaps been the most traumatic. That year her father was arrested, *Kristallnacht* occurred, her family fled to Berlin, she saw her mother for the last time, and she moved to a new country with a new language and new customs. After all that, she was forced to evacuate to yet another new place. Though the evacuation itself would not have been terrible, in context, it was one more change for a 10-year-old girl who had already experienced so much trauma. Inge stated, "It was another upheaval, and I hated it."[20]

After the four months of her evacuation ended, Inge returned to the Day family. However, the evacuation had not entirely served its purpose. Many of the children were evacuated to protect them from the bombing of the cities—yet in late 1939 and early 1940, the worst of the bombing on Birmingham was yet to come. The Blitz really began in late 1940, and thus, though Inge was evacuated, her four months in Ruddington did not prevent her from experiencing the terrifying nights of German bombing. Inge recalled:

> During the bombing, we were right in the line . . . . I've got quite a lot of memories of the bombing . . . there was shrapnel and stuff like that. And the railway was just at the bottom of the road, so getting at that really. There was a family of three, I think the mother and two daughters, they had a direct hit right opposite us.[21]

In fact, Inge remembered the day a bomb was dropped directly onto their house:

> Father Day, as I began to call him, and his daughter Louie . . . wouldn't go into the shelter . . . . They just sat—and as it turned out, a bomb came across the chimney, blew the fire out, which they were able to shuffle back straight away, and so save the house.[22]

To this day, Inge does not know why Father Day and Louie refused to go into the shelter—she thinks that it was perhaps a manifestation of their faith, but she is not sure. Though it was extremely dangerous and seemed ill advised at the time, Inge declared, "But for us it was providential."[23] Because the two of them stayed outside the shelter, the house was saved.

Wartime not only brought about physical danger, but also it brought disappointment for Inge. She finished her primary school, and she remembers not being able to attend a grammar school because the Day family did not have enough money. So she went to a secondary modern school instead, which she found very difficult. Nevertheless, at that school she was treated well: "I think they just accepted me: I never had any problem there."[24]

Top: John Beacham.
Bottom: Inge Beacham, 2017.

As the Years Passed

After the war ended, the difficulties continued. The Day daughters were older than Inge was and had all gone off to live on their own. It was just Inge with Mum and Dad Day. Then tragedy struck again: Inge lost her third parent. Dad Day became ill and died suddenly—not only was this loss painful for Inge, but also it meant that Inge had to move yet again. Without Dad Day, their little family no longer had a breadwinner, so Kate Day moved in with one of her daughters, and Inge went to live with another Christadelphian family, the Humphersons, who had also taken in a Jewish refugee named Mary.

When she was 18 years old, Inge Levy, after witnessing the love and care of the Christadelphians, and after believing the teaching of both the Old and the New Testaments, chose to be baptized as a Christadelphian. In 1947, *The Christadelphian* magazine carried the following announcement:

> BIRMINGHAM (Central).—The following baptisms have taken place at the Midland Institute: March 20, Winifred Jean Salisbury (on behalf of the Worcester ecclesia) and John Arthur Sacksen (for the South Birmingham ecclesia); March 27, Gladys Hilda Smith (sister of bro. Percy Smith), Ingebourg Sara Levy (a refugee who has made her home with bro. and sis. R. A. Day), and Pauline Mary Nowell (daughter of bro. and sis. W. Nowell). We rejoice that five more have put on the Saving Name of Jesus.—G. T. Fryer (rec. bro.).[25]

Though she had lived in the United Kingdom for nearly eight years, the middle name given to her by the Germans had stayed with her. Nevertheless, when Inge was baptized, for her, it was a new beginning. She felt as though she was starting a new life and beginning afresh with a new goal: the Kingdom of God.

As part of her baptism, Inge became a member of the Birmingham Central Christadelphian ecclesia, one of the largest in the world at the time. At the same time, the British government also granted her British citizenship.[26] It was at that ecclesia that she met John Beacham, and the two of them were married at the Smallheath Christadelphian Hall on March 3, 1956. Together, they had two daughters and a son, and they remained Christadelphians throughout the rest of their lives. After John's death, Inge continued to live in England in a Christadelphian Care Home, where she takes part in the regular activities and continues to attend the Sunday memorial service.

John and Inge both held to the fervent belief that God was working in their lives, and this belief has helped them face the difficulties that confronted them. Inge remembered, "John said I had been 'a brand plucked from the fire' (Zechariah 3:2),"[27] reflecting the idea that God had delivered her from almost certain death. Later in life, when John and Inge lost a daughter to cancer, they continued to hold to that conviction—believing that no matter how trying the circumstance, God is "working all things together for good" (Romans 8:28).

This is not to say that her experiences no longer trouble her:

> I listened to some of the stories on the television recently, and it just churns you up a bit. I mean, at one time, I couldn't have talked to you like this at all. It took ages .... You couldn't talk about it .... There was a brother and sister who were German, in Central ... they always wanted me to talk in German, but I hated it. I wanted to forget it, and that's what I did.[28]

Inge did not want to associate herself with Germany—she was furious over what the Germans had done to her and her family. Over 50 years after the atrocities, in the 1990s, Inge returned to her birthplace in Germany and saw the result of the Nazi efforts to erase the Levy household:

> We actually went back to where the house was, where I was born I think . . . . When I was young, we were about a hundred or so miles away from Poland. But the line had been redrawn, and it was now nearer to Poland . . . . We could see places where the bullets had hit the factory that was at the bottom of our road . . . the house wasn't really anything like . . . the gates were still there, strangely. It had been changed into a school in the years between. The business that my father had was completely gone.[29]

In witnessing these things, she stated, "Germany didn't matter to me in any way; in fact, I felt a bit anti."[30]

Thus, while Inge looks back and is grateful for the way in which her experiences have worked together, and the way in which she believes God has led her and cared for her, the experiences are not at all without pain. Though they took place decades ago, their memory and their legacy are still poignant.

Nevertheless, despite the terrifying experiences of her youth and the trying experiences of her adult life, Inge has held to the hope that one day, the Messiah, whom she believes to be Jesus, will return to the earth and set up his Kingdom, beginning in Jerusalem. Eventually, he will wipe away all tears, and sorrow and sighing will flee away (Revelation 21:4).

This hope, and the trust that God has been preparing her and her family for that Kingdom, brings her great peace: "I can see

God's hand at work, and he has been there to support me in all my difficulties."[31]

---

[1] "Timeline of Events," *United States Holocaust Memorial Museum,* accessed April 28, 2017, https://www.ushmm.org/learn/timeline-of-events/1933-1938/hitler-appointed-chancellor.

[2] "Boycott of Jewish Businesses," *United States Holocaust Memorial Museum,* accessed April 28, 2017, https://www.ushmm.org/wlc/en/article.php?ModuleId=10005678.

[3] "Antisemitic Legislation 1933–1939," *United States Holocaust Memorial Museum,* accessed April 28, 2017, https://www.ushmm.org/wlc/en/article.php?ModuleId=10007901.

4 Inge Beacham, interview by Sarah Watts, February 23, 2016.

5 Ibid.

6 "Law on Alteration of Family and Personal Names," *United States Holocaust Memorial Museum,* accessed April 28, 2017, https://www.ushmm.org/learn/timeline-of-events/1933-1938/law-on-alteration-of-family-and-personal-names.

7 "German Jews' Passports Declared Invalid," *United States Holocaust Memorial Museum,* accessed June 2, 2017, https://www.ushmm.org/learn/timeline-of-events/1933-1938/reich-ministry-of-the-interior-invalidates-all-german-passports-held-by-jew.

8 Inge Beacham, interview by Sarah Watts, February 23, 2016.

9 "Antisemitic Legislation 1933–1939," *United States Holocaust Memorial Museum,* accessed April 28, 2017, https://www.ushmm.org/wlc/en/article.php?ModuleId=10007901.

[10] Sara Rimer, "Reunion Recalls School for Jews in Nazi Germany," *The New York Times* (New York, NY), November 11, 1985, http://www.nytimes.com/1985/11/11/nyregion/reunion-recalls-school-for-jews-in-nazi-germany.html.

[11] Inge Beacham, interview by Sarah Watts, February 23, 2016.

[12] Inge Beacham,"Inge," in *Living Stones: Ordinary people - Extraordinary stories* (Birmingham: The Christadelphian Sunday School Union, 2015), 36.

[13] Inge Beacham, interview by Sarah Watts, February 23, 2016.

[14] Inge Beacham,"Inge," in *Living Stones: Ordinary people - Extraordinary stories* (Birmingham: The Christadelphian Sunday School Union, 2015), 35.

[15] Ibid, 35–36.

[16] Inge Beacham, interview by Sarah Watts, February 23, 2016.

[17] Ibid.

[18] Ibid.

[19] Inge Beacham, "Inge," in *Living Stones: Ordinary people - Extraordinary stories* (Birmingham: The Christadelphian Sunday School Union, 2015), 36.

[20] Ibid.

[21] Inge Beacham, interview by Sarah Watts, February 23, 2016.

[22] Ibid.

[23] Ibid.

[24] Ibid.

[25] G. T. Fryer, "Intelligence," *The Christadelphian*, May 1947, 89.

[26] Rachel Newman, e-mail message on behalf of Inge Beacham to the author, February 12, 2017.

[27] Inge Beacham, "Inge," in *Living Stones: Ordinary people - Extraordinary stories* (Birmingham: The Christadelphian Sunday School Union, 2015), 37.

[28] Inge Beacham, interview by Sarah Watts, February 23, 2016.

[29] Ibid.

[30] Ibid.

[31] Inge Beacham, "Inge," in *Living Stones: Ordinary people - Extraordinary stories* (Birmingham: The Christadelphian Sunday School Union, 2015), 37.

Ben Weiss

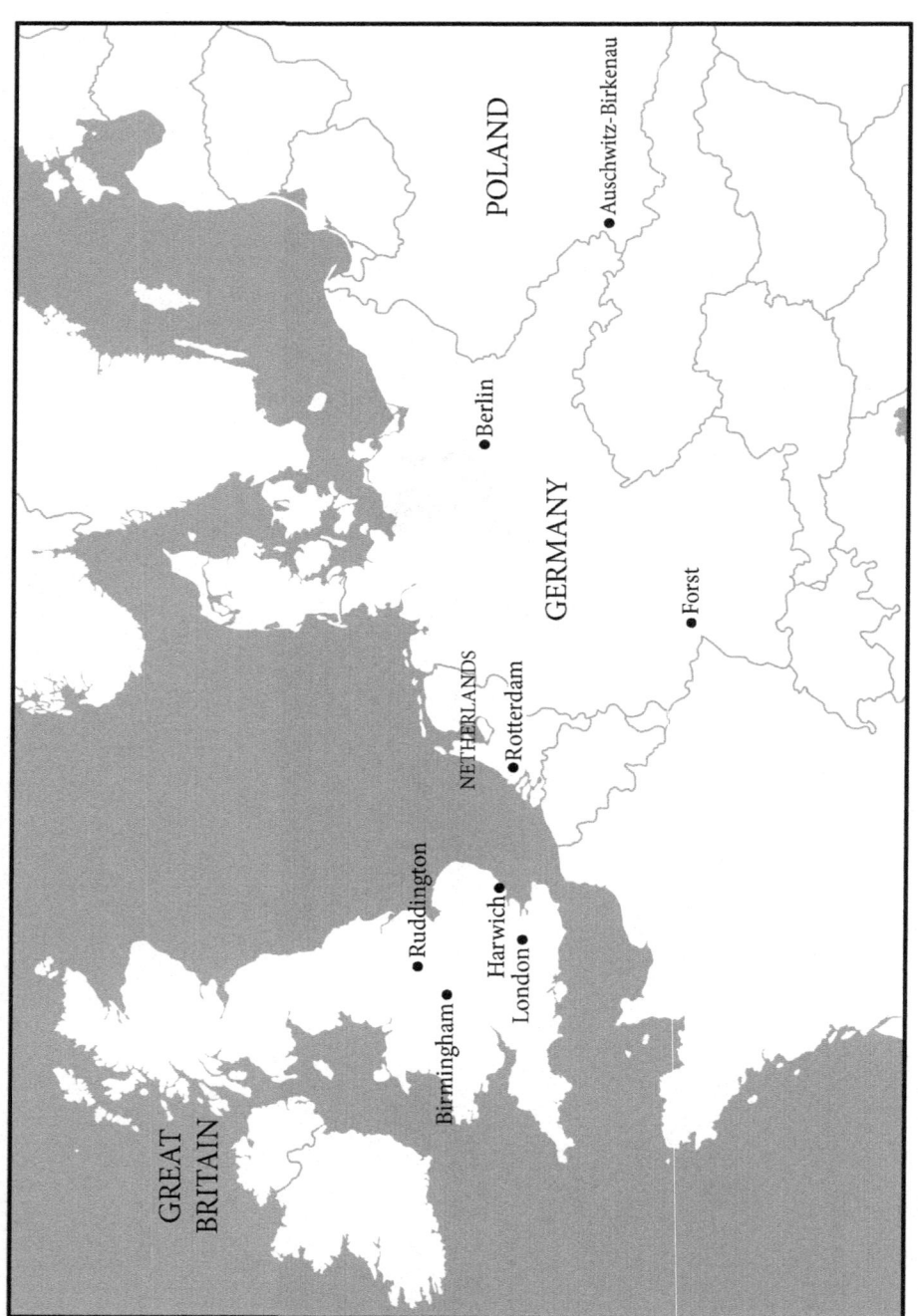

6

BEN WEISS

Gustav Stresemann is noted as the man "largely responsible for restoring Germany's international status after World War I."[1] In 1923, he became the foreign minister of the Weimar Republic, and it was in that position that he did his work of restoration—leading Germany through a number of the difficult reparation years, negotiating the Dawes Plan and the Pact of Locarno, and bringing Germany into the League of Nations. In 1926, for his work of reconciliation with France, he, along with French Foreign Minister Aristide Briand, was awarded the Nobel Peace Prize. In 1928, he made Germany a signatory of the Kellogg-Briand Pact, an international agreement led by France and the United States meant to eliminate war and to solve international disputes—and because of Germany's participation, Weimar Germany came to be seen as a nation that was reasonable and with which other modern powers could favorably negotiate. Finally, in 1929, he helped to negotiate the Young Plan—another attempt at stabilizing Germany's reparations—which brought Germany's payments to a level that the new democracy could easily meet.

Overall, Stresemann was remarkably successful in his attempts to restore Germany's reputation and political and economic stability. And as his success became more and more apparent, the revolutionary and radical nature of Nazism began to lose its appeal—why turn to the Nazis to restore Germany's greatness when that greatness was already being restored by the Weimar Republic? William Shirer, an American journalist and war correspondent who lived in Nazi Germany, describes this period in his classic history of Nazi Germany, *The Rise and Fall of the Third Reich*:

> Stresemann was succeeding in his policy of reconciliation with the Allies. The French were getting out of the Ruhr. A security pact was being discussed which would pave the way for a general European settlement (Locarno) and bring Germany into the League of Nations. For the first time since the defeat, after six years of tension, turmoil and depression, the German people were beginning to have a normal life . . . . The Nazis, in league with northern racial groups under the name of the National Socialist German Freedom movement, had seen their vote fall from nearly two million in May 1924 to less than a million in December. Nazism appeared to be a dying cause. It had mushroomed on the country's misfortunes; now that the nation's outlook was suddenly bright it was rapidly withering away.[2]

But as the 1930s approached, the situation in Germany began to change dramatically.

On October 3, 1929, Gustav Stresemann, at the age of 51, died of a stroke. Three weeks later, on October 25 and 29, "Black Monday" and "Black Tuesday," the "Dow Jones Industrial Average fell 13% and 12% back-to-back."[3] Those who had speculated and sold all that they had in order to pay a down payment to borrow money to purchase stocks—thinking that as the stock prices climbed, as they had done fairly consistently, they would pay off the loans with the money they had earned on the market and become wealthy with the extra—found that not only had they *not made money*, but also with the crash they had *lost* the money they borrowed. As such, they had lost everything they had—and were in debt.[4] This financial crisis, eventually called the Great Depression, would last for 10 years and would afflict both the United States and the nations of Europe—including Weimar Germany.

The end of 1929 was an end to the peace and stability that Gustav Stresemann had brought to Germany. And with that came the end of the prosperity that had staved off the popularity of the Nazis. Moreover, Hitler had predicted that Germany would eventually face an economic catastrophe.

Thus, when faced with the poverty, joblessness, and misery of the German people in the midst of the Depression, Hitler believed that his time had come. The German people were beginning to feel a desperate need for a change. And so he could write these words: "Never in my life have I been so well disposed and inwardly contented as in these days. For hard reality has opened the eyes of millions of Germans to the unprecedented swindles, lies and betrayals of the Marxist deceivers of the people."[5]

Beginnings

Ben Weiss was born in Berlin on August 6, 1929—just two months before Gustav Stresemann's untimely death and Wall Street's collapse. His childhood years were spent in the midst of a nation's economic chaos and, eventually, under the control of a maniacal tyrant. Thus, those years were filled with the consistent optimism of youth and the fondness of time spent as part of a happy family, yet plagued by the many restrictions the Nazi government placed on him, his siblings, and his parents. He was the middle child of Max and Golda Weiss—with his birth between that of his older brother Heinz (b. November 24, 1925) and his younger brother Charlie (b. February 6, 1936). Their family would remain together for the first nine years of Ben's life.

From left to right: Heinz, Golda, Ben, and Max Weiss in 1935, approximately one year before Charlie's birth.

Ben grew up in Berlin on Fehrbelliner Strasse. There, his family had an apartment, and his grandmother, whom he called Frimke, lived in the apartment above them. He and his brothers visited her regularly and enjoyed a close relationship. Ben's relationship with everyone in his family was strong—he cherished both of his brothers and looked up to his father, but, out of everyone, Ben was closest to his mother.

Ben's father, Max, was a tailor who had his shop in the front of their apartment building. His shop was filled with various bolts of cloth, and he often spent his time with pins in his mouth and a measuring tape over his shoulders. His specialty was suits, which he would make by hand from the bolts of cloth. As a treat, Max used to give his children samples of the past season's fabric; unlike what they could do with the cloth on the wall, they could cut this fabric, manipulate it, and twist it. In the excitement of youth, however, one season, Ben could not wait for the samples—and thus he approached his father's new cloth for the new season and cut up those samples instead. Needless to say, his father was not very pleased.

Some of Ben's favorite memories come from time spent at school. From the very beginning, Ben and his brothers attended a Jewish day school near their house. Ben was a good student who enjoyed studying, and he was also popular, sharing the company of his many friends.

But perhaps most striking is the fact that Ben remembers life, for the most part, before Hitler and the Nazis tightened their grip, as being *normal*. For the first few years, Ben and his brothers could just be kids—and they played together, laughed together, and competed with one another:

> The street next to ours was very steep. Often on our way home from school, I would stand at the top of the street and try and guess the type of car driving up the hill before we saw it. Most of the cars were Mercedes or Opels and we had to guess the model. I was very good at this game. On weekends, I played soccer on the

street in front of my father's shop with my brother and all of our friends. We were like any other German Jewish family of that time.[6]

Life was normal. Although there were certainly the everyday kind of frustrations that presented themselves, Ben loved his family, enjoyed his school, and played with his brothers and his friends, just as any other child his age.

Antisemitism

Adolf Hitler was appointed the Chancellor of Germany in 1933. As one of his first steps against the Jews, he called for a boycott of Jewish businesses on April 1, 1933—and thus, it's likely that Max's business was impacted that day. Pictures of the Führer soon became commonplace; his image could be seen in schools, libraries, shops, and even in the private citizens' homes. Nazi soldiers, noted by their bright red armbands with swastikas, were seen patrolling the streets— Ben and his older brother would often pass these soldiers on their walk to school. Rather than turning to look at them, however, Ben and Heinz would simply stare straight ahead and keep walking.

In September 1935, life began to change profoundly. At that point, the Reichstag passed the Nuremberg laws—a set of regulations that disenfranchised the Jews and stripped them of their German citizenship. Now every German Jew was affected—and it was abundantly evident that life would no longer be the same.

For Max, business began to change. Jews were clearly outsiders in Nazi Germany, and thus, many non-Jews stopped shopping at Jewish businesses. Max's tailor shop found that fewer and fewer customers were walking through the door—meaning that the Weiss family's money for food and supplies was much

Golda, Charlie, Heinz, Max, and Ben in front of Max's tailor shop, 1937.

more limited. The restrictions were felt, not just by his parents, but also by Ben and his brothers. Eventually, the government forced Ben's school to close, and he and his brother Heinz attended another Jewish school that was close by—yet Ben did not enjoy this school nearly as much as he did his first. Signs appeared all throughout the city—at the swimming pools, the cinemas, the parks, and restaurants—plainly stating that Jews were forbidden entry.

Despite all this, Ben's family tried to make the best of the situation and attempted to keep life as normal as possible for the children. The family continued to eat dinner together each night, they attended synagogue on *Shabbat*, and they celebrated the Jewish holidays with their friends and relatives. But at the same time, Max and Golda realized that the situation was becoming desperate:

> I never realized why Papa was so worried and why he and Mama were always whispering. They must have tried very hard not to let us know how scared they were. We didn't have much money and knew not to waste food, but we did spend money on postage stamps. In desperation, my parents sent many letters to relatives in the United States, hoping that they could help us get a visa and find us a new home where we could be safe.[7]

Kristallnacht

The situation worsened even further in November 1938:

> Around 8 p.m. on November 9, a group of men in Nazi uniforms appeared on our street. They began marching, stopping at all Jewish shops, homes and synagogues in the area. A massive attack was underway. In a brutal night of chaos, the Nazis

*Top: Max and Golda Weiss.
Bottom: Ben, Charlie, and Heinz Weiss.*

> destroyed everything in their path that could be identified as Jewish. They pulled the shutters off my father's tailor shop and shattered the windows. They threw cloth and half-made garments onto the floor, and smashed the large worktable. They looted my parents' bedroom, which was immediately behind the shop, overturning the large dresser and breaking the mirror. They destroyed our synagogue, along with many others. We watched in horror that terrible night as soldiers took my father away to Dachau.[8]

Dachau was the Third Reich's first concentration camp, beginning its operations in March 1933, and was built to house political prisoners. It was located in southern Germany, about 10 miles northwest of Munich. Because of its focus on those who politically opposed the Nazi regime, the first inmates were mostly German communists, Social Democrats (one of the major political parties in the Weimar Republic), and other enemies of the state. In its first year, the camp held approximately 4,800 prisoners. In 1937, the camp expanded, with the inmates being forced to undertake the expansion work. With the expansion, Dachau housed 32 barracks, which became the living quarters for tens of thousands of prisoners. Prisoners in Dachau were slaves, forced to do the Third Reich's bidding—and eventually, some were also subjected to terrifying medical experiments. By the time Dachau was liberated by American forces, there were 67,665 registered prisoners—43,350 of whom were noted as political prisoners, and 22,100 of whom were Jews. The remaining were categorized into other categories.[9]

Herman Hillman was one of the American soldiers who liberated the camp:

> When we came to Dachau, which was near Munich, we found the prisoners, the ones that were alive, in the

camp, wandering around, dressed in their black and white uniforms, in a daze, most of them emaciated and near death; walking skeletons, I called them. The crematoria were still warm. There were bodies piled outside of the crematoria ready for incineration. All the guards . . . had vacated the camp and ran away a day before as the camp was approached by the forerunners of the . . . American troops.[10]

Max was imprisoned in Dachau for six weeks, along with thousands of other Jews who had been arrested on *Kristallnacht*. During his arrest, his son Heinz turned 13—but with an environment of terror and Max's tenuous situation, Heinz's bar mitzvah was canceled.

After *Kristallnacht*

After *Kristallnacht*, life was very different for Ben and his brothers. Not only was their father missing, but Berlin had also become considerably more dangerous. The line between hatred of the Jews and state-sponsored violence against the Jews had been breached—so violence was much more prevalent. Ben was terrified of his walk home from school, despite the fact that his school was just around the corner. As he walked, it was not uncommon for Hitler Youth to laugh at him and yell, "Kill the Jews." At one point, he was stopped and harassed, eventually arriving home with bruises on his face and a black eye. He was nine years old.

Perhaps, though, the most frightening incident for Ben did not actually occur on his walk home from school. In early 1939, Golda had asked Ben to take his brother Charlie, who was just a toddler, for a walk. During the walk, Ben was confronted by a group of Hitler Youth who had a dog. They proceeded to set the dog loose on Ben, who fled—running with Charlie and his stroller as quickly as he could. The dog attempted to fasten its teeth onto Ben's leg, and the Hitler Youth chased them, but that time, Ben escaped from them unscathed. However, the Hitler Youth were not finished.

After chasing Ben and Charlie, the group lost interest, and instead, focused their attack on a man who was standing high on a ladder, painting window frames on a house on Ben's street. Running up to his ladder, they insulted him, and, placing their hands on the ladder, began to shake it.

The man lost his balance. Ben watched in horror as the painter fell off the ladder and thudded on the ground. He was killed instantly.

In complete shock, Ben tore home:

> I can't describe how afraid I was. I had never imagined anyone could do such a thing, and I got Charlie home as quickly as I could. I could barely tell Mama the story through my sobs. It was after this incident that my parents realized just how unsafe Berlin had become.[11]

During this period, it was not uncommon for Ben to find out that his friends had simply disappeared—their families had secretly fled the country during the night.

Plans for Escape

With the changes that had taken place in Berlin, Max and Golda realized how desperate the situation had become. It was imperative that they flee. Ben recalls that once Max returned from Dachau, his parents' whispers became increasingly frequent. In late January 1939, Max and Golda planned for their family to leave Germany to live with relatives in the United States. They sold pieces of their furniture to purchase train tickets, and they wrote letters in anguished attempts to acquire visas. But the visas never arrived. After months of waiting, it seemed clear that the entire family was not going to escape together—the plan was simply a broken dream.

Thus Max and Golda made an agonizing choice: they would send their two eldest boys away, in hopes that they could live in safety. On January 27, 1939, during *Shabbat* dinner, Max and Golda revealed their decision:

> It was Friday night. I remember it clearly. In my mind I can see us all sitting around the dining room table. My father, Max, sits down at the head of the table. Golda, my mother, starts lighting the Shabbat candles. My little brother, Charlie, who is not quite three, sits beside me. He is kicking my leg under the table. My older brother, Heinz, sits opposite my mother. As we begin to eat the challah and chicken soup, my father says, 'I have something important to say tonight. This is very difficult for us, but your mother and I have decided that the two of you, Heinz and Benno, will leave Berlin in the next few days. It's not safe here anymore for us Jews. We will follow as soon as we can.' This was the last Friday night dinner we were together as a family.[12]

Max and Golda had attempted to piece together a plan with the little knowledge they had of the situation for Jewish refugees outside of Germany. Originally, Ben and Heinz were to escape to Belgium—but then Max and Golda heard that two boys down the street had done the same thing, were caught when trying to enter Belgium, and had not been heard from since. On the other hand, they had heard that the Jewish Refugee Committee in Holland was actually helping children come into the country illegally—and that the Germans would allow children without passports to leave the country. Thus, Ben and Heinz were to flee together to Holland.

Heinz was 13 and Ben was 9. They had never traveled without their parents. They had never made major decisions without their parents. They had never been to Holland. Yet, in a passionate attempt to give their children life, Max and Golda knew that Ben and Heinz must leave.

When Ben heard the news, at first he was excited—it sounded like an adventure. They would be on their own! They could make their own choices, and no one could tell them what to do! Heinz, on the other hand, became very sober and said nothing.

They were to leave the following morning.

Leaving

Ben struggled to fall asleep that night. Even though Charlie was so young, Ben had become quite fond of him. The two of them shared a room together, and in the next few hours, Ben was going to have to say goodbye. How he would miss his little brother!

His thoughts then drifted to what he would pack for the journey—and at that point, he fell asleep.

The next morning, Ben's family ate breakfast together, and for a long time, no one spoke. Finally, Max gestured toward two tweed knickerbocker suits that he had just finished making. "These are for you," he said. Ben tried on his suit, feeling proud and thinking that he looked much older than nine years old.

On the floor of the kitchen was their suitcase, which had been packed by Max and Golda. It contained clothes, toys, books, and, perhaps most importantly, pictures of Max, Golda, and Charlie. Before they left, Ben added a few books to those that

Ben and Heinz in Germany.

his parents had already packed—stuffing the suitcase so full that he and Heinz had to sit on it to close it.

With that, Max turned to Heinz and said: "Benno is only nine years old. He needs you to look after him. I want you to remember something. Do not come back to Berlin. Whatever happens, it is not safe here for Jews. We will follow you as soon as we can."[13]

Golda had been watching her children in silence, taking in the scene. But with those words, she could no longer contain herself. The tears began to flow freely.

Ben looked at his mother's glistening face. He felt a powerful urge to run to her.

Max, however, reminded her that she must be strong: "Come now, Golda, don't let the boys see you so unhappy. They might not want to leave if you seem so sad. You know it's for the best. We must let them have their chance at life."[14]

Max then continued to counsel Ben and Heinz: "If you are turned back from the border, follow the guard's orders. But at the first chance you get, when the train stops, get off and try again. Hide on the train if you have to, but get out of Germany any way you can. Once you are out of Germany, you will be safe. Try to find the Jewish Refugee Committee. They will give you food and somewhere to sleep. We will come and meet you as soon as we can."[15]

Max gave both boys their birth certificates—the only legal identification documents they each possessed. Ben placed the certificate within a hidden pocket on the inside of his suit. Both Ben and Heinz were also given 10 marks—Max would have given them more, but 10 marks was all that was allowed. Finally, Ben was given a pocket watch and a pen, most likely so that he could write to his parents wherever he was.

Ben walked to his bedroom one last time, looked around the room, considered how Charlie would now have the room all to himself, and earnestly hoped that all five of them would be together again soon.

Then it was time to leave.

The Weiss family walked to the train station, *Anhalter Bahnhof*, in the middle of Berlin. They arrived at 6:30a.m. Ben's thoughts were a flurry of how to say goodbye to his family and when he would see them again.

Max walked up to the ticket counter and purchased five tickets—two tickets to Holland and three platform tickets, which would allow Max, Golda, and Charlie to accompany Ben and Heinz to the train. As they waited for the train, none of them spoke, but when the train finally arrived, Golda once again broke down, but this time in loud sobs. Working quickly, Max took the boys into the train and returned to his doleful wife, attempting to comfort her. As Ben looked at his mother, the tears began to well in his own eyes.

Max then helped Golda into the train car to say her goodbyes. "Don't make the children sad," he urged her, knowing that it was imperative that Ben and Heinz stay on that train. "Be brave like the children."[16]

With that, Golda Weiss suddenly stopped crying, dried her eyes, and reminded them: "Don't let them turn you back, boys. We will follow as soon as we can."[17]

Ben simply did not understand. How could his mother be crying over them at one point and then so quickly decide that they needed to leave?

With a final goodbye and the admonition to write frequently, even that night, Max, Golda, and Charlie left Ben and Heinz on the train. The two boys were now alone.

Golda and Charlie.

We stayed by the window for a long time, waving while the train pulled out of the station. I'll never forget Mama and Papa holding Charlie up so he could wave too, his little face smiling, and his little hand waving goodbye. We watched until they were as small as ants, and we kept waving long after they disappeared. This is the last image I have of my parents and my little brother, and I'll never forget it.[18]

Heinz wiped tears from his face, although he clearly did not want Ben to see them. He had to be brave for Ben.

The Weiss Family

It was decades before either Ben or Heinz learned of their family's fate. Shortly after the war, Ben and Heinz encountered a man who had been their neighbor in Berlin, and he explained to the brothers that he had been deported on the same train as their family. He told them that their family had been gassed as soon as they had arrived, in March 1943. But he had no proof, other than the fact that he thought he had seen them.

As such, for years Ben wondered what had *really* been his family's fate. Was what he had been told in fact true? Or had his neighbor just been mistaken? His parents had been determined to follow the two of them—and they had engineered their sons' flight, had they not?

Only in 1987, almost 50 years after he and Heinz had fled Berlin, did Ben find concrete proof of his family's fate. In January, a letter arrived at Ben's house from the Red Cross, following up on an enquiry he had placed years prior. Now, however, the records of the prisoners at Auschwitz were available. The Red Cross confirmed Ben's worst fears.

Max Weiss lived another 22 months after Ben and Heinz's flight from Berlin. At some point in 1939, he was conscripted into forced labor at a factory in Berlin.[19] He perished on November 25, 1940,[20] leaving behind his wife and his son Charlie, who was almost five. Max was 42.

After Max's death, Golda and Charlie continued living in Berlin. They stayed in the city for another two years until

March 1943. They were deported together from Berlin on March 12, 1943,[21] to Auschwitz-Birkenau, where it is believed they were murdered by poison gas upon arrival. Golda was 37 years old, and Charlie had just turned 7.

Kleve

Hours passed. The seats on the train were cold and hard. Ben had already eaten the sandwiches his mother had packed, he had already gone through some of the books he had brought, and he had exhausted his desire to look out the window. Not knowing what else to do to occupy his time, he began to get scared and longed to go home.

Soon, however, the train stopped at Kleve, a town on the western border between Germany and Holland. They had reached their destination, and now they had to cross the border. It was night.

Ben and Heinz walked around the train station, not sure what to do. Heinz carried their suitcase. After a while, an older man approached them and asked whether they were attempting to leave Germany. Not sure how to respond, Heinz decided to be honest, stating that they were endeavoring to enter Holland but did not know the way. The man explained that they were still in Germany and that to get into Holland, they would need to take a streetcar. If they were turned back, however, he explained that they still had hope. The German border guards would bring them back to the station in Kleve, and from there, they could purchase a ticket on the next train to Berlin. If they got off the train at its first stop, they could take another train that would lead them to the border guards at Nijmegen, Holland. They would then have another chance.

This man's kindly advice ultimately saved their lives.

Ben and Heinz boarded the streetcar and eventually got off at the border. There, the guards accosted them, asking them why they were attempting to get into Holland and where their parents were. Before they had an opportunity to answer, however, the guards began talking among themselves. They were Germans, and they decided that if the Dutch border guards were willing to take them in, they, the Germans, would let them go. Thus, after they had given the Germans their birth certificates for examination, a guard walked them over to the border and gave a nod in the direction of Holland. It was time for them to cross and to meet the Dutch border guards.

Ben and Heinz walked into Holland alone, in the dark. Suddenly a bright light shone into their eyes, and a man yelled, "Halt!" Ben was petrified and began to shake.

Showing the guards their birth certificates, Ben and Heinz waited to hear the verdict. It was negative. The guards, after marveling at their young ages, turned them back and scolded them for attempting to enter a foreign country without the proper papers. Upon hearing this, Ben had to keep blinking his eyes to hold back his tears.

They were turned back. Just as the older man had said would happen, the German guards took the two of them back to the train station and had them wait for the next train back to Berlin.

But the two brothers were not going to return to Berlin: "I remembered what Papa had said just before we left. We should not let them turn us back. We would have to try to get into Holland another way."[22]

Holland

When Ben and Heinz boarded the train, one of the German guards spoke to the conductor and impressed upon him that the two boys were not to leave the train until they had arrived in Berlin.

On the train, Ben could no longer hold in his tears. It had been an intensely long day, and he was overwhelmed with disappointment.

After some time had passed, when the train began to slow, Heinz got up and looked down the corridor—the conductor who had been watching them had moved into the next compartment. Heinz told Ben that this was now their chance—when the train slowed down, they were to jump off and attempt to catch a train to Nijmegen, as the older man had instructed.

Before the train had come to a complete stop, Heinz had grabbed Ben's arm. The two then jumped from the doorway onto the platform at the station. From there, they sprinted as quickly as they could, although Ben struggled to keep up with Heinz. They no longer had their suitcase to weigh them down; they had left it on the train. They thought that at least if they were seen on the platform and their suitcase was still on the train, it would look as though they were planning on returning to the train.

Soon the train pulled away without them, and their pictures, their clothes, their toys, and their books went with it.

They then approached the ticket counter and purchased two tickets to Nijmegen.

The train was about to leave, but they hurried and made it aboard. But the nightmare continued. As they were looking for a compartment, they realized that there were Nazi guards searching the train and checking passengers' papers. As Ben and Heinz walked faster to stay ahead of the guards, Heinz noticed that there was a compartment with a broken light. The entire room was black. The two of them decided to hide in that compartment, curling up underneath the seats:

> We were in total darkness and immediately slid to the floor and hid under the seats. I couldn't see Heinz; I could just hear his breathing getting heavier. Each time he took in a breath, I thought of us getting caught. We heard footsteps coming closer, getting louder and louder. My heart pounded in my chest. It was beating so fast that I thought it was going to explode. Hot tears fell down my cheeks as the footsteps stopped outside our compartment. Then the guard walked in, the thud of his boots echoing on the floor beside us. Heinz and I held our breath. We thought we were going to burst. After several agonizing seconds, the footsteps started again. They grew quieter as the guard walked away. We let out our breath as quietly as we could. Finally, the train started. We had been lucky again.[23]

Eventually, their train arrived at the border. Exiting the train, they stood in a long line of people waiting to cross the border. The scene was overwhelming, and waiting simply made it worse. Sweat began to trickle down Heinz's forehead.

When their turn finally came, they braced themselves for another interrogation—questions about their parents, questions about their destination, and questions about possible relatives in Holland. Yet no questions came. The border guards simply looked at them and nodded for them to keep walking.

It could not be. Ben and Heinz stood rooted to the spot—not willing to give in to hope. Then someone nearby motioned for them to continue moving. The two brothers looked at each other. And they walked into Holland.

Nijmegen and Wijk aan Zee

Relief flooded over both Ben and Heinz. They had been successful—they had found safety. As the minutes passed, the two of them simply stood, basking in the freedom, until eventually, a small man approached them and asked whether they were refugees from Germany. They replied in the affirmative and asked whether he could help them. He could, he said, and after taking them for a ride in a taxi, brought them to a house where they were asked a number of questions, most likely from workers in a refugee agency, in German and not Dutch. From there, they were brought to another house—to a home of a kindly man and his wife, who allowed them to wash up, fed them, and taught them to play cards. It was here that Ben and Heinz wrote their first letter to their parents, letting them know that they had made it to safety in Holland.

However, after three days, on February 2, the refugee agency moved Ben and Heinz from that family to a convent in Wijk aan Zee, a coastal city about an hour and a half northwest of Nijmegen.

Life at the convent was quite different from life with the kindly family in Nijmegen. At the convent, the boys were told that they would only be allowed to write letters once a week—specifically on Fridays. The letters would be censored by the Mother Superior, so they were admonished not to complain of their treatment. The convent, however, would pay the postage. If their parents sent any parcels, those parcels would be confiscated. It was crucial that they obey all of the rules, particularly that they make their bed exactly as instructed.

There was a very tight schedule at the convent, including an hour-long nap after lunch. Everything was extremely precise.

> I . . . thought that Heinz and I should run away. This place was like a prison . . . . The routine was exactly the same every day. After morning bed-making, we went downstairs where a teacher taught us Dutch. In the afternoons after lunch, we had our sleep. We were only allowed to sleep on our left sides. If we accidentally moved to our right, we were woken up and forced to turn over.[24]

The weekends, however, were entirely different. Then, they played football (soccer), climbed trees, and were allowed to act like children.

Though Ben wanted to run away from the convent, Heinz told him that they must wait and must stay where they were. After six weeks of enduring the weekdays in anticipation of the weekends, Ben and Heinz were informed that they would soon be leaving.

On March 9, 1939, the morning they were scheduled to leave the convent, Ben noticed that his clothes had been packed for him and that he had more clothes than those with which he had arrived. From one of his parents' letters, he knew that they had sent more clothes, but because parcels were confiscated, he did not know what had happened to them. He hoped that this extra bulk of clothes was from his parents.

Later that morning, Ben and Heinz walked with the Jewish Refugee Committee workers to the train station, which reminded him of the similar walk he had made with his parents and Charlie just a few weeks earlier. The thought brought his tears back again, and he held onto the hope that his parents, just as they had said so many times, would follow him and Heinz out of Germany. Perhaps they would even be at the train station.

But they were not. Instead, Ben was told that he and Heinz were being transferred to an orphanage in Amsterdam—the title of which caused yet more foreboding over his family.

Amsterdam

The orphanage offered a sharp contrast to the convent. The orphanage staff allowed the boys to write letters freely, any time they wanted, and no one censored them. Nonetheless, Ben found himself wistfully thinking about the convent's immaculate grounds; there was nothing clean about the orphanage:

> It was awful. Water dripped into the room through a cracked fan. There was dust everywhere. The floors were dirty and the beds untidy . . . . The windows were filthy, the walls needed to be painted, and the ceilings were grey and dirty. The dining room was also very dirty and the tablecloth had large holes in it.[25]

That night, when Ben climbed into bed, he made another upsetting discovery: the leak in the ceiling was not just an unpleasant addition to a dirty room but also dripped straight onto his bed. Before drifting off to sleep, Ben spent time in bed feeling sorry for himself. At least in the convent, things were clean.

On their third day at the orphanage, Ben and Heinz were taken to the barber, where their heads were shaved and they were given striped uniforms. Ben felt as though he looked like a convict—and this thought perpetually brought him to tears. Were they actually criminals? They had indeed passed into Holland illegally: were these clothes simply reflecting what the boys thus deserved?

Once again, Ben desperately wanted to run from this place—but the thought that his parents and Charlie were attempting to join them kept him put. If they ran away, without some kind of permanent address, it would be nearly impossible for his parents to find them.

After a few more weeks at the orphanage, Heinz ran up to Ben to give him exciting news: they were moving again. In the excitement of the moment, Ben did not think to ask *where* they were going, only *when*.

On April 18, 1939, the matron of the orphanage called out the names of eight people who were to be leaving. Just as they had before, they walked to the train station. On the way, Ben counted the number of weeks that they had stayed in each place—they had been in the convent for six weeks and then in the orphanage for six weeks. Now they were starting all over again, walking to the train station, as they had done twice before.

On May 15, 1940, slightly more than a year after Ben had left the orphanage, the Germans occupied the Netherlands.[26] After the war, Ben discovered that the orphanage where he and Heinz had lived for six weeks had been liquidated by the Germans—and that the children there had all been sent to concentration camps. The eight boys who had been sent out on April 18, 1939, were the only survivors.

Ben and Heinz in England, 1939.

To England

When Ben and Heinz were on the train, they had no idea where they were bound. There was only one other boy in their compartment, their friend from the orphanage, named Eli. The three of them discussed where they might be headed, and they considered the possibility of running away. Ben had a map in his pocket, and upon examining the map, he thought that perhaps they could run from Holland all the way to Iraq or Turkey, and from there to Palestine. But for fear of being caught by the police, they resigned themselves to their fate.

After about four hours, the train stopped. They had arrived at the Hook of Holland. They still had no idea what awaited them. All that was known was that they were now leaving Holland and were going to another country called England:

> There were lots of children, all refugees, and none of us knew what would happen to us. I was very worried. I kept as close to my brother as possible. We asked everyone around us if they knew where we were going. England, was the answer. How did our parents arrange this? We never found out. As we walked towards the crowd, we saw a big ferry in port, full of children. Finally, we were told to get on board. Hesitantly, I followed the children in front of me.[27]

Each time they were transferred, Ben felt wistful: although they were safe, each move took them farther and farther away from their parents. As Holland faded from view, he wondered, as he had done so often for the last 12 weeks, whether he would ever see his parents again and ever hold them again. And what of Charlie?

Arrival in England

Ben does not recall many details of the trip from Holland to England, except that he and the seven other boys from the orphanage played games together to keep themselves occupied, that they were fed soup and bread, and that many of the other children became seasick. Thankfully, this sickness did not afflict either him or Heinz.

That evening, on April 18, 1939, the boat docked in Harwich. Ben and Heinz had fled from Germany to Holland and now were in Great Britain. They were miles from the Germans—and miles from their family.

Eventually, Ben and Heinz disembarked from the boat and waited on the dock. Many adults had come to the dock to claim one or more of the children. Ben and Heinz simply waited—hoping for their name to be called and wondering to whom they would go this time.

It would not be a convent, nor would it be an orphanage. Rather, it would be a hostel for young refugees in Felixstowe— a port city just a few miles across the bay from Harwich, but approximately an hour's drive away.

Life in England

The hostel's warden was also a refugee, and being from Vienna, he spoke German, which added to Ben's sense of comfort. For the first time since leaving the family in Holland, Ben's surroundings were accommodating, and he was treated respectfully. He stated:

> The hostel warden and his wife were responsible for us, and made our life very pleasant. It was a nice change after the strict rules and lack of care we had lived with for nearly three months . . . . For the first three weeks after our arrival, we were allowed to play and just have fun . . . . Letter writing was not controlled or censored, and we finally heard from our parents. It was a huge relief, and a great source of joy when we got their letter. They were pleased that we were now safe in England and had been able to find a place where we were happy.[28]

War would not come for another four months, so Ben, Heinz, and his parents wrote freely to one another. Max and Golda sent pictures, both of family and of Berlin, just to help the boys remember their home. The mail's arrival was one of the highlights of Ben's day, and he read his parents' letters over and over. These were his lifeline.

Unlike children in Germany, who only attend school in the mornings, children in England attend school in the morning and afternoon. This gave Ben and Heinz many opportunities to practice their English, and they soon picked up the language. They not only began speaking English but also began making English friends, and visiting their friends at their homes. Life in England was extremely different from the life they had had in both Germany and Holland: "Days passed in England, happy days that made all the bad days seem to fade away. Our hair grew in again and we felt much more like ourselves."[29]

But this was not to last. As Ben had learned in the last few months, things can change in an instant.

On May 29, 1939, six weeks after their arrival in Felixstowe, Ben and Heinz were moved again. This time they were going to a place called Barham House, which was in Claydon, approximately 45 minutes northwest of both Felixstowe and Harwich. In his book about the Kindertransport, *...And the Policeman Smiled,* Barry Turner gives a description of Barham House:

> Barham House, just outside Ipswich, on the Essex-Suffolk border, started life as an overspill camp for Dovercourt. It had accommodation for 200 boys.

There was no mistaking Barham House. Built as a Victorian workhouse, it had a grey, forbidding look which must have deterred all but the neediest applicants. Its defects were emphasised by its proximity to Shrubland Park, a splendid Palladian mansion with a long drive and imposing gatehouses, which first-time visitors sometimes mistook for the RCM [Refugee Children's Movement] building. They were soon put right.[30]

Barham House comprised a number of houses, all named after a variety of British politicians,[31] to which the refugee boys were assigned based on their ages. For the first time since fleeing Germany, Ben and Heinz were separated: Ben was placed in Baldwin House, and Heinz was placed in Brentnall House. For some reason though, Ben was content with the separation. As it turned out, Ben recognized a few boys in Baldwin house—a handful he had met at the convent in Holland and two he had seen on the ferry to Harwich.

One of Ben's primary concerns upon arrival at Barham House was familiarizing himself with the rules. Each time he moved he had new rules to learn—and he hoped that the rules would not be too repressive. As he found out, although Barham House may not have looked pleasant and inviting, the rules were quite bearable: He would attend school every weekday and only in the mornings, attendance was not taken at school (and yet everyone of his or her own volition seemed to attend every day), and cleanliness and respectful behavior were rewarded by a point system. The boys were also able to earn money, which was critical to them because they could use it to buy their own clothes and toys (rather than using the ones that belonged to the camp) or go into town to watch a movie. At one point during his stay at Barham House, Ben became a prefect, for which he earned two pence a week. As a prefect, he had to make sure that the other boys in his house made their beds and kept their living spaces clean.

Once again, Ben began to grow accustomed to life in this new place:

> Our afternoons were free. We built things, played games, and spent time with our friends. The days passed quickly; soon we were well into the summer and nearing my tenth birthday. I wrote home often. Heinz and I were both enjoying ourselves and the very difficult days faded a bit from our memories.[32]

And this time, he was able to stay at the camp for longer than six weeks. Finally he could begin to grow some roots and make stronger friendships. He and his friends occupied themselves with all sorts of activities: there Ben learned to ride a bike and swim; there, Ben, only 10 years old and without any idea of the health implications of smoking, first made a cigarette out of dried leaves and toilet paper and began smoking. It was also there that Ben attempted to turn a blanket into a parachute and jumped off one of the fire escapes on the third floor.

War

On September 3, 1939, Great Britain declared war on Germany.

> The first change for us was that letters across international borders now had to go through the Red Cross, and would be censored. Suddenly, home seemed much further away. We heard air raid sirens and wondered if we were going to be bombed.[33]

For the first few weeks, life went on as usual. The boys at Barham House continued to have pillow fights. They continued to swim. They continued to play table tennis. And they continued to follow the local soccer team's winnings. Letters from Max and Golda, however, as they now needed to be sent through one of Golda's friends living in neutral Spain, came less frequently.

And then, near the end of September, the boys at the hostel were given an order: they were to dig trenches in which they could hide in the case of a German invasion. At the beginning, Ben enjoyed the work—digging holes was fun for a 10-year-old boy. But after a while, his arms began to become sore, and he grew tired of the task.

Finally, after a few days of digging, the trenches were completed. After this, though, the boys were given another order: the hostel had become infested with rats and mice, which were eating the hostel's food—food that was precious during wartime. Thus, each boy was given rodent traps and charged to kill as many rats and mice as possible—one penny

Ben and Heinz in England, 1940.

would be paid for a dead mouse and two pennies for a dead rat. Ben, however, was never able to catch either.

In November, Heinz turned 14. Soon after his 14th birthday, he told Ben that he was going to leave the hostel and move to Birmingham. There he was going to take a position as a tailor's apprentice to follow in his father's footsteps. Now Ben and Heinz would truly be separated, and it would be many months before they would see each other again. As Ben went with his brother to the train station, he became overwhelmed with sadness: they had endured so much together, and Ben did not know the next time he would see his brother.

Birmingham

Heinz moved to Birmingham and eventually found himself as one of the first refugees living in a hostel named Elpis Lodge—a hostel with an unusual name—*Elpis* being the Greek word translated as "hope." At the hostel's dedication, Rabbi Abraham Cohen gave the name the following explanation:

> The name which has been given to this house, Elpis Lodge, signifies the Abode of Hope, and above all I do hope our generous Christadelphian friends will have there ward [sic] for their act of generosity; that the boys, when they leave these portals after being in our charge, will go forth in the world imbued and enlightened with the hope of a better future.[34]

At the same time, the fact that the Greek word *Elpis* was used, rather than any other language, is also significant because Elpis Lodge was the hostel founded and funded by the Christadelphian ecclesias of Birmingham and Coventry, and one of the first Christadelphian books ever published was titled *Elpis Israel,* or *The Hope of Israel.* Indeed, this hostel was meant to be a tangible manifestation of the Christadelphians' belief in that hope of Israel. This was affirmed, once again, at the dedication of Elpis Lodge, this time in the words spoken by Sidney Laxon, one of the Christadelphians who had been heavily involved in making Elpis Lodge a reality, and E.W. Newman, a Christadelphian who became Elpis Lodge's treasurer:

> Bro. Laxon, in reply, explained the grounds of Christadelphian interest in Jewish affairs. They considered friendship for the Jews a privilege not only for the nation which showed it but for the individual who promoted it. The faith of Christadelphians was rooted in the Law which Jesus said he came not to destroy but to fulfil.
>
> Bro. Newman also replied, explaining that the contributions of Christadelphians were made anonymously, and quoting the note in the January issue of *The Christadelphian* recording the receipt of a packet containing £350 for that Hostel.[35]

Perhaps a unique aspect of Elpis Lodge was that it was entirely funded by the Christadelphians, and various Christadelphians frequented the hostel to help teach the boys diverse skills, such as shorthand and gardening. But a Jewish warden named Dr. Hirsch, whom the Christadelphians had appointed, oversaw the hostel's daily operations. Dr. Hirsch ran Elpis Lodge on Orthodox lines.

The hostel opened on Sunday, April 21, 1940,[36] and the first group of boys was brought there on May 1.[37] Heinz was likely part of that group. In July of 1940, *The Christadelphian* magazine reported this:

> The sixteen boys at Elpis Lodge, the Birmingham Hostel for Jewish Refugee Boys, are settling down into

> a happy community, healthy and full of good spirits. All have been found work: four in jewellery, three as tailors; and the occupations of others include toolmaker, upholsterer, garage hand, electrician, wood-worker, baker, etc. One boy is a junior clerk to a firm of chartered accountants, and is studying to take his matriculation.
>
> In placing the boys in the trades they are now learning, Dr. Hirsch (the Warden) has been at pains to find out their natural aptitudes, and has taken into account their family history. Some of the Viennese families, for instance, have been tailors for generations, and one boy's grandfather is a tailor's cutter of considerable repute in Vienna. The father of the boy who is doing wood-work is a turner of chessmen. The boy learning upholstery hopes some day to join his brother, who is an upholsterer in the Argentine.[38]

As it would appear, at 14 years old, Heinz came to Elpis Lodge and was likely one of the three boys who became tailors. Heinz continued to live in Elpis Lodge until 1942. Of that time, Ben recalls this: "We wrote to each other often, as he settled down in his new life in Birmingham. He said that the work was interesting and, from his letters, he seemed happy."[39]

Moving

While Heinz was living in Elpis Lodge, Ben heard rumors that he was to be moved again. All Germans living in England were considered enemy aliens; thus, they were not allowed to live by the sea, where they could possibly be privy to the British navy's training and pass on valuable information to the Germans. Thus, Ben and about 30 others from Barham House were to be moved to a hostel in Leeds—unfortunately, the hostel was not yet ready to house them.

Because the hostel was not ready—but the government dictated that they be moved farther inland—Ben and his peers were taken to Wallingford, which was a prison near Oxford, as a six-week, temporary place for them to be overseen. Though they were in prison, they were separated from the inmates, and life was bearable. Finally, he was moved to Leeds. By that point, he had lived in three separate places in Holland and four in England.

In Leeds, Ben lived in a hostel on Stainbeck Lane. Unlike any of the previous hostels, this was a strict Orthodox Jewish hostel, with its own synagogue. Ben and the other boys there attended synagogue three times a day for prayers, and Ben had to wear a *kippah* at all times.

Ben stayed at this hostel for three years. During that time, he began to seriously acknowledge that he might never see his parents, or Charlie, again. As always, mail delivery was a highlight. But letters from his family came very infrequently these days, and because of Max's death in 1940, of which Ben was unaware, they were only from Golda. The last letter Ben ever received from his mother came in 1941.

In August 1942, Ben turned 13 and celebrated his *bar mitzvah*. Heinz made the two-hour trek north to be there for the event: it was the first time Ben and Heinz had seen one another in two years.

In mid-1943, Ben left both school and the hostel, wanting to be closer to Heinz, believing that he should start working so that he could support himself, and wanting to find a different type of environment in which to live. Ben wrote:

> I had been in England since 1939 living in various hostels at that time, mainly in Leeds, with many other

Ben's bar mitzvah, 1942.

boys. I had been separated from my brother but we had kept in contact by letter. In August 1942 I was bar mitzvahed and Heinz came to visit me, he had been living at Elpis Lodge in Birmingham for some time. He realised that I was not happy in the hostel in Leeds, it was extremely Orthodox and we were never brought up that way. When Heinz returned to Birmingham he arranged for me to join him.[40]

At that point, Heinz left Elpis Lodge and moved to a different hostel in Birmingham so that Ben could take Heinz's place. Thus, Ben came to live at Elpis Lodge.

Elpis Lodge

When asked about Elpis Lodge, Ben responded quite positively. His own words effectively convey his feelings about his time there:

After all this planning I arrived in Birmingham at Elpis Lodge around May of 1943 and I was very happy there. Of course it was also nice to be able to see Heinz often as he lived not too far away.

I turned 14 in August of that year and then had to go to work. My first job was with a dentist who made false teeth. He was most unpleasant to work for and as he also paid me very little, only 15 shillings a week. This was not enough to live on so I found employment at a munitions factory where the pay was 3 pounds a week. This munificent amount was enough to enable me to eventually find my own accommodation and I could move out of Elpis Lodge after about 9 months. I had had enough of living in hostels, at least 6 or 7 since I had left Berlin and my family. Over the years I stayed in Birmingham I kept in touch with the boys and we were all good friends, I would love to hear any news of them.[41]

The war of course affected us all, the black-outs, the shortages of food, in fact shortages of most things at that time. Everything was rationed, not only food but also clothing, but we never went hungry at Elpis Lodge. I do remember that a house a few doors away from us was bombed, and that we spent a lot of time in the air raid shelter.

We boys lived in dormitories, about 8 boys to a room. We made our own beds but there seems to have been someone who cleaned and did the laundry. The clothes we wore were communal, supplied partly by Marks & Spencer and the Jewish community. I have no idea who paid for the food we ate, of course rationing made for a very limited variety but whatever we were given was always tasty.

I also have a fond memory of Dr. Hirsch and his wife, Frau Doctor Hirsch and their two children Hannah and Rudi. The Hirsches ran the Hostel and I only have happy memories of those days. There was never any pressure for any of us boys to become Christadelphians but we were all aware of the fact of their financing the hostel and their kindness to us of the Kindertransport."[42]

Ben lived in Elpis Lodge until 1945, just before the war ended. From Elpis Lodge, Ben moved to London, where Heinz had moved and also gotten married.

After the War

After the war ended in May 1945, Ben and Heinz were jubilant, but their elation was tempered by the fact that they had heard nothing from their family in four years.

> At long last the destruction, fighting and killing were over, but I was still scared. What would I find out? How would I find my parents and little brother? What would happen if I didn't find them? What would my

Ben and Rita, 1953.

brother and I do? I had been hoping for so long that one day we would be a family again.[43]

Yet, no matter whom they asked, they could never find proof of what had happened to their parents and to Charlie—until 1987, when Ben received the letter from the Red Cross. In the months that succeeded the war, Ben was plagued with guilt—how could he and his brother have survived but the rest of their family perished?

In 1949, at a Jewish discussion club in London, Ben met a young English girl named Rita. Four years later, in 1953, they were married, and they have been happily married ever since. They now have three daughters, seven grandchildren, and two great grandchildren. Heinz and his wife had three children and six grandchildren.

For years, when Ben would recall his experiences, it was difficult for him to grapple with the fact that his parents sent him away. It was only once he had his own children that he began to see the love that enveloped his story of survival:

> For many years, when I thought about being sent away I became very upset. As a teenager, I remember being very annoyed at my parents. I thought that they hadn't really loved us at all. They had just tried to get rid of us. How can parents who love you one day just send you away into the unknown? I couldn't understand what they had done. But as I became an adult with children of my own, I began to realize that theirs was the supreme act of kindness and selflessness.[44]

The Holocaust was one of the darkest times in human history. Yet through love, kindness, and selflessness, some light was able to shine through that darkness. Ben's survival is a testament to that fact.

Though they lived in many places and were overseen by many different hostels, both Ben and Heinz were able to find a place in Birmingham—a place they were protected, encouraged, and respected. This place, Elpis Lodge, came about because the Christadelphian ecclesias of Birmingham and Coventry chose to act, inspired by their beliefs, on behalf of the Jewish people. Beliefs impact actions—and though the Christadelphians were a small religious group, these actions made powerful, profound imprints on the lives they touched. Once again, this is a reminder to us to examine our own beliefs and to consider whether they are inspiring us for good or for ill.

---

[1] "Gustav Stresemann," *Encyclopedia Britannica Online,* accessed April 28, 2017, https://www.britannica.com/biography/Gustav-Stresemann.

[2] William Shirer, *The Rise and Fall of the Third Reich* (New York: Simon and Schuster, 1960), 112.

[3] "Oct. 28–29, 1929: Stock Crash," *The Wall Street Journal* (New York, NY), October 27, 2014, http://blogs.wsj.com/wsj125/2014/10/27/oct-28-29-1929-stock-crash/.

[4] Pierre Berton, *The Great Depression: 1929-1939* (Toronto: Anchor Canada, 2001) 37.

[5] Adolf Hitler, quoted in William Shirer, *The Rise and Fall of the Third Reich* (New York: Simon and Schuster, 1960), 136.

[6] Susy Goldstein, Gina Hamilton, and Wendy Share, *Ten Marks and a Train Ticket* (Toronto: The League for Human Rights of B'nai Brith Canada, 2008), 16.

[7] Ibid, 18.

[8] Ibid, 21.

[9] "Dachau," *United States Holocaust Memorial Museum,* accessed April 28, 2017, https://www.ushmm.org/wlc/en/article.php?ModuleId=10005214.

[10] Herman Hillman quoted in *Memories of Liberation,* ed. Violet Zeitlin (Philadelphia: Gratz College), 3.

[11] Susy Goldstein, Gina Hamilton, and Wendy Share, *Ten Marks and a Train Ticket* (Toronto: The League for Human Rights of B'nai Brith Canada, 2008), 24.

[12] Ibid, 12.

[13] Ibid, 28–29.

[14] Ibid, 29.

[15] Ibid, 30.

[16] Ibid, 34.

[17] Ibid.

[18] Ibid.

[19] Christoph Kreutzmüller, *Jewish Book Council,* March 11, 2016, http://www.jewishbookcouncil.org/_blog/The_ProsenPeople/post/max-wisens-tailor-shop.

[20] "Datei:Stolperstein Fehrbelliner Str 20 (Mitte) Max Wisen.jpg," *Wikipedia,* accessed April 28, 2017, https://de.wikipedia.org/wiki/Datei:Stolperstein_Fehrbelliner_Str_20_(Mitte)_Max_Wisen.jpg.

[21] "Gedenkbuch - Opfer Der Verfolgung Der Juden Unter Der Nationalsozialistischen Gewaltherrschaft in Deutschland 1933-1945," *Das Bundesarchiv,* accessed April 28, 2017, http://www.bundesarchiv.de/gedenkbuch/de1180821.

"Gedenkbuch - Opfer Der Verfolgung Der Juden Unter Der Nationalsozialistischen Gewaltherrschaft in Deutschland 1933-1945," *Das Bundesarchiv,* accessed April 28, 2017, http://www.bundesarchiv.de/gedenkbuch/de1180822.

[22] Susy Goldstein, Gina Hamilton, and Wendy Share, *Ten Marks and a Train Ticket* (Toronto: The League for Human Rights of B'nai Brith Canada, 2008), 40.

[23] Ibid, 43.

[24] Ibid, 57.

[25] Ibid, 63.

[26] "German Wartime Expansion," *United States Holocaust Memorial Museum,* accessed April 28, 2017, https://www.ushmm.org/wlc/en/article.php?ModuleId=10005481.

[27] Susy Goldstein, Gina Hamilton, and Wendy Share, *Ten Marks and a Train Ticket* (Toronto: The League for Human Rights of B'nai Brith Canada, 2008), 70.

[28] Ibid, 76.

[29] Ibid, 77.

[30] Barry Turner, *. . . And the Policeman Smiled* (London: Bloomsbury, 1990), 165.

[31] Günther Abrahamson, "Günther Abrahamson," in *I Came Alone: the Stories of the Kindertransports,* ed. Bertha Leverton and Shmuel Lowensohn (Sussex: The Book Guild Ltd., 1990), 10.

[32] Susy Goldstein, Gina Hamilton, and Wendy Share, *Ten Marks and a Train Ticket* (Toronto: The League for Human Rights of B'nai Brith Canada, 2008), 79.

[33] Ibid, 85.

[34] Rabbi Cohen, quoted in John Carter, "An Abode of Hope," *The Christadelphian*, June 1940, 258.

[35] John Carter, "An Abode of Hope," *The Christadelphian*, June 1940, 259.

[36] Ibid, 258.

[37] John Carter, "Refugee Boys' Hostel," *The Christadelphian*, June 1942, 230.

[38] John Carter, "Birmingham Refugee Boys' Hostel," *The Christadelphian*, July 1940, 334.

[39] Susy Goldstein, Gina Hamilton, and Wendy Share, *Ten Marks and a Train Ticket* (Toronto: The League for Human Rights of B'nai Brith Canada, 2008), 88.

[40] Ben Weiss, e-mail message to author, May 31, 2016.

[41] Ibid.

[42] Ben Weiss, e-mail message to author, June 11, 2016.

[43] Susy Goldstein, Gina Hamilton, and Wendy Share, *Ten Marks and a Train Ticket* (Toronto: The League for Human Rights of B'nai Brith Canada, 2008), 95.

[44] Ibid, 29–30.

MAX HARPER

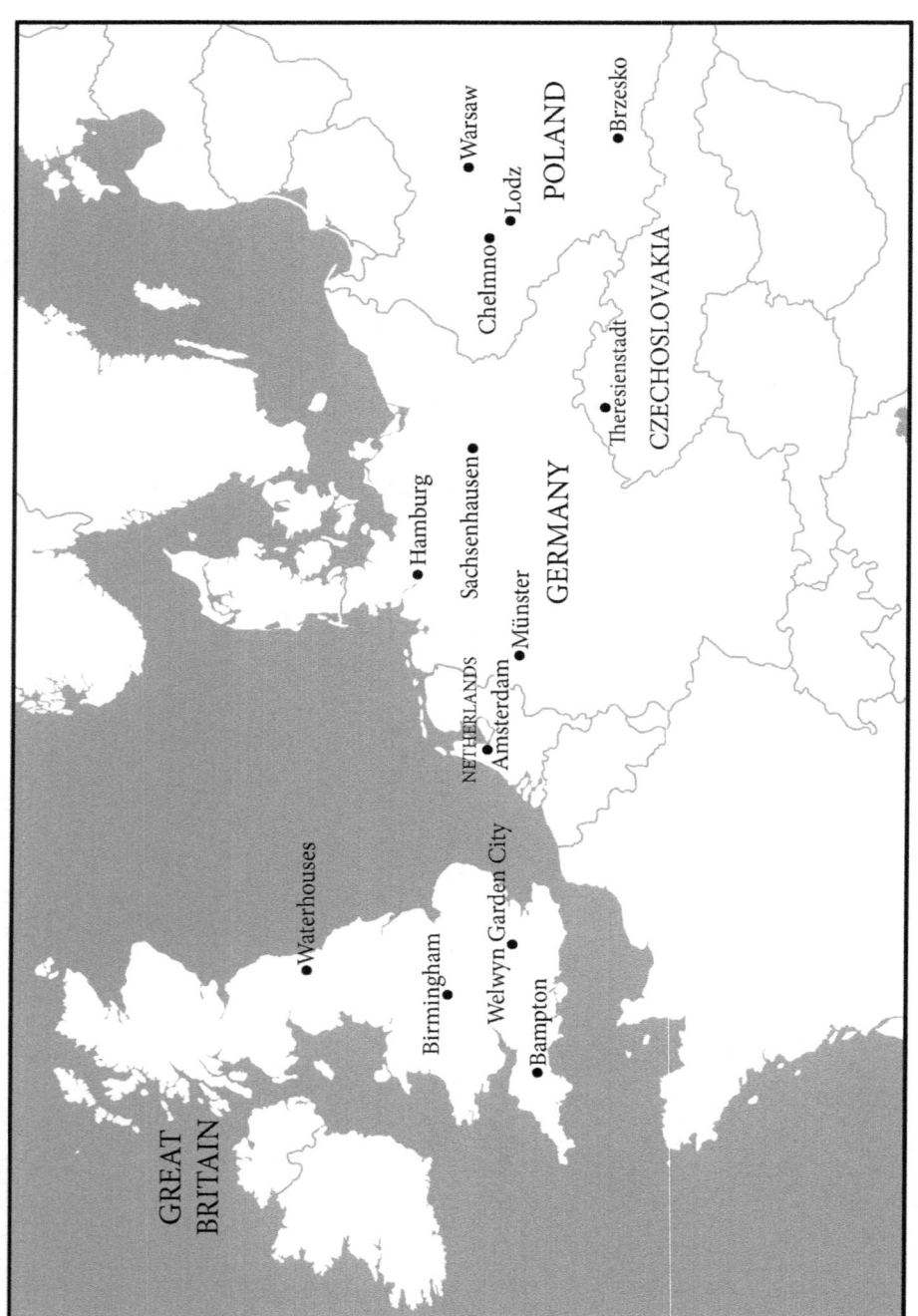

7

Max Harper (née Koenigsbuch)

Hamburg, Germany, is often termed the Venice of the North[1] because it is a city divided by branches of the Elbe River, which ultimately, 75 miles northwest, connects it to the North Sea. It is this connection to the sea that has led to Hamburg becoming Germany's largest port today,[2] and it is this connection to the sea that brought many Jews to Hamburg over the centuries.[3]

Jews have been living in Hamburg since the late 1500s. The first Jews to arrive there originally came from Portugal and Spain, and shortly thereafter, by 1600, German Jews came to the area. In 1648, Ukrainian and Polish Jews came to Hamburg to escape the persecution occurring in their own countries. Yet life was not perfect for Jews in Hamburg either. Coming from Spain and Portugal, the first Jews in Hamburg were *conversos*,[4] Jews who had been forced to convert to Catholicism, yet still had wanted to remain Jews. In Hamburg, these Jews took care to conceal their actual religion, specifically because they were afraid of what might happen to them if the Christian population knew that they were in fact Jewish. And when that news finally spread—after they were seen practicing Jewish customs—their fears were justified: some Hamburg residents demanded that the Jews be expelled from the region. This expulsion was staved off for a number of years by the city council, which pointed out that the Jews' presence in the city had yielded an economic benefit. Thus, the

Jews were simply given the tax of 1,000 marks per year—a tax levied in 1612. In 1617, the tax was increased to 2,000 marks.[5]

Despite this tax levy, the region's Christian clergymen still clamored for the Jews' removal from the area—an expulsion that took place in 1649, only a year after the Polish and Ukrainian Jews had fled to Hamburg for refuge. At that point, many of the Jews of Hamburg made their homes in Amsterdam. Regardless, a number of the Jews who had been forced out of the city were eventually allowed to reside there again—and Hamburg again became a place with a flourishing Jewish community. In 1656, just seven years after the expulsion, a number of Jewish refugees from Vilna were welcomed to the area. Finally, at the end of the seventeenth century, in 1697, the tax on the Jews of Hamburg was suddenly and unexpectedly raised again—this time to 6,000 marks—prompting a number of Jews to again leave the area.[6]

Starting in 1811, and as part of Napoleon's conquests, the city of Hamburg was ruled by the French, at which point, for the first time in the history of the Hamburg Jews, Jews were given full and equal rights among the rest of the city's population. This period of freedom, however, was very brief—the French were driven from the city, and Hamburg again became independent in 1814, revoking any rights that the Jews had been given during French rule. Finally, in 1850, the Jews of Hamburg were granted citizenship.[7]

The Jewish community in Hamburg has historically been one of the larger ones in Germany. In 1800, there were approximately 6,400 Jews living in the city—who accounted for about 6% of the city's population. By 1866, that number had almost doubled, to 12,550, and by 1933, it had grown to 19,000, although by that time, it was only 1.7% of the population of the city.[8] In the 1930s, Hamburg was the second largest city in Germany, and had the fourth largest Jewish community. By that point, many of Hamburg's Jewish residents had acculturated and become well integrated into city life.[9]

Max Harper was born in Hamburg in 1931.

Additionally, 1931 was one of the years in the late 1920s and early 1930s in which the fortunes of the Nazi party appeared to change. In 1929, the start of the Great Depression caused many Germans to again look for hope elsewhere than the Democratic Weimar Republic—making some radical Nazi views more appealing. By 1930, the Reichstag elections demonstrated the German people's dramatic shift toward Nazism. Peter Hoffman, in his book *German Resistance to Hitler*, gives the numbers for the elections from 1924–1930:

> The Nazi Party was catapulted to national importance in the Reichstag elections of September 1930. After receiving 6.6 percent of the popular vote, or 32 Reichstag seats, in May 1924, the Nazis had won only 2.6 percent of the popular vote, or 12 Reichstag seats, in the elections of May 1928. In September 1930, they increased their support to 18.3 percent, for 107 Reichstag seats.[10]

This made the Nazis the second largest party in the Reichstag.[11] William Shirer explains the effect of this:

> The month of September 1930 marked a turning point in the road that was leading the Germans inexorably toward the Third Reich. The surprising success of the Nazi Party in the national elections convinced not only millions of ordinary people but many leaders in business and in the Army that perhaps here was an upsurge that could not be stopped. They might not like the party's demagoguery and its vulgarity, but on the

other hand it was arousing the old feelings of German patriotism and nationalism which had been so muted during the first ten years of the Republic. It promised to lead the German people away from communism, socialism, trade-unionism and the futilities of democracy. Above all, it had caught fire throughout the Reich. It was a success.[12]

Therefore, by 1931, business leaders began to back Hitler and his party.

> That the Austrian upstart, as many of them had regarded him in the Twenties, might well take over the control of Germany began to dawn on the business leaders after the sensational Nazi gains in the September elections of 1930. By 1931, Walther Funk testified at Nuremberg, 'my industrial friends and I were convinced that the Nazi Party would come to power in the not too distant future.'[13]

Walther Funk was the editor of a leading German financial newspaper, the *Berliner Boersenzeitung*, who left his job to join the Nazis and serve as a connection between the Nazi Party and business leaders.[14] Thus the Nazi party continued to gain increasing support—and from the businesses, increasing financial strength.

In 1931, the future for Germany's Jews was growing steadily and relentlessly darker.

Beginnings

Max Harper was born on December 23, 1931, as Kurt Max Koenigsbuch. Max's father was Aron Adolf Koenigsbuch (b. April 21, 1893, in Brzesko),[15] and his mother was Elisabetha Koenigsbuch (b. April 12, 1896, in Münster).[16] His older brother, Rolf Koenigsbuch, was born two years prior to Max on May 26, 1929. But Max would not remember any of the time in which he lived with just them as a carefree, happy family, undisturbed by the perils of Nazism. Because he was born at the very end of 1931, and Hitler was appointed chancellor of Germany in January 1933, Max's memories of childhood are tainted by the dark cloud Nazism had brought over German Jewry.

Elisabetha, Rolf, Max, and Aron Koenigsbuch.

When asked about anything he remembered from his childhood, specific memories consisted of confrontations with the Nazis: "My father owned a factory . . . he used to make uniforms for the German army . . . they just took the factory away from him, and they said, 'a Jew has no right to own a company and so on.'"[17]

Max then jumped to a memory of *Kristallnacht*—which occurred when he was just six:

> The S.S. came into our house—my mother saw them coming, so she hid us under the kitchen table with the long table cloth hanging down to the floor. And they came in; they threw all the cabinets down looking for gold and silver—stealing it from the people"[18]

After *Kristallnacht,* Max and his family were forced to leave their house: "I remember when I lived in Germany . . . the place we lived in, a Nazi officer moved into the building, and he threw us out. He didn't like Jewish people living in the same building as him."[19]

When discussing these things, another memory came to Max's mind:

> Before the Nazi officer threw us out of that house in Hamburg . . . just before we were thrown out, there were a couple of Nazis pushing an old guy back and forward on the street . . . pushing him from one to the other, you know what I mean?[20]

From his birth to a time shortly before his eighth birthday, when he fled Germany on the Kindertransport, Max's memories of his childhood are far from idyllic. They recall scenes from a childhood broken and scarred by antisemitism and the ability of many to act upon that hatred with impunity.

Rolf's experiences were the same—though he was older than Max was when the Nazis came to power in Germany, and thus could remember more. Rolf also had the benefit of recording his testimony in 1955, when memories were fresher—although he could still recall only a few of the details of the Koenigsbuchs' life before the Nazis:

> My father, Aaron[21] Koenigsbuch, was a business man, as far as I remember a successful one, who owned a

clothing business dealing in special clothing for seamen and other lines. I believe, but will have to make enquires before stating so, that he also owned the factory producing the wares he was selling . . . . My mother, Elisabetha Koenigsbuch, nee Von de Walde, was a housewife. She was in ill-health, suffering from heart trouble and had the assistance of a maid-cook, and a nurse to look after me.

My brother, Kurt Max Koenigsbuch, was born in December 1931 in a Hamburg clinic. I remember the time of his birth and remember driving with my father to visit my mother and brother at the Clinic. We resided at No. 4, Werderstrasse, Hamburg, in a large block of flats. We lived in the ground floor flat."[22]

The Isebek Canal.

The Koenigsbuch apartment was located only a few feet from Innocentia Park, a beautiful green space in the midst of the city. The Isebek Canal was just a few blocks from their home. The nearest synagogue, the Alte und Neue Klaus synagogue, located at 11a Rutschbahn, was less than half a mile from their flat. The synagogue held seating for 160 and was specifically a *Beit Midrash*—a place in which study of the Talmud took place throughout the day.[23] Only slightly farther south, just over half a mile away, was one of Hamburg's largest synagogues, the Bornplatz synagogue. This house of worship had seating for 1,100.[24]

The Bornplatz synagogue.

In Rolf's testimony, it is at this point, after the brief description of his brother's birth and his early life, at which his memories begin to include the Nazis. Just as with Max's memories, Rolf's childhood recollections were tainted and colored by Nazi persecution: "We were a happy family and lived comfortably until the beginning of the Nazi regime."[25]

Everything changed when the Nazis came to power—the happy and comfortable family life, as was the case in each of these stories, was shattered. At that point, January 1933, Rolf was three and Max was one.

Nevertheless, Rolf recalled a terrifying picture of that time:

> In 1933 my family was one day ordered to join the family on the top floor of the block of flats we occupied. They were Jewish, as were my family. From a window of this flat I remember seeing men in brown shirts and breeches (S.A. Men) sniping with rifles from the doorways of shops in the streets opposite.[26]

From 1933 until 1936, Rolf's memories are silent—but remembering 1936, he told the same story as Max about their father's company, but with a few added details:

> One day, while with my father at his business, a man came into the shop and advised my father to close.
>
> A large gang of Nazi hooligans were entering all shops in the area and dragging proprietors and customers into the street for manhandling. I saw a woman dragged through the streets by her hair. My father hurriedly closed the shop and took me home.

In the same year of 1936 my father was forced to give up his business to a member of the Nazi party who, no doubt, just felt that he would like to own the business. I remember that little or nothing was given to my father for the business, in fact after that we became very poor.[27]

Aron Koenigsbuch, like all the parents in this series who owned their own businesses, was the victim of Aryanization—the transfer of Jewish-owned businesses to non-Jewish Germans throughout the Third Reich. It took place in two stages: the first, from 1933–1938 was "voluntary," in which the Nazis sought to either bankrupt Jewish businesses or intimidate Jewish business owners into selling their companies for a fraction of what they were worth. This was accomplished through unofficial boycotts—in which advertisements were printed denouncing Germans who bought from Jews, and guards were posted outside Jewish businesses to harass customers. Jews owned 50,000 shops in Germany in 1933—and after this first stage of Aryanization, by 1938, only 9,000 remained; 41,000 had been stolen, and Aron Koenigsbuch's uniform company was among them. The second stage of Aryanization took place after 1938—at that point, businesses were simply stolen from their Jewish owners, without any kind of compensation.[28]

Consequently, in the middle of this Aryanization process, Aron Koenigsbuch sold his business for close to nothing—essentially forced to give away his livelihood.

Nevertheless, though the Koenigsbuchs were impoverished by this sale, Aron was able to find employment as a chauffeur for a friend. Again, however, tragedy struck—this time in the form of an accident. Aron was sitting in the car, waiting for his friend. Suddenly, the car was rear-ended by a truck carrying pigs. The crash crushed the car, pinning Aron between the seat and the steering wheel. Rolf stated:

> I remember being told of the accident on my return from my first day at school. My father was taken to hospital and I believe suffered from concussion. It was the end of his employment and of his means of providing for the family for a long time.[29]

Aron, who had been sitting in a parked car, was not responsible for the crash—and in fact, such was subsequently determined in a German court of law. Nevertheless, the truck's driver was a member of the Nazi party, and Aron was a Jew. Therefore, despite being the victim of the crash, Aron was given no compensation for his injuries or for his inability to work any longer.

Rolf and Max Koenigsbuch.

This was a calamity for the Koenigsbuch family, who now had no source of income—and no prospects for one either, with their major breadwinner needing to be hospitalized. Elisabetha, as Rolf recalled, was ill herself, and so her opportunities were also limited. Furthermore, the family also needed to pay hospital bills, which, Rolf remembered, they could not afford. Fortunately, a friend, Mr. Kurt Moses, graciously foot the bill for them. Subsequently, Mr. Moses was murdered by the Germans, according to Rolf, "in a concentration camp." The *Gedenkbook*, or the Memorial Book of the German Jews who perished as victims of the Nazis from 1933–1945, lists two men by the name of Kurt Moses from Hamburg. One perished in Hamburg in 1940 but had been imprisoned in the Sachsenhausen concentration camp for a few weeks after *Kristallnacht*,[30] and the other was deported from Hamburg in 1942 and was murdered in the Theresienstadt concentration camp[31] in 1943.[32]

Kristallnacht

Though Max described some of the events of *Kristallnacht*, recalling that his mother had him and his brother hide under the table, Rolf's memories barely touch on the pogrom. His description is succinct: "My father was arrested in our home and taken to a concentration camp."[33]

That night, seven synagogues in Hamburg were destroyed.[34] The Alte und Neue Klaus synagogue—the closest one to the Koenigsbuch's apartment, survived the pogrom, although the inside was looted.[35] The Bornplatz Synagogue was set on fire, yet its structure remained intact. Despite that fact, after *Kristallnacht*, the congregation was forced to pay for its demolition and then to sell the property. Eventually, a bunker was built on the property.[36]

And then, on *Kristallnacht,* over 1,000 Jewish men were incarcerated in Fuhlsbüttel prison. From there, a few were sent to Sachsenhausen concentration camp, approximately 35 miles north of Berlin, where they were detained for a number of weeks.[37]

At the time of his testimony, 1955, Rolf did not know the exact camp to which his father was sent, but he suspected Buchenwald. Now however, it is known that Aron Koenigsbuch was among those who were arrested and taken to Sachsenhausen, where he was imprisoned from early November 1938 to January 17, 1939.[38] There he was prisoner number 10767.[39]

Yet the Koenigsbuchs had no idea what Aron's fate would be—and if he would ever be released. Thus, Max and Rolf, after "the Night of Broken Glass," suddenly found themselves without a father, and Elisabetha, with her heart condition, without a husband.

After *Kristallnacht*

But time would not stand still—hence their situation continued to worsen.

> While my father was imprisoned, a number of events happened. The school which my brother and I attended was surrounded by S.S. men and several of the children beaten in the gymnasium into which everyone was ordered to go. Shots were fired at the windows of the classrooms. My brother and I were rescued by a non-Jewish lady who was a friend of the family. She persuaded the men in charge of the outrage to let us go with her, and she took us home in a taxi. When the remainder of the children were released I do not know. Most of the teachers, however, were missing when we

> resumed schooling, having been arrested. That same day I saw two S.S. men who were busy smashing up a synagogue next to the school falling off the dome of the synagogue to their deaths. I was amongst those who clapped heartily.[40]

Rolf was nine years old when he witnessed these things. Max had just turned seven.

After the events at the school, Rolf, Max, and Elisabetha were forced to move—as Max recalled. Rolf's recollection added a few extra specifics however. The Koenigsbuch family had lived in their apartment for over 12 years, and as Rolf related at the beginning of his testimony, they lived on the ground floor. After *Kristallnacht,* a member of the Nazi party moved into the same building—but his residence was on the top floor. Regardless, he objected to living even on the same block as a Jew; therefore, the Koenigsbuchs had to leave.

They moved from their apartment on Werderstrasse to one on Agathenstrasse. It was a short move—the two homes were only a little more than a mile apart. But Elisabetha Koenigsbuch, with her husband locked up in Sachsenhausen, had to find a way to fund this relocation.

> We moved to Agatenstrasse [*sic*] No. 3, Hamburg, which was to be my last home in Germany. My father knew nothing of this because he was still imprisoned. My mother had to move the whole family and belongings across the city with the money she had saved for food. My brother and I did not go short but I remember well that my mother had little or nothing to eat for many days . . . . My father was released nine weeks after his arrest and about a fortnight after our move.[41]

Eventually, Aron Koenigsbuch returned home. During that time, the Koenigsbuchs received notice that all of their jewelry was to be confiscated by the Gestapo—thus, the family handed over a cigar box full of gold and silver trinkets. At the same time, Aron was also able to find employment, this time as a carpenter. Rolf recalled that as a result, "We were able to eat better." They were not allowed "luxuries" such as sugar and butter, but they "managed."[42]

It was likely around this time, perhaps because of what Aron had seen in Sachsenhausen, that plans began to be made to send the two boys out of Germany and to safety in England.

The Kindertransport

In June 1939, the two boys were given startling news: they were moving to England in five days. Neither of them had known of the plans for their travel, and everything took place very suddenly. It was a flurry of activity as they, along with their parents, attempted to determine what should be taken on the journey.

Five days later, they boarded a train and said goodbye to their parents.

Rolf had just turned 10 and Max was 7.

Within four years, the boys were orphans.

Max's Family

In the 1930s, there were approximately 19,000 Jews living in Hamburg.[43] Of these, 300 committed suicide during Nazi rule, and at least 8,877 were murdered. After the Holocaust, a new Jewish community was started in Hamburg—as of 2007, there were 3,100 Jews living in the city, and though it was 60 years after the war had ended, that number was less than 20 percent of the Jews who had lived in Hamburg before the Nazi tyranny.[44]

Aron and Elisabetha Koenigsbuch were two of those who perished.

After being released from Sachsenhausen, Aron returned home and lived in Hamburg with Elisabetha until October 25, 1941—over two years after the boys had been sent to England. On that day, both Aron and Elisabetha were deported to the Lodz ghetto.[45]

Lodz is approximately 85 miles southwest of Warsaw and centrally located in Poland. When the Germans conquered the city, they renamed it Litzmannstadt, after a German general who had captured the city during World War I. As such,

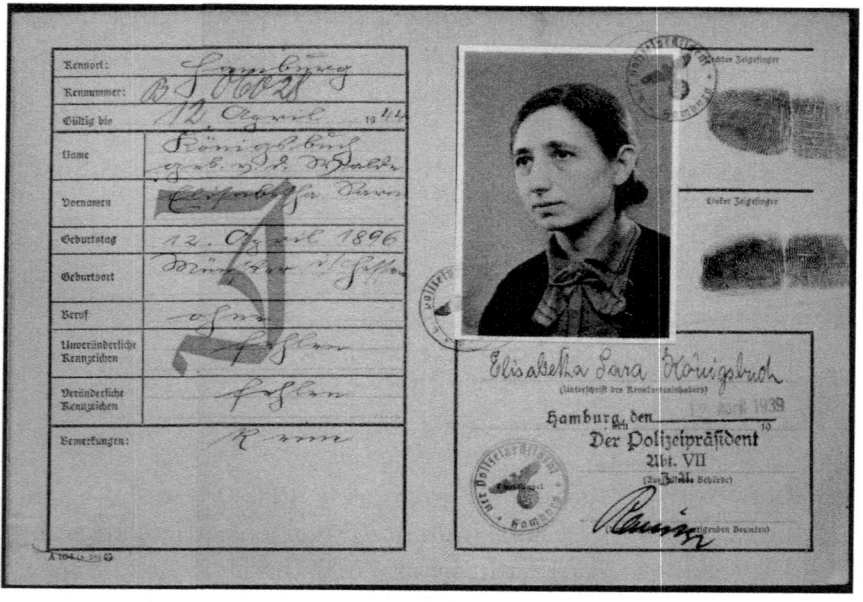

Elisabetha Koenigsbuch's *kennkarte* (identity card), 1939. Note the large "J" stamped on the left, as well as her middle name "Sara."

264

occasionally the Lodz ghetto is called the Litzmannstadt ghetto. The ghetto itself was established in February 1940, approximately six months after the Germans had captured Lodz. Around 160,000 Jews were forced to live in the ghetto, separated from the rest of the city's inhabitants by barbed wire. The head of the Jewish council in Lodz, Mordechai Chaim Rumkowski, believed that industrial productivity could render the ghetto indispensable to the Germans and consequently could spare the lives of the ghetto's inhabitants, so the Lodz ghetto became a major center of production during the Holocaust.

Nevertheless, ghetto life was characterized by overcrowding, starvation, hard labor, and primitive facilities—most of the ghetto lacked running water and a sewer system. More than 20 percent of the ghetto's inhabitants perished as a direct result of the squalid living conditions there. In January 1942, the Germans began deportations from Lodz to Chelmno, one of the Holocaust's death centers. There, the Jews were gassed with carbon monoxide in the back of vans. From January to September 1942, approximately 70,000 of the ghetto's inhabitants were murdered in this way.[46]

Chaim Kaplan, confined in the Warsaw ghetto, heard of the situation in Lodz and made the following entry in his diary on March 23, 1942:

> The administration of Lodz decided to abolish the ghetto in two or three days. That is always its way, to surprise the wretched deportees and cast confusion in their ranks; and the main point is that they not manage to remove their property in the time of emergency, so that the regime will be the 'legal' inheritor. In line with that custom it called upon the Chairman of the Judenrat, Chaim Rumkowski, decreeing with the full severity of the law, that he was required to abolish the

ghetto in two or three days. Immediately after the announcement it began its thievish work: it stole all the cash from the council treasury (estimated at two million zlotys) and plundered all the food supplies and all the raw material that had been brought in to sustain the ghetto. The hand that had given returned to take away. The deportation began. The details of it are not well known to me, because I am far from the scene of the deed. Now Lodz is tantamount to foreign soil, and there is no contact between it and the other Jewish settlements in the Generalgouvernement. The local chroniclers will certainly record them in full detail for coming generations. Here I only emphasize the existence of the signs of that dread decree. Now the post office no longer sends letters from Jews to the inhabitants of the Lodz ghetto, as if they no longer were living. And letters from there no longer arrive here.[47]

Thus the Jewish community of Lodz, the second largest Jewish community of Poland,[48] was eradicated.

Aron and Elisabetha Koenigsbuch were two of the many who perished from the horrendous conditions within the ghetto. Yet, for a time, Aron's work in the ghetto saved both his life and that of his wife—or at least prolonged their lives for another few months. After having arrived in Lodz in October 1941, in May 1942, the Koenigsbuchs were among those chosen for deportation. In response, Aron wrote a letter—one of the last he would ever write:

Aron Königsbuch
Litzmannstadt-G[hetto], d[en] 8.V.42
Kranachstr. 24/58

To the office of new settlers, here

Ref.: Request for departure IX/661-62

I hereby ask politely for the request to depart to be canceled for <u>me</u> and <u>my wife</u> [emphasis in original] Elisabetha Koenigsbuch, because I have been working as a specialist in the carpenter department since 23.3.42. Work attestation of the department is attached.

Attachment: 1 Work attestation.[49]

Attached to the letter is the following note:

The Elders of the Jews in Litzmannstadt
Labor Department, Department of Carpentry
Zimmerstr. No. 12.

Litzmannstadt, 8 May 1942

Ltz. 2102/42 TA.

Regarding Case No. IX 661-62

Certificate

We hereby certify that Königsbach Aron, residing at Jewish St. 24/58, is hired in this department as a carpenter and is necessary to us for production.

This certificate is issued for the purpose of submission to the Deportation Commission.

Director of the Labor Department
[Signed][50]

The letter is stamped with the word *Uwzglednione*, or "Accepted" in Polish. Because of his work, Aron and Elisabetha avoided the death otherwise awaiting them at Chelmno.

Nonetheless, on August 3, 1942, less than three months after his request to avoid deportation had been accepted, Aron Koenigsbuch died of tuberculosis in the Lodz ghetto.[51] He was 49 years old. Elisabetha lived in the ghetto for another year but perished in the same way her husband had—of tuberculosis on December 7, 1943.[52] She was 47.

In his testimony, only a little over a decade after his parents' death, Rolf stated the following:

> They were taken without belongings and sent to a concentration camp in Poland where they died. I was assured of their death by the Red Cross whom I contacted just after the war. I first learned of their arrest through a Red Cross letter of 25 words.[53]

Twenty-five words is less than two lines of text—and Rolf and Max would have likely received the 25 words shortly after their parents' deportation, or when they were no more than 13 and 10 years old. Four years later, the boys were told that their parents were dead.

And in 1955, Rolf and Max apparently still had no certainty regarding *where* their parents had died: "I believe the camp in which they died was somewhere near Lodz, Poland."[54]

Thus, Aron and Elisabeth were dead, and Rolf and Max had been sent to live in a foreign country and had to learn a new language and adapt to a new culture. The Holocaust struck hard at the Koenigsbuch family—and not just at the immediate family. Many of the family's relatives were victims

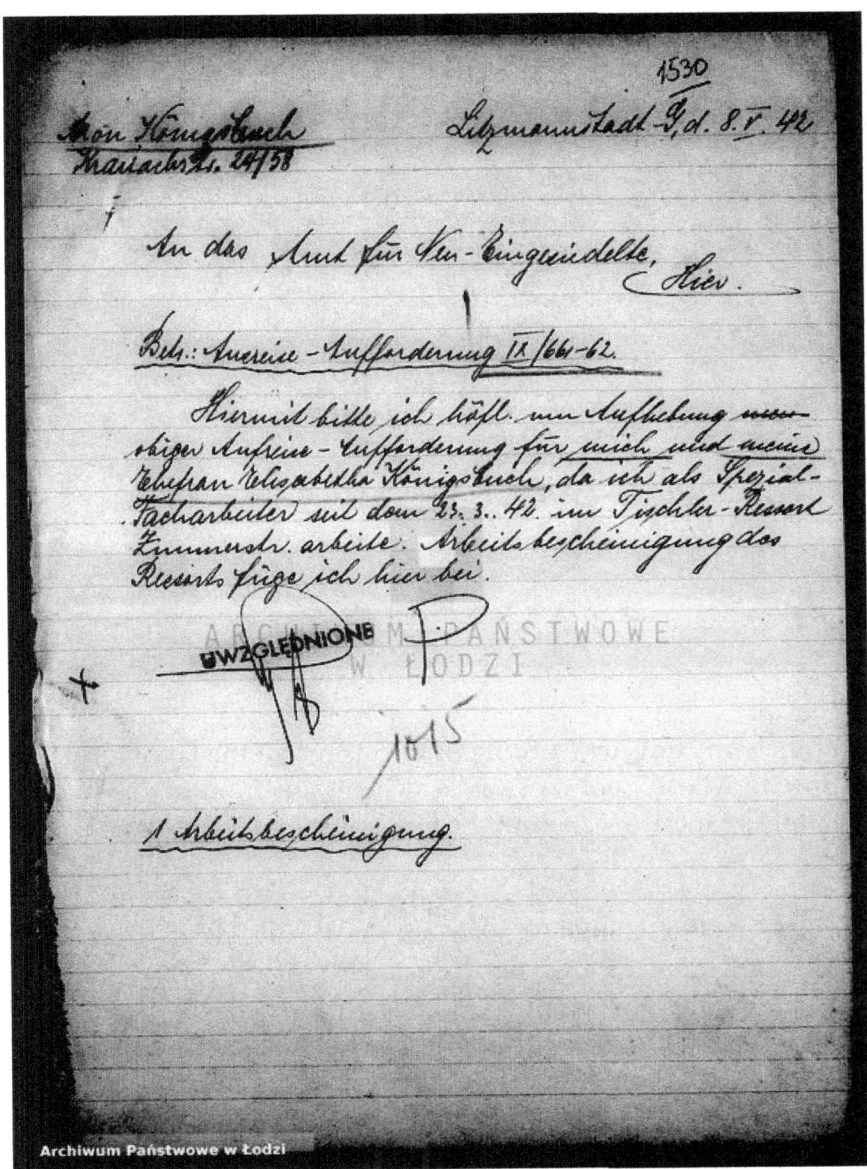

Aron Koenigsbuch's request to be excused from the deportation, 1942.

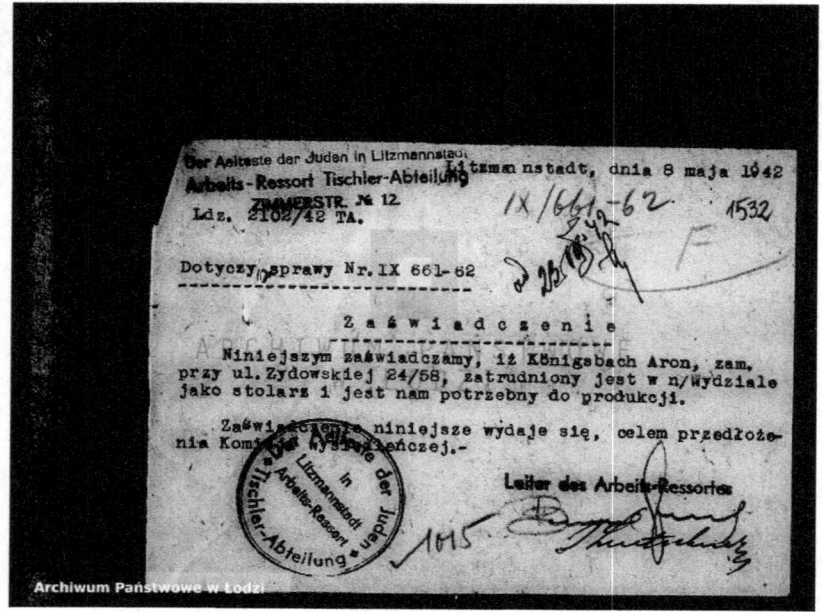

Work attestation attached to Aron Koenigsbuch's request to be excused from the deportation, 1942.

of the same tragedy. Writing of the history of the family, Jacob Rosen, whose mother was a Koenigsbuch, described the family's experience in both the Holocaust and its aftermath:

> So far I established that members of the KOENIGSBUCH clan survived Auschwitz, were on Schindler's List, on the Kindertransport, were hidden in the Netherlands, escaped to Sweden via Denmark, served in the British Police in Mandatory Palestine and the British Army, were illegal immigrants to Palestine, fought during the [Israeli] War of Independence and were killed in action as soldiers and officers in the Israeli Defense Forces.[55]

Yet tragically, despite the uniqueness of the Koenigsbuch family experience—children sent on the Kindertransport, and individuals escaping to Sweden from Denmark—the death and destruction that also came upon the Koenigsbuchs—with children being separated from their parents, individuals having to live in hiding, some perishing in Lodz, and others deported to Auschwitz—was heartbreakingly similar to that of many other Jewish families throughout Europe. Although the tragedy of the Holocaust is indeed a tragedy of individuals, the number of individuals who suffered is staggering—and thus the sheer enormity of the Holocaust cannot but help make this tragedy even more poignant.

England

Yet Max and Rolf escaped.

And in June 1939, the two boys arrived in England.

In England, they moved from place to place. Max believes that he initially came to live in a home in Welwyn Garden City, a town approximately 20 miles north of London.[56] From there, Max and Rolf came to live with the Argle family in Waterhouses, a small village in Stoke on Trent, 140 miles northwest of Welwyn Garden City. The files of the Jewish Refugee Committee state the following about Rolf while in Waterhouses:

> July 1941 – Has a very happy carefree home with the Argles in lovely country . . . is a rather reserved quiet boy.
>
> October 1941 – Seems to have settled well in the household. He helps with the animals out of school and leads a healthy outdoor life. He gets on well with

the village people who tend to be a little biased against refugees.[57]

But there was also a religious concern. The refugee committee noted the following: "Rolf refused to attend classes arranged by Jewish Emergency Com. wanted to go to Methodist Sunday school . . . . It is now suggested he takes correspondence course."[58]

It appears as though Rolf was doing well at the home in Waterhouses, although there was some type of religious concern. Nevertheless, despite the report stating that Rolf has "a very happy carefree home," Max has vastly different memories of their time with the Argles. He states:

> I think it was Stoke on Trent, at a place called Waterhouses, and there the people that looked after my brother and me weren't very kind people . . . they had us sleep in the chicken house. Yeah, it was part of the chicken house, converted into bedrooms. . . . I think we were allowed in for meals only. I remember that my father gave me a silver watch before we left for England. And I didn't want to lose it. It was an old silver watch like a pocket watch, and I asked these people to look after it. When we left there, they claimed they never had it.[59]

In 1942, the boys complained about how they were treated, and consequently were moved from Waterhouses to the town of Bampton, in Devon, approximately 200 miles from Waterhouses, in the southwestern portion of England. In Bampton, the brothers lived with Mr. and Mrs. Hyams in a home called "The Old House." At first, things were good, with the committee making the following note (specifically about Rolf, although Max was living there too):

> June 1943 – excellent health, attending Bampton Senior Council School, boy happy and well cared for.[60]

Approximately a year later, however, it seems that the relationship between Rolf and the Hyams had declined.

> October 1944 – talked to Mrs. Hyams: according to Mrs. Hyams Rolf has tried to move into private digs (after a uqarrel [sic] with the Hyams). For prestige reasons Mrs. Hyams has made it clear to him that he could not do that, living in digs, when his brother is still with the Hyams. So he stayed on.[61]

For reasons unknown, Rolf no longer wanted to live with the Hyams. Moreover, at school in Bampton, Max was bullied and called the "German-Jew"[62]—so the pull for him to stay in Bampton was also not strong. Accordingly, the notes of the refugee committee for December 1944, shortly after Rolf's quarrel with the Hyams, state, "Mrs. Hahn-Warburg ... taking up the questions of move into a hostel for both boys."[63]

Accordingly, in January 1945, both boys moved to Birmingham, in the Midlands of England, to a hostel called Elpis Lodge.

Elpis Lodge

Elpis Lodge was founded in 1940, so by the time Max and Rolf came to live there, it had been operating for nearly six years. And by January 1945, the war was almost over—and it was beginning to be felt that the need for the hostel was not nearly as great as it had been originally.

Consequently, that year, in November 1945, *The Christadelphian* magazine printed an article reflecting upon the six years in which the hostel had been in operation and explaining that the Representative Council for Birmingham Jewry and the Refugee Children's Movement in London had jointly agreed that the Christadelphian ecclesias of Birmingham and Coventry had met their commitments for the hostel and that the financial support they had given to it over the last six years could cease. In other words, it was felt that the hostel was no longer essential. Therefore, the remaining £275 in the hostel's treasury was split between the Chief Rabbi's United Appeal Fund and The Women's Appeal for Jewish Women and Children. The hostel's structure and its furnishings were donated to the Refugee Children's Movement.[64]

At that point, the Refugee Children's Movement assumed financial responsibility for Elpis Lodge, so for the first few months Max and Rolf lived at Elpis Lodge, the Christadelphians were still the sponsors. But as 1945 came to a close, the ownership of the hostel changed.

With the Christadelphians ending their work in Elpis Lodge, Dr. Albert Hirsch, the man whom the Christadelphians had chosen to run Elpis Lodge, wrote a letter to express his gratitude:

> On this occasion I would like to express our heartiest thanks to you personally as well as to the subscribers of *The Christadelphian* and *The Path* for their continuous interest and their spiritual and material help. You have been so closely connected from the beginning with the magnanimous foundation of 'Elpis Lodge' that it will hardly be necessary to give you any details. Still I would like to say that you have enabled 48 boys, most of whom are to be regarded as orphans, to be properly trained in a trade or employment best suited for them, that you have given them the opportunity of being instructed in the English language, of being introduced

> into the cultural life of this country and educated in the religion of their parents. I need not say how much we were pleased about articles in *The Christadelphian* and *The Path* concerned with 'Elpis Lodge' and how often we ourselves found consolation and encouragement in your magazines. We are very grateful indeed for all your good work which we highly appreciate. I am sure that every boy who has been educated in 'Elpis Lodge' will keep his gratitude for his lifetime.[65]

Max and Rolf were able to stay in Elpis Lodge until 1948, longer than they had lived in any other place since they had fled to England from Germany. They had moved from one place to another, and here, in this hostel named "an abode of hope," they had found a place they could settle in for more than three years.

Later

In 1947, two years after the war had ended, Max and Rolf became British citizens. Eventually, both also joined the British army. Max recalled: "I was in the royal engineers. . . . I served with them for five years. Part of the five years I served in Korea for 18 months, in the Korean war. That was just a rough sort of thing for my life."[66]

On the other hand, Rolf was stationed on the Malay Peninsula, thus after years of being together, and without any family remaining, the two brothers were separated. Nevertheless, for a moment in time, during their five years in the army, the circumstances came together for them to meet again:

> He was stationed in Singapore, and when our ship docked in Singapore, he knew we were coming on the ship, so he got me—I had a leave for four hours for compassionate reasons to see him, so he came aboard,

and he took me around Singapore for four hours. I applied for compassionate leave because he was my only living relative at the time, you know?[67]

After serving in the army, Max returned to England and met his wife, Ada Potts. Yet he still wanted to see the world. Although he had traveled quite a bit during his lifetime, he still longed to see more. As such, before they were married, Max and Ada agreed that they would make their home in Canada. They came over in 1956. Max states:

> I saved up enough money for the fare, and we spent our honeymoon on the boat coming over . . . I had £100 in my pocket when I came to Canada. That lasted a long time. I think it lasted over three months. My grocery bill in '56 was eight dollars a week.[68]

Max and Ada settled in the Toronto area. Rolf had also been interested in making his home in Canada, so that same year, but a bit later, Rolf followed Max and Ada.

For a number of years, the brothers lived happily together in the Toronto area. Yet, approximately four decades after they had fled Germany together, their family was again struck by early death—Rolf was diagnosed with multiple sclerosis, and in 1981, passed away.

Max is now 85 years old and still lives in Canada. He and Ada have one son, Stephen, and three grandchildren, Megan, Michael, and Aidan.

Conclusion

Max and Rolf had their lives spared when a place was found for them on the Kindertransport. Yet when they came to England, they continued to move from place to place, until

Max and Ada Harper, with their son Stephen and three grandchildren – Megan, Michael, and Aidan.

coming to live in Elpis Lodge in January 1945, and staying there for more than three years.

Elpis Lodge was a place of hope for many. Despite all that they had suffered in continental Europe, there, in that place that had come into being because of a small Christian group's belief in the promises made to Abraham, the two brothers found comfort.

A few months after the Christadelphians had transferred the ownership of Elpis Lodge to the Refugee Children's Movement, E.W. Newman, the Christadelphian who had served as the treasurer of Elpis Lodge, received the following letter from a young man who had lived in Elpis Lodge and subsequently immigrated to Palestine:

> Now I have the opportunity to thank you for everything you have done for me. All the happy years I spent at the Hostel under the able guidance of Dr. and Mrs. Hirsch I must admit there was little we went without. In all the ways in which you helped us, I do not think there could have been a better place in a foreign country, except being together with our families.
>
> My father is very sorry he cannot add a few lines, as he does not speak any English, but he will always be grateful to you for having made a man out of me. You can imagine how he felt when he saw me after seven years' separation. I left at the age of eleven and then return[ed] a full-grown youth of eighteen. I will never be able to thank you enough for what you have done for me.[69]

And yet, the opening of a hostel—of a place where Jewish boys such as Kurt Max Koenigsbuch and Rolf Koenigsbuch, who were orphaned as adolescents, could find some solace—was something that not only the refugees found invaluable, but an opportunity that the Christadelphians were grateful to have seized. In the same magazine article that explained that Elpis Lodge would pass to the care of the Refugee Children's Movement, the editor of *The Christadelphian* magazine, John Carter, expressed the community's feelings:

> We venture to think that the brethren and sisters who have contributed to the maintenance of the hostel . . . will feel that at a time when Israel's need was so great, the establishment and maintenance of this hostel out of funds contributed solely by Christadelphians has thoroughly justified itself.[70]

Indeed, in the hindsight of 70 years, it can unquestionably be said that it has.

---

[1] "The Jewish Traveler: Hamburg," *Hadassah Magazine,* November 2008, http://www.hadassahmagazine.org/2008/11/29/jewish-traveler-hamburg/.

[2] "Port of Hamburg," *Port of Hamburg,* accessed April 6, 2017, https://www.hafen-hamburg.de/.

[3] "The Jewish Traveler: Hamburg," *Hadassah Magazine,* November 2008, http://www.hadassahmagazine.org/2008/11/29/jewish-traveler-hamburg/.

[4] Ibid.

[5] "Germany: Hamburg," *Jewish Virtual Library,* accessed April 6, 2017, http://www.jewishvirtuallibrary.org/hamburg.

6 Ibid.

7 Ibid.

8 Ibid.

9 "Hamburg," Yad Vashem, accessed April 6, 2017, http://www.yadvashem.org/odot_pdf/Microsoft%20Word%20-%206350.pdf.

10 Peter Hoffman, German Resistance to Hitler (Cambridge: Harvard University Press, 1988), 9-10.

11 William Shirer, The Rise and Fall of the Third Reich (New York: Simon and Schuster, 1960), 138.

12 Ibid, 141.

13 Ibid, 142.

14 Ibid, 143.

15 "Last Letters from the Lodz (Lodsch) Ghetto," JewishGen, accessed April 28, 2017, http://www.jewishgen.org/databases/jgdetail_2.php.

16 Ibid.

17 Max Harper in discussion with the author, April 25, 2016.

18 Ibid.

19 Ibid.

20 Ibid.

21 Despite the fact that Rolf's father's name is spelled in this way here, his letter from the Lodz ghetto spells his name "Aron."

22 Rolf S. Koenigsbuch, Personal Experiences. Weiner Library P II.a. No. 175.

23 "Hamburg - 11a Rutschbahn, Alte und Neue Klaus Synagogue," Synagogue Memorial "Beit Ashkenaz," accessed April 6, 2017, http://germansynagogues.com/index.php/synagogues-and-communities?pid=58&sid=603:hamburg-11a-rutschbahn-alte-und-neue-klaus-synagogue.

24 "Hamburg - 8 Bornplatz (Rotherbaum Locality)," Synagogue Memorial "Beit Ashkenaz," accessed April 6, 2017, http://germansynagogues.com/index.php/synagogues-and-communities?pid=58&sid=601:hamburg-8-bornplatz-rotherbaum-locality.

25 Rolf S. Koenigsbuch, Personal Experiences. Weiner Library P II.a. No. 175.

26 Ibid.

27 Ibid.

28 "Aryanization," Yad Vashem, accessed April 6, 2017, http://www.yadvashem.org/odot_pdf/Microsoft%20Word%20-%205775.pdf.

29 Rolf S. Koenigsbuch, Personal Experiences. Weiner Library P II.a. No. 175.

30 "Gedenkbuch - Opfer Der Verfolgung Der Juden Unter Der Nationalsozialistischen Gewaltherrschaft in Deutschland 1933-1945," Das Bundesarchiv, accessed April 7, 2017, https://www.bundesarchiv.de/gedenkbuch/en932657.

31 For more information on this camp, see Hana Holman's biography, Part of the Family - Volume 1, 154.

32 "Gedenkbuch - Opfer Der Verfolgung Der Juden Unter Der Nationalsozialistischen Gewaltherrschaft in Deutschland 1933–1945," Das Bundesarchiv, accessed April 7, 2017, https://www.bundesarchiv.de/gedenkbuch/en932655.

33 Rolf S. Koenigsbuch, Personal Experiences. Weiner Library P II.a. No. 175.

34 "Hamburg - Introduction," Synagogue Memorial "Beit Ashkenaz," accessed April 7, 2017, http://germansynagogues.com/index.php/synagogues-and-communities?pid=58&sid=599:hamburg-introduction.

35 "Hamburg - 11a Rutschbahn, Alte und Neue Klaus Synagogue," Synagogue Memorial "Beit Ashkenaz," accessed April 7, 2017, http://germansynagogues.com/index.php/synagogues-and-communities?pid=58&sid=603:hamburg-11a-rutschbahn-alte-und-neue-klaus-synagogue.

36 "Hamburg - 8 Bornplatz (Rotherbaum Locality)," Synagogue Memorial "Beit Ashkenaz," accessed April 7, 2017, http://germansynagogues.com/index.php/synagogues-and-communities?pid=58&sid=601:hamburg-8-bornplatz-rotherbaum-locality.

37 "Hamburg - Introduction," Synagogue Memorial "Beit Ashkenaz," accessed April 7, 2017, http://germansynagogues.com/index.php/synagogues-and-communities?pid=58&sid=599:hamburg-introduction.

38 "Gedenkbuch - Opfer Der Verfolgung Der Juden Unter Der Nationalsozialistischen Gewaltherrschaft in Deutschland 1933-1945," Das Bundesarchiv, accessed April 7, 2017, https://www.bundesarchiv.de/gedenkbuch/en902033.

39 Monika Liebscher, archivist at Sachsenhausen Museum, e-mail message to author, May 24, 2017.

40 Rolf S. Koenigsbuch, Personal Experiences. Weiner Library P II.a. No. 175.

41 Ibid.

42 Ibid.

43 "Germany: Hamburg," Jewish Virtual Library, accessed April 7, 2017, http://www.jewishvirtuallibrary.org/hamburg.

44 "Hamburg - Introduction," *Synagogue Memorial "Beit Ashkenaz,"* accessed April 7, 2017, http://germansynagogues.com/index.php/synagogues-and-communities?pid=58&sid=599:hamburg-introduction.

45 "Gedenkbuch - Opfer Der Verfolgung Der Juden Unter Der Nationalsozialistischen Gewaltherrschaft in Deutschland 1933-1945," *Das Bundesarchiv*, accessed April 7, 2017, https://www.bundesarchiv.de/gedenkbuch/en902033.

"Gedenkbuch - Opfer Der Verfolgung Der Juden Unter Der Nationalsozialistischen Gewaltherrschaft in Deutschland 1933-1945," *Das Bundesarchiv*, accessed April 7, 2017, https://www.bundesarchiv.de/gedenkbuch/en902036.

46 "Lodz," *United States Holocaust Memorial Museum*, accessed April 7, 2017, https://www.ushmm.org/wlc/en/article.php?ModuleId=10005071.

47 Chaim Kaplan, "Scroll of Agony," in *The Literature of Destruction*, ed. David Roskies (Philadelphia: The Jewish Publication Society, 1989), 445.

48 "Lodz," *YIVO Institute for Jewish Research*, accessed April 7, 2017, http://www.yivoencyclopedia.org/article.aspx/%C5%81odz.

49 Aron Koenigsbuch, letter to the office of new settlers, May 8, 1942. Translated by Fritz Neubauer. Copy of translation in possession of the author.

50 Work attestation for Aron Koenigsbuch. Translated by Jenny Levin. Copy of translation in possession of the author.

51 "Last Letters from the Lodz (Lodsch) Ghetto," *JewishGen*, accessed April 28, 2017, http://www.jewishgen.org/databases/jgdetail_2.php.

52 Ibid.

53 Rolf S. Koenigsbuch, Personal Experiences. Weiner Library P II.a. No. 175.

[54] Ibid.

[55] Jacob Rosen, "The Search for Koenigsbuch on the Internet," *Sharsheret Hadorot,* August 2005, XIII.

[56] Max Harper in discussion with the author, April 25, 2016.

[57] World Jewish Relief case files for Rolf Koenigsbuch, note for October 1941.

[58] Ibid.

[59] Max Harper in discussion with the author, April 25, 2016.

[60] World Jewish Relief case files for Rolf Koenigsbuch, note for June 1943.

[61] World Jewish Relief case files for Rolf Koenigsbuch, note for October 1944.

[62] Megan Harper, e-mail message to author, March 1, 2016.

[63] World Jewish Relief case files for Rolf Koenigsbuch, note for December 1944.

[64] John Carter, "The Ecclesial Visitor," *The Christadelphian*, November 1945, 129.

[65] Albert Hirsch, quoted in John Carter, "The Ecclesial Visitor," *The Christadelphian*, November 1945, 129.

[66] Max Harper in discussion with the author, April 25, 2016.

[67] Ibid.

[68] Ibid.

[69] Quoted from John Carter, "The Ecclesial Visitor," *The Christadelphian,* August 1946, 125.

[70] John Carter, "The Ecclesial Visitor," *The Christadelphian*, November 1945, 129.

RITA DEVLETIAN

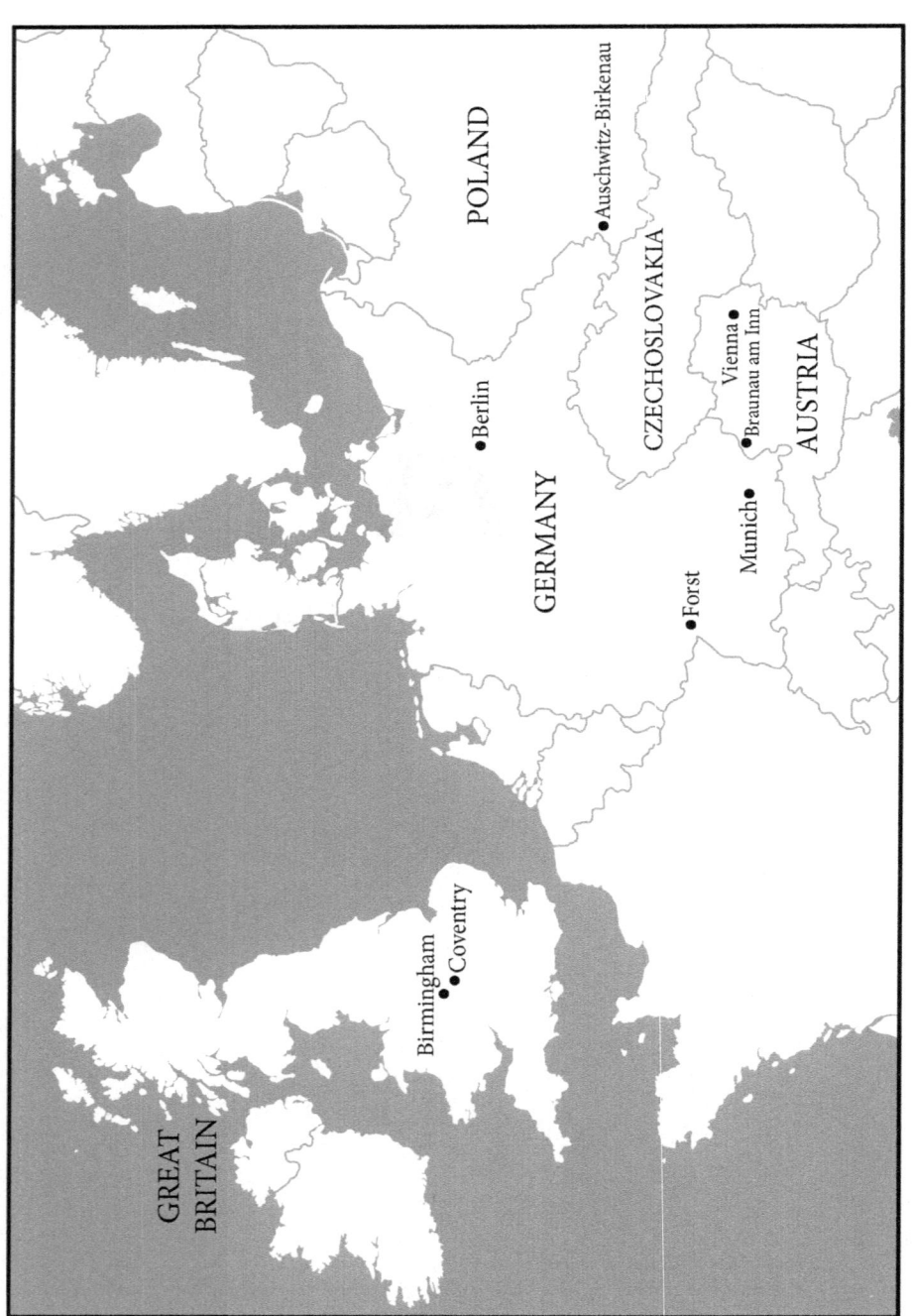

8

Rita Devletian (née Levy)

For over one thousand years, Austria was unified with the German states under the rule of the Holy Roman Empire. Austrians spoke German, and many Austrians considered themselves Germans. Although Austria was formally separated from the German states throughout the 1800s, many Austrians continued to keep their German identity.

Adolf Hitler was born in 1889 in Braunau am Inn, a town on the border between Germany and Austria. Though it was located on the border between the two nations, the town was clearly within Austria's territory. Both of Hitler's parents, Alois and Klara, were born in Austria and were thus Austrian citizens. Adolf Hitler was not born in Germany, nor were his parents Germans. He grew up with Austrian citizenship but spoke German and saw himself as an ethnic German—a nationalism that appears to have crystallized and become more essential to his ideology after he was influenced by certain political thinkers during his stint in Vienna.[1]

From February 1908 to May 1913, Hitler lived in Vienna, where he attempted to attend the Vienna Academy of the Arts, but failed. In May 1913, Hitler fled from Vienna to Munich, in an attempt to avoid arrest for evasion of mandatory military service to Austria.[2]

The First World War broke out in July 1914, and Hitler found himself living in Germany. For those few months, between Hitler's move to Munich and the eruption of war, he supported himself on income earned from his watercolors and sketches, but with the declaration of war, Hitler enlisted in the army. Being in Germany, he served in the German army. Despite his nationalism, this move eventually caused him problems in German politics, and after his service, his antisemitism appears to have become a clear part of his ideology.

Though Hitler saw himself as ethnically German and was a clear German nationalist, he was an Austrian citizen. Joining the German army meant that his Austrian citizenship had to be relinquished[3]—and thus, after the beginning of World War I, Adolf Hitler became stateless. He no longer had Austrian citizenship, nor was he offered German citizenship.

After the war ended, Hitler failed to apply for citizenship in Germany.[4] As his influence grew, he continued to remain stateless, yet his lack of citizenship appeared to be irrelevant, considering that his desire, along with that of his followers, was to overthrow the current government in Germany. Hence he staged the Beer Hall Putsch in 1923.

Nevertheless, the importance of gaining power through legal means was demonstrated in this failed revolution. After the Beer Hall Putsch, Hitler realized that to achieve rule over Germany, he would have to do so legally.[5]

Thus, German citizenship became essential. Without it, Hitler could not be elected to public office. Perhaps even more important, without it, Hitler could have been deported from Germany at any time.[6] And because of his revolutionary spirit, gaining citizenship was not going to be easy. In September 1930, *The New York Times* reported: "He failed to apply for

German citizenship when he was still a political nonentity, and since he has become the avowed enemy of the present republican form of government, his applications for citizenship have been constantly rejected."[7]

The German government was not going to give citizenship to a man who was an avowed enemy of the state—and so another legal means for Hitler to gain citizenship had to be devised. Under German law at the time, German citizenship would be conferred upon an individual if that individual was appointed to a government position.[8] After a failed attempt in 1930 to gain an appointment in Thuringia,[9] Hitler, two years later, was given a position in Brunswick, another German state. On February 25, 1932, Adolf Hitler became a German citizen, as reported one day later by *The New York Times*:

> Adolf Hitler became a German citizen today through his appointment to the post of Attaché at the Berlin Legation of the State of Brunswick . . . . A decree authorizing his enfranchisement was signed by Dr. Kuechenthal, the Premier of Brunswick, who belongs to Dr. Alfred Hugenberg's Nationalist party, and Dietrich Klagges, the Minister of the Interior, one of Herr Hitler's chief aides.[10]

The appointment could not have come too soon for Hitler, who was already a candidate in the German election for president—which would take place in March of that year. Rather than making Hitler a martyr just before the election, the federal government of Germany accepted his appointment and his citizenship.

With German citizenship conferred upon him, one of the major barriers to Adolf Hitler's becoming the master of Germany, by entirely legal means, was removed.

Though Hitler failed to win the election that March, he did indeed receive a surprising number of votes—so many in fact that a second vote was cast the following month.

The stage was set for Hitler to become a major player in German politics, and for his assumption of power just one year later in 1933.

Beginnings

Erna Rita Levy, known as Rita, was born just one month before Hitler received his German citizenship. Oddly enough, she was a German citizen before he was. Yet, though she had her citizenship longer than he did, with the Nuremberg Laws of 1935, he would take that citizenship from her, and four years later, in 1939, would force her to flee the country of her birth.

The circumstances surrounding Rita's birth are traumatic and set the stage for the experiences she would have throughout her childhood and the rest of her life. Rita was born on January 6, 1932, to Gerhard and Mary Levy in Forst,

Gerhard and Mary Levy.

Top: Rita and Inge Levy.
Bottom: Mary Levy.

Gerhard and Mary Levy.

Germany. She was born extremely premature, and the Levys' doctor, Dr. Hesse, who also happened to be a close family friend, sadly told Mary that Rita would not survive. Nevertheless, the Levy family's live-in help, Detta, cared for Rita, nursing her to health and taking her with her wherever she went—even when Detta went to visit her mother in Dübin.

At that time, the Levys already had one daughter, a three-year-old named Inge, whose story was detailed in chapter five. As both Inge and Rita remembered, Gerhard Levy owned a department store, and Rita explained that he had inherited the store, being the eldest son in the family.

Because Rita was so young when she left Germany, her memories of Forst and her childhood home appear in just tiny snapshots. She remembers that her family was well off, because the department store was quite a large one, and that they had servants who lived with them. Additionally, the entrance hall

Forst, Germany. The building on the far left is the Levy department store.

in their house contained a fountain which flowed into a round pool filled with goldfish. On the side of the house, there were grapevines, and the girls could actually pick the grapes from their window. The garden behind the house was "so large, you could get lost in the trees,"[11] and it included a pool, over which large fruit trees dropped their fruit. Mirroring the opulence of the house, a three-car garage was part of the property.

Although Rita can remember bits and pieces of where she grew up, most of her memories are of specific instances in which she was mischievous. She was the youngest child in the family, and she was quite a spitfire—she recalls that she loved to slide down the banister that began at the servants' quarters in the house. Sometimes she would run to the pool in the entrance hall and fish out gold fish—though she does not remember what she would do with them after catching them. Another time, in the winter, when the pool in the garden froze, despite Inge's admonition not to step onto the ice, Rita ventured out underneath the canopy of the trees' branches. Eventually, the inevitable happened, and just as her older sister had forewarned her, Rita fell into the freezing water. She was rescued by her mother, scolded, and spanked, yet in response to her punishment, she merely laughed—she was so numb and her clothes so heavy laden with water that she could not feel the blows. The threat of spanking, however, was often held over her head: "I was a very bad eater. So at each meal time, my father would have twigs from the trees to spank me with on the table; if I ate I could burn them, if not I got it."[12]

While she does not ever recall actually being spanked for this reason, she does remember being allowed to burn the sticks. Another memory continues to demonstrate her childhood incorrigibleness: at one point, both Rita and Inge had to go to the dentist—an activity most children would rather skip. Being the older sister, and wanting to be a good example to her fearful younger sibling, Inge offered to go first to prove to Rita that there was no reason to be afraid of the dentist. Yet, while Inge was in the dentist's chair, Rita realized that this was her opportunity to escape from the dentist's clutches. Giving insight into her personality as a child, Rita says, "I went to the toilet and crawled through the window and ran home."[13]

Many of Rita's memories involve her sister—and although Inge and Rita loved one another, with Rita's big personality, they experienced the frustration and rivalry that often characterizes relationships between siblings, but perhaps magnified:

> I remember riding my sister's bike when she had chicken pox or some other childhood disease. She came running out, yelling at me, threw me off her bike, and we got into a bad fight till I bit her hard through

her nightgown, drawing blood. She still has the marks today.[14]

In one of the more ironic cases of sibling bantering, she remembers going on vacation as a family, with all of them piling into the family car. About ten minutes into the trip, Rita felt her stomach churning—which her sister thought was quite entertaining and thus took this opportunity to tease her. Yet, in a beautiful case of irony, though carsickness is not contagious, soon, Inge too felt her stomach begin to churn, and the two of them took turns throwing up over the back of the car.

In another case, Rita had to have her tonsils removed. She was petrified of the idea, and so when she was in the doctor's office, she held onto her mother and refused to let go—until her mother tickled her, causing her to lose her grip. After that, Rita remembers having her legs and arms held behind her while someone approached her with a large needle—and then, once again, the main part of this memory concerns her sister. After the operation, one of the main things that Rita can remember is the pleasure she felt after the surgery—not at all because her mouth was healing or because the surgery was over, but because she had to eat soft foods, meaning that she could eat ice cream for meals while Inge could not!

Yet, the two sisters did enjoy one another's company—a fact that would be confirmed by their heartbrokenness at being separated upon their arrival in England. Thus, in one of the more pleasant memories, Rita recalled that around Christmas time, she and Inge loved to walk to her father's department store to admire the huge Christmas tree that was showcased in the store's hall. Typically, after their excursions to the store, they would walk across the street to enjoy a frankfurter together.

Though it might seem odd to consider a department store that was owned by a Jewish family having a huge Christmas tree, Rita actually recalls that at home, their family had both a tree and a Chanukah menorah.

Other than the few paragraphs above, Rita has no memories of her childhood—and even fewer memories of her parents: "I can hardly remember my father, my mother more."[15]

Antisemitism

Though Rita's childhood memories of her parents have mostly been forgotten, there are scars from other experiences Rita had and that cannot be erased, no matter how much she has attempted to leave the past behind.

As early as April 1933,[16] Hitler began to exclude Jews from schools and universities. Eventually, this anti-Jewish legislation began to touch Rita's family—for years, her uncle had wanted to become a lawyer. He had begun his education and was working toward his goal, but he became one of the victims of these early laws; suddenly, the door was closed and the path blocked. He was forbidden, because he was Jewish, from continuing his education at the university. At that point, Rita and Inge's father welcomed him as a partner into the family business.

But not even the family business could be a refuge from Hitler. In 1938, Rita and Inge's uncle again came into disrepute with the Nazis—for reasons unknown to both sisters. With charges against him, and with a very dismal future ahead of him in Germany, their uncle fled the country to Palestine. Unfortunately, though Rita and Inge originally faced the prospect of their uncle being arrested, the situation became even more dire. Not being able to find their uncle, the Nazis instead chose to arrest their father. Thus, in 1938, before

Kristallnacht, and before many of the Jewish men had been taken to concentration camps, Gerhard Levy was arrested.

Neither Inge nor Rita would ever see him again. At this point, Rita was only six years old.

Tragically, though Mary Levy had urged Gerhard to attempt to get his family out of Germany, Gerhard's story was another of misplaced confidence on the German government's loyalty to those who had fought for Germany in the First World War. Gerhard was insistent that nothing would happen to him. Rita recalls his saying, "'I fought for Germany in the last war, even got wounded; they will not do anything to us.' So we stayed."[17]

The situation for the girls at school also deteriorated. It became clear that they were different from their peers when, unlike everyone else who said "Heil Hitler" to begin their school day, Rita and Inge were forbidden from saying the phrase because they were Jews. Yet, socially awkward situations transitioned to dangerous situations—when their German peers decided to start throwing rocks at them on their way home from school. Once again, Rita's fiery personality manifested itself: "Kids [started] throwing stones at us and calling us names on the way home from school. Inge tried to ignore it.... I wanted to fight them, while Inge was trying to drag me along."[18]

By the summer of 1938, Rita and Inge had already experienced more hatred, troubles, and difficulties than most would experience throughout their childhoods and even into their adult lives. And yet *Kristallnacht* was just around the corner.

Kristallnacht

The memory of what ensued on *Kristallnacht* has never left Rita. Her father was in prison, and her mother was out for the evening with Dr. Hesse and his wife, Charlotte. The Hesses had two boys, Frank and Peter, who were approximately the same ages as Inge and Rita, and the four of them, along with the Levys' cook, were in the Levys' house at the time. Rita recalls that the children were simply being children, playing and having fun—and then suddenly, everything changed:

> We were going around and around the kitchen table, including the cook, singing 'Doing the Lambeth Walk,' when the front door smashed open, and the Gestapo came in and started breaking anything they could get their hands on. They had clubs and pistols, and told us children they were looking for weapons . . . . the cook had taken to her heels the minute she saw them, leaving us alone with these men. We followed them from room to room.[19]
>
> They went from room to room . . . smashing doors, windows, mirrors . . . even ripping all our clothes, all the time asking us where the guns and weapons were. The house was a wreck. Then they left as quickly as they had stormed into our house. I don't remember any of us crying; I think we were just in shock.[20]

With the cook gone, there were no adults around. As mentioned in a previous chapter, 10-year-old Inge mounted her bicycle and pedaled through the night, through the darkness and through the destruction, to the Hesses' house, presumably attempting to find their mother. When Inge arrived, Mary Levy was no longer with the Hesses, but Inge remained with them, not venturing into the night again.

The Levys' childhood was falling to pieces. First their father had been taken, and now their home was ruined. When Mary Levy returned home, she was in shock over what had happened. Clearly, there had been no expectation whatsoever of the danger headed toward them that night—otherwise the children would not have essentially been left alone.

That night, Mary Levy and the Hesses came together once again, reuniting Inge with her mother and sister. But the night was not over:

> Within a short time, we were on the train going to Berlin.[21]
>
> We had nothing left to pack.... My mother got off the train to buy us something to eat, when the whistle blew, I remember screaming ... to get my mother back on the train, she was as if she was in shock, didn't remember where to go, I remember ... how scared I was she wasn't going to make it.[22]

In Berlin, Mary, Inge, and Rita stayed with friends, and Inge attended the Leonore Goldschmidt School—which made it possible for Inge and Rita to flee to England. Eventually, however, though Inge continued to attend school, both Inge and Rita, instead of staying with their mother, were moved to a home for Jewish children—a place in which Rita made a lasting memory:

> I don't remember too much about that time, only that we were eating cauliflower soup, when I saw on my spoon, on my way to my mouth, a huge thick caterpillar rear its black head up. I didn't eat cauliflower again for over 50 years.... It's funny the things you remember.[23]

The Kindertransport

Eventually, Rita and Inge left Berlin for England. For a while, even though it was possible for them to go to England, Mary

Levy held onto her children—keeping them in Berlin and refusing to allow them to leave. For them to leave her, she had one major requirement that had not yet been met: rather than being sent to a hostel or children's camp, she insisted that her children be sent to a family. They would not leave Germany until they had a family to live with:

> My sister and I were going to different families; the others were going into an orphanage. This apparently was why we left so late; my mother had been trying desperately to keep us out of the orphanage, which she did. The families were not Jewish, but both were Christadelphians, their belief made them take us.[24]

Inge was to live with Roland and Kate Day, and Rita was to live with William and Priscilla Hoverd. Both the Days and the Hoverds lived in the Birmingham area, and both families were Christadelphians. As such, while the girls were not going to live together, they would at least live in the same area as one another and would likely see one another at Christadelphian gatherings and events.

The girls boarded the train and waved goodbye to their mother. They had no idea when they would see her again. As Mary Levy faded into the distance, Rita and Inge would only have one another, but even they would be parted. Rita recalled, "I was devastated to leave Inge."[25]

Perhaps that devastation manifested itself in Rita's behavior becoming even more outlandish. The train ride was calm, and the two arrived in Rotterdam, Holland, without any mishaps. But on the boat from Holland to Harwich, Rita once again displayed her childhood spunk—taking not only her hat and throwing it out the window but also her removable orthodontic braces.

At the time, she was seven—a very lively seven-year-old.

The two girls arrived in England on July 26, 1939, approximately one month before Britain declared war on Germany and transportation between the two countries ceased indefinitely.

Rita, Mary, and Inge Levy, just before the two girls left on the Kindertransport, 1939.

Rita's Family

It was extremely important to Rita to know what had happened to her family; thus, after the war ended, she set about researching their fate. Here is what she discovered:

Gerhard Alexander Levy was born on January 25, 1898. The Nazis arrested him in 1938, when he was 40 years old. After the war, Rita learned of her father's fate: "We had received news through the Red Cross . . . that my father had been released from prison, sent to a work camp and had died there of double pneumonia, but nothing about my mother."[26]

Rita and her grandmother Selma in the United States.

Gerhard Levy died in a Nazi work camp in 1941. He was in his early 40s and had not seen either of his daughters for three years.

Mary Levy (née Schwartzhaupt) was born on December 21, 1907. She was only 30 years old when her husband was arrested and sent to prison, as well as when her house was destroyed during the horrors of *Kristallnacht*. She was 31 years old when she waved goodbye to her two daughters and sent them off to a foreign country and foreign families—not knowing whether she would see them again.

And news about her was not forthcoming.

After the war, Rita did not hear anything about her mother. However, she did hear about her mother's mother, Selma Schwartzhaupt, and her mother's sister, Aunt

Hilda. Apparently, Grandmother Selma and Aunt Hilda had been able to escape Germany through the help of another of her mother's siblings, Uncle Fred. Uncle Fred, who had lived in the United States since 1922, was able to provide an affidavit for Selma and Hilda, thus they fled through Spain and then Portugal, ultimately arriving in the United States in 1941. Selma and Hilda survived the Holocaust.

Because there was no news after the war about Mary Levy, and because Rita found out that her grandmother and aunt had survived—having been aided by her mother's brother, Uncle Fred, Rita put the pieces together and determined that her mother must still be alive: "I was sure she would be with my Grandmother. That was the only reason I wanted to leave Britain."[27]

Thus, in July 1947, after the war was over, Rita decided to reunite with her mother in the United States. Her grandmother and her uncle prepared her papers, and she traveled over the Atlantic to New York City. From there, she made her way to Washington, D.C., where her grandmother, Aunt Hilda, and mother were living.

This was the moment Rita had anticipated for years. After being separated from her mother when she was seven, at sixteen years old, she and her family would be reunited.

But when the time came, there, thousands of miles from where she had started her journey to reunite with her mother, Rita realized the horrific truth: her mother was not there. And she never would be.

Although Uncle Fred had been able to save his other sister, Hilda, and his mother, Selma, for some reason, one that Rita still does not know to this day, he was not able to get Mary out of Europe. Instead, separated from her husband, who was in a work camp, Mary went into hiding in Berlin. She remained in hiding until 1944.

From there, Rita still does not know exactly what happened to her mother—but she has been given two stories. The first came from someone who had provided a hiding place for Mary. They stated that as the Allies continued to make inroads into the Nazi empire, Mary decided to leave her hiding place—she was looking for something, although Rita's source did not know what exactly Mary was looking for. Perhaps Mary did not know either—with the years in hiding, the bombs falling on the city, and the separation from both her husband and her daughters taking their toll on her mind. Eventually, at a railway station in Berlin, someone spotted Mary Levy, recognized her as a Jew, and put her on one of the last trains to Auschwitz.

The other version of the story came from an official document Rita read. It stated that Mary Levy's hiding place had been given away, she was discovered, and she was sent on the train to Auschwitz.

Here is what Rita knows for certain: "The only thing I know is that she went directly to the gas chambers."[28]

Mary Levy, Inge and Rita's mother, was murdered by the Nazis before she turned 40 years old; by the time Rita came to the United States, Mary had already been dead for four years.

The truth of the Holocaust and the destruction of Rita's family is a tragedy that Rita Devletian has not, and cannot, come to terms with:

> Believe it or not, I am still looking [for peace]. Like my Grandma in every newsreel she would watch, and start up with, 'look there's my Mary, did you see her? Did

you see her?' even going so far as to get the Red Cross involved to find her, when it was already documented that she was killed in Auschwitz![29]

While her grandmother still held onto the hope that Mary was alive, Rita's hopes had been shattered—but like her grandmother, she cannot move on. Disillusioned and broken, Rita, now in her 80s, still grapples with the terror and devastation that Hitler brought upon her family.

The Christadelphians

Rita Levy, seven years old, was brought to the Hoverds' house in the Birmingham area. At the time, both William and Priscilla Hoverd were in their 50s—and old enough to have been Rita's grandparents. They had five children: David, Priscilla, Edna, Stephen, and Monica. David was the eldest. Tragically, he had died in a motorcycle accident before Rita arrived. Neither Priscilla nor Edna lived at home any longer, as both were married; Priscilla had a one-year-old son, also named David. Stephen and Monica were both still at home, although they were quite a bit older than Rita. Typically, William and Stephen were away at work during the week and only came home on weekends, leaving Rita at home with Priscilla and Monica.

Life with the Hoverds was interesting. As in so many cases, Rita became part of the family—choosing to call Mr. and Mrs. Hoverd "Dad" and "Mom" and even sharing a bed with one of her "siblings." Yet, just as she and Inge had engaged in sibling rivalry and frustrations, she shared these types of experiences with both Stephen and Monica.

Monica, the youngest girl in the family, who at this point was a teenager, shared a bed with Rita—yet all the trauma Rita had experienced had caused her to start wetting the bed again: "I

From left to right: Priscilla Hoverd, Rita Levy, Inge Levy, and William Hoverd in the Hoverd's garden, 1939, shortly after Rita and Inge arrived.

slept with Monica, and she hated my cold feet up her back, and the fact that I started wetting the bed again, and laid in it till it was dry, then lied about it."[30]

Nevertheless, despite the difficulties associated with a teenage girl's attempting to empathize with a child, Rita and Monica learned to love one another. The same was true of Rita's relationship with Stephen. The two of them got along well—often heckling one another, although they too had their fair share of arguments and typical sibling frustrations:

> Stephen and I were always carrying on. He was away with Dad all week, and one day I got into his piggy bank—boy did I get into trouble. He locked me in his room . . . and said I had to stay there till I realized what I had done. No food, no drink, and after maybe four to five hours (can't remember how long), I started screaming [that] if they don't let me out, I will jump out the window . . . . Mom came running up the stairs, opened the door, and saw me with my leg . . . out of the

window. Boy was she upset, but Stephen was furious with Mom for letting me out, saying she should have let me jump.[31]

Thus, Rita became part of the Hoverd family—experiencing all that one of their children would experience, including the sibling rivalry. But at the same time, Rita's situation was entirely different. Rita was a spirited child who had faced difficulties that even many adults would never encounter, and needed, in her words, someone who would be "tough"[32] on her. But the Hoverd family was really no longer in the childrearing stage, Mrs. Hoverd was in ill health, and Mr. Hoverd, whose strictness was able to keep Rita in line, was often away at work. Rita explained some of the difficulties that resulted:

> I guess Mom . . . was around 49 to 55, don't know exactly, and had Rheumatoid arthritis, with ulcerated

From left to right: David Harper, Norman Harper, Rita Levy, Inge Levy, Priscilla Hoverd (married to William Hoverd), Priscilla Harper (née) Hoverd (married to Norman Harper). On the far left is the air raid shelter, where the family would often sleep.

legs, when I arrived. I really led her a miserable life. I would lock her out, when she went to get coal in for the fire, she would run from one door to the other, which I then unlocked one at a time, and she was out there in the cold with her bad legs. She would tell me to go up to bed, I would usually be standing by the fire . . . and tell her 'make me!'[33]

Unfortunately, Mrs. Hoverd's condition made it difficult for her to control Rita. In another instance, Rita explained the circuitous route on which she would lead "Mom" when going to and from the Christadelphian meetings on Wednesday nights:

Poor Mom; I used to take her on a shortcut to the meetings on Wednesdays . . . . At the bottom of our garden was the railway, so I made her go over the fence, then walk along the railroad, then over the fence again, and then on to the meetings. She never complained. After the meeting, it was usually dark and with the blackout, very dark, so we went home the normal way, but since she had no sense of direction, I used to take her round and round. She never realized we were home, till I finally took her by the hand and led her up the front steps. Don't forget, she was older, and had really bad legs with ulcers, arthritis in her hands.[34]

Yet, even as Rita grew older, her mischievousness continued. As Christadelphians, the Hoverds did not encourage their children to go to the movies—for fear that the images on the screen and some of the themes of the movies would encourage the children to engage in improper activities. Unfortunately, even without going to the movies, Rita found a way to get into mischief:

> In England we used to go scrumping (stealing fruit from people's gardens). Anyway, from there it isn't far to doing other things. Not far from where I lived there was a huge . . . movie theatre; of course I wasn't allowed to go, being Christadelphian, but we (a bunch of boys and I) went into the parking lot and let down at least one tire from most of the cars. We never waited to see them come out and find their flat tires . . . . I kept doing it even after the boys got too scared.[35]

They were difficult circumstances, and Rita's childhood spunk remained unchecked. Now, as an adult, she can look back and understand the tragedy of the situation—but at that time, she simply could not understand or process all that had transpired:

> They were much too good to me. I wouldn't have put up with me for two minutes. I would have sent me packing. I was not just a brat, I was absolutely a living terror, there are really not enough words I can use against myself.[36]

> I would have sent me to that orphanage a month after I arrived at the Hoverds; I was absolutely rotten. But these people were too good, only thought about 'Poor little thing' and what I had gone through. Actually as a child, at least for me, I had no idea what I was doing there, or where my parents were.[37]

And yet, there was also a pleasant side to life with the Hoverds. As Rita said, they were indeed very good to her. They were kind, thoughtful, and compassionate. Though they could not speak German, Rita remembers their always carrying a dictionary with them to help facilitate communication. And she also attempted to be helpful—she would help Mrs. Hoverd with the chores in the house. Although at one point, Rita noticed that Mrs. Hoverd was following her and redoing everything she had just done!

Rita's time with the Hoverds, despite its difficulties, brought Rita into a family that cared for her and included her in everything they did together. In fact, one of Rita's favorite things about life with them was going to the weekly Bible classes on Wednesday nights:

> Mom and Dad Hoverd had a Bible night every Wednesday. I used to love them. First classical music and then reading from the Bible. They were lovely, sitting by the fire, all cozy and warm. I would go to the meetings with Mom; I got so good that I was teaching the little ones about the Bible.[38]

Even after Rita left England to find her mother, she missed both the Hoverds and the Christadelphians she had met at the meetings: "I should have stayed in England; the only reason I left was because I was sure my mother would be in America too. I missed the family . . . plus everyone at the meetings. They all knew me, and I think liked me."[39]

While living with the Hoverds, Rita attended the local Christadelphian functions, going to the meetings on Sunday and the Bible classes on Wednesday night. She enjoyed her time with the Christadelphians, feeling accepted by them and loved. Though she lived with a Christadelphian family for seven years and did the daily Bible readings, and even though her sister, Inge, was eventually baptized as a Christadelphian, Rita was very clear that she never felt any pressure to join the community: "No there was never ever any pressure to become a Christadelphian, which I really appreciate now. Then I don't think it would have mattered. As a child you don't think of these things."[40]

It was important for Rita that she remained Jewish. Nevertheless, she still spoke highly of the Christadelphians as a community:

> There are not many religions that hold the family together like the Christadelphians.[41]

> I always thought it a great thing that the Christadelphians have such faith in God; I wish I did. Although I prayed every night that I was at the Hoverds, I stopped after finding out that my mother wasn't with my Grandmother.[42]

Rita lived with the Hoverds for most of the war. Unlike Inge, Rita was not evacuated—with Mrs. Hoverd saying that Rita had been through enough and did not need to go through another change. Unfortunately, however, when it was felt that Mrs. Hoverd could no longer handle Rita, she was sent to a Jewish boarding school for refugees in Kent. Rita lived there from 1945 until 1947, when she came to the United States.

The Hoverds, in their compassion and in their fervent beliefs, though they were no longer in the childrearing stage, chose to open up their home and their family to a seven-year-old Jewish girl who did not understand what was happening to her life and her family. And while the situation was not always ideal, wartime does not make for ideal situations. The Hoverds did what they could—and in doing so, saved a life. For that, Rita will never forget their kindness:

> I wonder all the time what kind of person I would have turned out to be had the war not broken up our family. Would I have been such a terrible child had I been in a normal environment? The Hoverds were so good to me, and all I brought them was trouble, but they never gave up on me. I will never forget them.[43]

During the War

Despite the trauma of living with a new family, Rita was also living through the worst war in history. At one point, because of the bombing in Birmingham, she remembers having walked through the street and seeing body parts strewn on the ground before her. However, the war, rations, and the bombing did not quench her spirit and, in fact, likely accentuated her desire to act out.

> We went every night about 7 p.m. to the shelter at the end of the garden. I slept through everything. In the morning . . . I would find the shrapnel lying on the grass in the garden . . . . The first or second time we left the shelter in the morning, by turning around, we could see Coventry burning. Everyone was crying and carrying on, but somehow for me, I wasn't even scared. I remember enjoying going down to the shelter and having to sleep there.[44]

But it was not merely that Rita was not scared. In fact, she continued to employ the antics that she had used with Mrs. Hoverd to the war effort. At that point, every day, bread and milk was delivered to each house and was placed on the front porch next to a pile of sandbags and a bucket of water, which were put there to extinguish a fire in case the house were bombed.

Rita and her friends enjoyed walking by the houses, finding the bread that had been delivered, and dropping it into the bucket of water. They did this from house to house until they were eventually caught.

In another memory, she and her friends were made to take old newspapers to school—somehow these papers were used for the war effort. One day, Rita became frustrated with always having to carry papers—so she suggested to her friends that they drop off the papers at the train station.

But they were not simply going to drop them off. They planned to bring them to the train station, pile them up in a corner of the staircase, and, to ensure that no one found the papers, *light them on fire*. Add to that that the train station was made of wood.

It was an idea that would only sound clever to a child.

And so, Rita and her friends took the papers, dropped them into the stairwell, and set them on fire. After the fire was extinguished, Rita and her friends, who all went to school together, were called into the headmistress's office: "We all got the ruler over our knuckles, although I was smart enough to pull my hand away, and she hit herself in the knee instead."[45]

The next day, Rita was called again into the headmistress's office and told that she had to take a special exam—one that would determine whether she could be transferred to another school. It seems the headmistress wanted to find another school for Rita to attend.

Rita passed the exam and then transferred to an all girls Grammar school. There, she had another incident—and although it was again related to the war, this time she was not the initiator: "One of the girls kept calling me a Nazi pig. I fought with her and knocked her front teeth out; I was scared... now I was really in trouble."[46]

But in fact, something astonishing happened—rather than giving Rita consequences, the headmistress phoned the other girl's parents and had the girl removed from the school, saying that prejudice was not allowed at school.

After the War

After the war was over, Rita moved to the United States to find her mother. After learning of her mother's murder, Rita stayed in the United States with the Hesses, the family friends from Germany, who had been able to flee Europe and find safety in the United States. She later married and had three children.

Nevertheless, life remained broken. Though Rita had been shown kindness by the Hoverds, she had undergone great trauma, particularly in discovering that her mother, whom she had thought was alive, had been dead for years.

Rita continued to try to make the best of life, but struggled. After a few years, she and her husband divorced. The future began to look grim, and the desire to continue living began to wane.

Over the years, Rita had kept in contact with the Hoverds, and continued to see them as her family. Stephen was her big brother,[47] the one she "turned to when she was in any trouble,"[48] and though they had their share of sibling bantering, they genuinely cared for each other. Thus, Rita contacted Stephen, as well as Inge, who were both still in England, and arranged for her children to spend a few months in England with Stephen's family and Inge's family, not telling either her intentions. At the time, Stephen Hoverd and his wife had their own children, and a small three-bedroom house, but they were willing to take Rita's children because of the strength of their relationship with her.

After the children were gone, Rita attempted to take her own life—stating that she wished that God had allowed her to die with her parents.

Inge and Rita together again in Berlin, 1990s.

But life continued. After her attempt at suicide, she awoke in a hospital bed and was told by the doctors that she needed to leave to get into a better environment immediately. She needed to restart. But where would she go?

Rita arranged to move to Israel, where she worked on a kibbutz. Eventually, after living there for about 10 years and being joined by two of her children, she moved to Germany. Now, decades later, Rita lives in Spain, and though she has recovered from the depression she experienced in the United States, her life is one of countless that has been irreparably broken by the antisemitism, bigotry, and lies of Hitler and the Nazis.

Her life has been trauma filled. Yet, considering all that she has undergone—the tragedies, the heartache, the pain—throughout her life, she looks back at her time with the

Hoverds, and her continued contact with them afterward, as a glimmer of light amid intense darkness. Despite the challenges, they showed her love, compassion, and patience in the face of others who wanted her dead.

And for Rita, that relationship has been one of immeasurable worth.

---

[1] "Adolf Hitler: Early Years, 1889–1913," *United States Holocaust Memorial Museum*, accessed April 28, 2017, https://www.ushmm.org/wlc/en/article.php?ModuleId=10007430.

[2] "Adolf Hitler and World War I: 1913–1919," *United States Holocaust Memorial Museum*, accessed April 28, 2017, https://www.ushmm.org/wlc/en/article.php?ModuleId=10007431.

[3] "Fascists Glorify Pan-German Ideal," *The New York Times* (New York, NY), September 15, 1930.

[4] Ibid.

[5] William Shirer, *The Rise and Fall of the Third Reich* (New York: Simon and Schuster, 1960), 169–170.

[6] "Citizenship for Hitler," *The New York Times* (New York, NY), July 15, 1930.

[7] "Fascists Glorify Pan-German Ideal," *The New York Times* (New York, NY), September 15, 1930.

[8] Citizenship for Hitler," *The New York Times* (New York, NY), July 15, 1930.

[9] "German Citizenship Acquired by Hitler," *The New York Times* (New York, NY), February 26, 1932.

[10] "German Citizenship Acquired by Hitler," *The New York Times* (New York, NY), February 26, 1932.

[11] Rita Devletian, "Biography," typescript, 2.

[12] Ibid.

[13] Ibid, 3.

[14] Ibid, 2.

[15] Ibid.

[16] "Antisemitic Legislation 1933–1939," *United States Holocaust Memorial Museum*, accessed April 28, 2017, https://www.ushmm.org/wlc/en/article.php?ModuleId=10007901.

[17] Rita Devletian, "Biography," typescript, 1.

[18] Rita Devletian, e-mail message to author, May 22, 2016.
[19] Rita Devletian, "Biography," typescript, 3.
[20] Rita Devletian, e-mail message to author, May 22, 2016.
[21] Rita Devletian, "Biography," typescript, 3.
[22] Rita Devletian, e-mail message to author, May 22, 2016.
[23] Rita Devletian, "Biography," typescript, 3.
[24] Ibid.
[25] Rita Devletian, e-mail message to author, May 22, 2016.
[26] Rita Devletian, "Biography," typescript, 6.
[27] Ibid.
[28] Rita Devletian, e-mail message to author, May 25, 2016.
[29] Rita Devletian, e-mail message to author, May 23, 2016.
[30] Rita Devletian, "Biography," typescript, 4.
[31] Rita Devletian, e-mail message to author, June 2, 2016.
[32] Rita Devletian, e-mail message to author, May 28, 2016.
[33] Rita Devletian, "Biography," typescript, 4.
[34] Rita Devletian, e-mail message to author, June 2, 2016.
[35] Rita Devletian, e-mail message to author, May 30, 2016.
[36] Rita Devletian, e-mail message to author, May 22, 2016.
[37] Rita Devletian, "Biography," typescript, 4.
[38] Rita Devletian, e-mail message to author, May 28, 2016.
[39] Ibid.
[40] Rita Devletian, e-mail message to author, June 6, 2016.
[41] Rita Devletian, e-mail message to author, July 2, 2016.
[42] Rita Devletian, e-mail message to author, July 7, 2016.
[43] Rita Devletian, e-mail message to author, June 13, 2016.
[44] Rita Devletian, "Biography," typescript, 4.
[45] Ibid, 5.

[46] Ibid.

[47] Rachel Newman, Stephen Hoverd's daughter, e-mail message to author, June 1, 2016.

[48] Rachel Newman, Stephen Hoverd's daughter, e-mail message to author, July 19, 2016.

RITA GLANZ

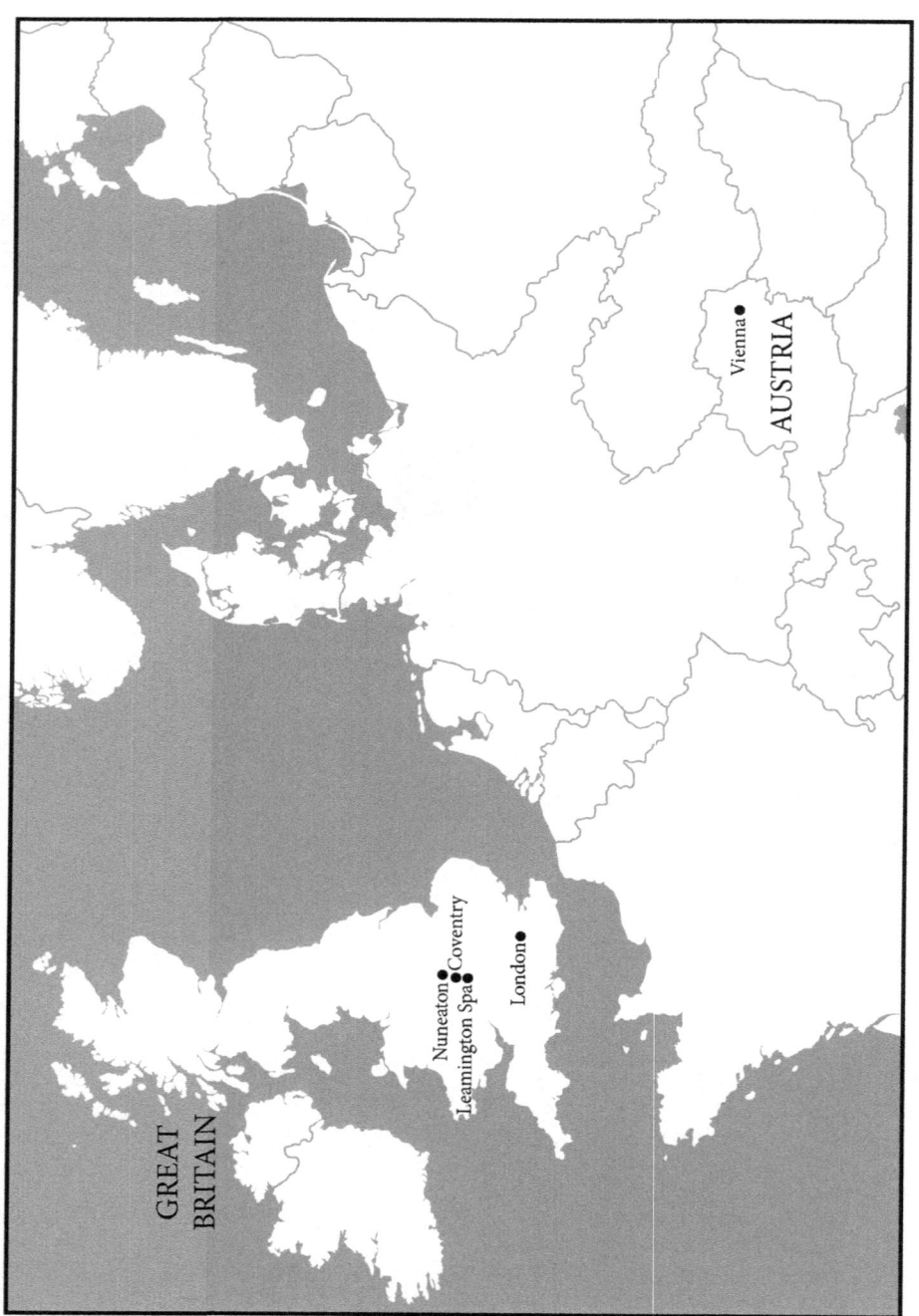

9

Rita Glanz (née Billig)

Paul von Hindenburg was born in Posen, Prussia, on October 2, 1847. By the time of the Great War, 1914, he had gone into retirement. But he was called out of it to serve the Fatherland as superior of Major General Erich Ludendorff, chief of staff of the German eighth army[1] and considered one of Germany's greatest strategists. Together, Hindenburg and Ludendorff were tasked with driving a Russian invasion from East Prussia—which they did successfully—and for which Hindenburg, rather than Ludendorff, earned the nation's adoration. Eventually, Hindenburg's influence in the army was greater than that of Emperor Wilhelm II, and, as such, he was appointed to the rank of field marshal—the highest ranking officer.[2] In 1916, the emperor gave Hindenburg control of all German forces and appointed Ludendorff as his jointly responsible chief aide.[3] In the spring of 1918, German victory seemed imminent. Yet, in the next few months, everything changed. In July 1918, the Allies mounted a counteroffensive that was remarkably successful—pushing the Germans back through Belgium and completely reversing the war's outcome.[4]

By the autumn of 1918, it appeared a German victory was hopeless. Ludendorff, supported by Hindenburg,[5] demanded an armistice—yet when he learned of the conditions of the armistice the Allies demanded,[6] he retracted his claim and instead declared that the war must continue. Nevertheless, by that point, continuing to fight was not something German political leaders were willing to do—so Ludendorff offered his resignation to the emperor, who accepted it on October 18, 1918. Much to Ludendorff's chagrin, however, while accepting his resignation, Wilhelm II issued an order to Hindenburg: remain at your post.[7] The army's command no longer provided the appearance of unity, and it seemed as though Ludendorff had caused many of the difficulties. Therefore, when the armistice was signed and revolution broke out in November 1918, Hindenburg remained in Germany,[8] while Ludendorff fled to Sweden in "false whiskers and blue spectacles."[9]

Consequently, with the end of World War I, Hindenburg allowed Ludendorff to shoulder the blame for Germany's surrender, while he attempted to promote own reputation as a national hero.[10] Nevertheless, by February 1919, Ludendorff had returned to Germany to make a farcical claim—one that would both resuscitate his reputation and prime the German nation for the advent of Adolf Hitler. The claim? The German forces had lost the war, not because of their defeat on the battlefield but because they had been stabbed in the back by malevolent forces at home.[11] Eventually, Hindenburg proclaimed the same notion.[12] But who were those malevolent forces back home? Who had truly caused Germany's defeat? It was the "November criminals," as Hitler would refer to them—those who had agreed to the armistice in November 1918 and had set up a new government—in other words, the leaders of the Weimar Republic, the new democracy in Germany.[13] *The Rise and Fall of the Third Reich* says this on the subject:

> The culprits, they never ceased to bellow, were the 'November criminals'—an expression which Hitler hammered into the consciousness of the people. It mattered not at all that the German Army, shrewdly and cowardly, had maneuvered the republican

320

government into signing the armistice which the military leaders had insisted upon, and that it thereafter had advised the government to accept the Peace Treaty of Versailles. Nor did it seem to count that the Social Democratic Party had accepted power in 1918 only reluctantly and only to preserve the nation from utter chaos which threatened to lead to Bolshevism. It was not responsible for the German collapse. The blame for that rested on the old order, which had held the power. But millions of Germans refused to concede this. They had to find scapegoats for the defeat and for their humiliation and misery. They easily convinced themselves that they had found them in the 'November criminals' who had signed the surrender and established democratic government in the place of the old autocracy. The gullibility of the Germans is a subject which Hitler often harps on in *Mein Kampf*. He was shortly to take full advantage of it.[14]

The Social Democratic Party of Germany had led the new government—albeit reluctantly. Nevertheless, the party leaders became the "November criminals." In *Mein Kampf,* however, Hitler made a further association with the "criminals"—because in his mind, they were not simply those who had led the Weimar Republic in 1918.

Miserable and degenerate criminals!

The more I tried to achieve clarity on the monstrous event in this hour, the more the shame of indignation and disgrace burned my brow. What was all the pain in my eyes [Hitler had temporarily lost his sight in October 1918 due to a British gas attack][15] compared to this misery?

> There followed terrible days and even worse nights—I knew that all was lost. Only fools, liars, and criminals could hope in the mercy of the enemy. In these nights hatred grew in me, hatred for those responsible for this deed...
>
> Kaiser William II was the first German Emperor to hold out a conciliatory hand to the leaders of Marxism, without suspecting that scoundrels have no honor. While they still held the imperial hand in theirs, their other hand was reaching for the dagger.
>
> There is no making pacts with Jews; there can only be the hard: either—or.[16]

For Adolf Hitler, the "November criminals" were not merely the leaders of the Social Democratic Party. They were the Jews—because, as he explained earlier in *Mein Kampf*, "Only a knowledge of the Jews provides the key with which to comprehend the inner, and consequently real, aims of Social Democracy."[17]

This "stabbed-in-the-back" philosophy gave Adolf Hitler, as well as the rest of Germany, a scapegoat for Germany's misery—a scapegoat that for Hitler was clearly connected to the Jews.

Hindenburg, however, also found this idea appealing—he too blamed Germany's defeat on those who had stabbed the Fatherland in the back. Thus, blame for Germany's tragic years after of the war was directed elsewhere—and by June 1919, he retired once again, at the age of 71, to cultivate his reputation as a national hero.[18]

The next few years were tumultuous. In 1922, economic hardship led the Weimar government to declare that it could no longer pay reparations to the Allies. In response, in 1923, France and Belgium sent 60,000 troops into the Ruhr district of western Germany. The economic situation consequently plummeted even further—and the German government attempted to alleviate the situation by simply printing more money, leading to a period of massive hyperinflation.[19] At that point, any Germans who had saved their money discovered that their savings was worthless. Those on a fixed income, such as retirees, suffered profoundly. It is not a coincidence that at this same time, November 1923, stirred up by the chaos of 1922 and 1923, and supported by Ludendorff,[20] Adolf Hitler attempted to overthrow the Bavarian state government (and eventually the entire Weimar Republic) in his Beer Hall Putsch—and failed. Hitler was arrested.

In 1925, France and Belgium finally removed their troops from Germany—after a new Reichsbank president had taken steps to stabilize the currency[21] and Germany had accepted a new reparation plan called the Dawes plan.[22] It was also at this point that Hindenburg chose to come out of retirement yet again. In April 1925, after the death of Germany's Social Democrat president, Friedrich Ebert, Paul von Hindenburg ran for president in Weimar Germany. Ludendorff ran against him.[23] Hindenburg won the election. He was 77 years old.

During the years of Hindenburg's first term in office, the situation in Germany went up and down. At the beginning, the German economy began to flourish—but with the onset of the Great Depression, everything came crashing down. The economic situation had helped make the radical Nazi ideology more appealing to the masses, so the Reichstag election of 1930 brought them 107 seats, making them the second largest party in the Reichstag.[24] As the years progressed, the fortunes of the party looked increasingly positive—thus Hitler ran for president in 1932.

He didn't win. Hindenburg, running as the war hero and the incumbent, took the majority of the vote, despite that he turned 85 in 1932. Hitler had lost his opportunity.

Yet less than one year later, Hindenburg made a decision that would drastically change the course of German history—and world history. In January 1933, Hindenburg used his power as president of the Weimar Republic to appoint a new chancellor.

The man he appointed was none other than Adolf Hitler.

The Timeline

Rita Billig was born just two months later, on March 18, 1933, in Vienna, Austria, not in Germany. Just three months after her birth, in June 1933, the Nazi party was outlawed in

Rita Billig.

Austria.[25] For five years, until the *Anschluss,* Rita would live in Vienna in relative peace.

In July 1939, at the tender age of six, she fled to safety in Great Britain, along with her brother Ernst, who was four, on the Kindertransport. Their destination was Coventry—both had been sponsored by Christadelphian families in the area. Rita went to live with Harry and Freda Morgan, and Ernst went to live with Harold and Marjorie Moore.

In 1946, Rita and Ernst moved to Birmingham, Alabama to live with an aunt and uncle who had survived. From there, Rita moved to New York, eventually marrying William Glanz, another Jewish refugee who had fled the Nazis. The two of them made the United States their home, having two children and two grandchildren.

Memories

Now, Rita is in her 80s and is afflicted with dementia. Some things, mostly short-term memories, are nearly impossible to recall. Yet, memories of her childhood, and particularly her feelings about her time in England with the Morgans, remain with her.

Because of her specific situation, it is perhaps best for her to simply tell her memories; her family's full story will be told in her brother Ernst's story (Chapter 10). The memories below are from an interview that I conducted with Rita in 2016:

> I remember where we used to live. The apartment, and then we crossed the street and there was the Danube. The park, and then you walk down steps and there was the Danube river . . . it was beautiful. But I hate them all. I hate those people. I can't forgive them.

Top: Rita and Freda Morgan at the beach.
Bottom: Rita and Harry Morgan at the beach.

> I was adopted by Christadelphians in England . . . they were wonderful, wonderful people.
>
> Harry and Freda Morgan . . . didn't have any kids of their own, and I lived with them for seven years . . . . They couldn't have treated me better if I was their own. I mean, you know, in England, we didn't have much food, and it was, you know, during the war, and they used to give me stuff and do without so I would have something. It was, they were remarkable people.
>
> I can't remember what happened this morning—but I remember so vividly back then. Maybe because I'm 83 already [laugh].

I asked her what she called the Morgans:

> Aunt and Uncle—because well, I didn't know at the time that my mother was dead.

And then if she ever felt pressure to become a Christadelphian:

> No, I left when I was 13. But they didn't push me or anything. Just we went to the meetings every Sunday; I belonged to the Sunday school there. And even when we moved to Nuneaton, we still used to go to Coventry to the meetings.

After living with the Morgans for seven years, she moved to the United States to be with her aunt and uncle:

> I came from England. Well, I used to live in Coventry, and then we moved to Nuneaton because it was getting bad in Coventry—the bombing. We moved to Nuneaton, and then I heard from an aunt and uncle who had gotten out of Vienna. They lived in

> Birmingham, Alabama. . . . It was terrible. Well, especially in those days [people in Alabama] were very prejudiced.

Although her aunt and uncle were considerate and tremendously caring people, adjusting to the new situation, and even just the humid weather, was extremely difficult for Rita, who was just entering her teens. Rita missed what she had back in Coventry.

As one of the closing questions, I asked her, "If you could say one final thing to the Morgans, what would you say?" She responded:

> To my folks? I can't imagine what—they were so wonderful. They used to give me, you know we were rationed. They used to give me their share sometimes. It was amazing. They were just wonderful, wonderful, wonderful people. I can't believe it.[26]

Sixteen years earlier, before the onset of dementia, Rita wrote the following recollections in a book published by the Kindertransport Association. It adds a few details but also confirms what she said in her interview:

> The years have passed, and memories fade, however some memories will remain forever. I remember my mother crying, they had taken my father away. Three days later he was released; he came home took a few belongings and left. He went to Switzerland, and was interned in a labor camp. We did not see him again until March 1947.
>
> My brother and I were left with my mother and a nurse. At that time I was not aware that my mother was dying of cancer. My last memory of her was

standing at the top of the stairs hugging us and saying to me 'don't ever leave him,' referring to my four year old brother. We were then put on a train, we had labels pinned on our clothes. Everything was a blur after that, as we were both crying.[27]

After that, Rita recalled an orphanage in London and a separation from her brother. This is difficult to place, as it seems she and her brother rode on the train from London to Coventry with two Christadelphian brethren, along with Suse Rosenstock (see Suse's story in *Part of the Family - Volume 1*) and Hannelore Zack. It is likely that in Coventry she was separated from Ernst and perhaps it is from there that the following memory stems:

> My next memory is of the orphanage in London, and two people talking to me, of course I didn't know a word they were saying. Finally someone came who spoke German and explained that they were going to take me, and friends of theirs would come and get my brother. I remember holding on to the bed and screaming that I could not leave my brother. But I was hustled into a car, and off we went to Coventry, the following day, as promised I did see my brother again, and was able to see him every weekend after that.
>
> I was adopted by the two most wonderful people, Harry and Freda Morgan, and my brother by Harold and Marjorie Moore. We lived with these families all through the war until May of 1946 when again we were torn away from everything we had grown to love, and sent to America to an Aunt and Uncle we hardly knew in Birmingham, Alabama.
>
> Of course we acclimated, and the years have passed. I am married, and have two children and two

grandchildren, and live in Old Bridge, N.J. My brother is married and has three step children, and lives in Huntington, West Virginia.[28]

The Morgans

For Rita, though certain things are difficult to remember, one memory that has been imprinted indelibly in her mind is the Morgan family's kindness. Over and over she described them as "wonderful." Multiple times she mentioned that they would go without so that she would never lack. At one point, she even referred to them as her "folks."

Harry Morgan was born on December 30, 1902, and Freda Morgan was born on September 2, 1904.[29] Thus, when Rita

Rita in front of the Morgan's house in Coventry, before they moved to Gypsy Lane in Nuneaton.

came to their home in 1939, Harry was 36 and Freda was 34. They did not have any children.

Harry and Freda were baptized together as Christadelphians in 1933,[30] and thus they had been Christadelphians, believing in the Hope of Israel, for six years by the time that Rita came into their home. As the years passed, they remained Christadelphians, with Harry becoming the recording brother of the Nuneaton ecclesia for a few years in the 1960s and 1970s, and both of them eventually passing away in the 1980s at the Christadelphian Care Home in Leamington Spa.[31]

Conclusion

In her write-up for the Kindertransport Association, Rita stated, "Some memories will remain forever." In her interview she stated, "I can't remember what happened this morning—but I remember so vividly back then."

What a gift, then, that the Morgans, a Christadelphian family from Coventry, helped make those memories ones in which Rita, despite being taken from her culture, her language, and her parents, knew that she was loved and respected. Because of beliefs the Morgans held so dear, hope and light were brought into the world of a little six-year-old girl who had known so much darkness.

---

1 "Erich Ludendorff," *Encyclopedia Britannica Online,* accessed April 19, 2017, https://www.britannica.com/biography/Erich-Ludendorff.

2 "Marshal," Encyclopedia Britannica Online, accessed April 19, 2017, https://www.britannica.com/topic/marshal.

3 "Paul von Hindenburg," Encyclopedia Britannica Online, accessed April 19, 2017, https://www.britannica.com/biography/Paul-von-Hindenburg.

4 Deborah Dwork and Robert Jan van Pelt, Holocaust - A History (New York: W. W. Norton & Company, 2002), 47.

5 William Shirer, The Rise and Fall of the Third Reich (New York: Simon and Schuster, 1960), 31.

6 "Terms of the Armistice with Germany," The National Archives, accessed April 19, 2017, http://www.nationalarchives.gov.uk/pathways/firstworldwar/transcripts/aftermath/armistice_terms.htm.

7 "Erich Ludendorff," Encyclopedia Britannica Online, accessed April 19, 2017, https://www.britannica.com/biography/Erich-Ludendorff.

8 Ibid.

9 William Shirer, The Rise and Fall of the Third Reich (New York: Simon and Schuster, 1960), 34.

10 "Paul von Hindenburg," Encyclopedia Britannica Online, accessed April 19, 2017, https://www.britannica.com/biography/Paul-von-Hindenburg.

11 "Erich Ludendorff," Encyclopedia Britannica Online, accessed April 19, 2017, https://www.britannica.com/biography/Erich-Ludendorff.

12 William Shirer, The Rise and Fall of the Third Reich (New York: Simon and Schuster, 1960), 31.

13 Ibid, 31-32.

14 Ibid, 31.

15 "Adolf Hitler Wounded in British Gas Attack," History.com, accessed April 19, 2017, http://www.history.com/this-day-in-history/adolf-hitler-wounded-in-british-gas-attack.

16 Adolf Hitler, Mein Kampf (Boston: Houghton Mifflin, 1971), 205-206.

17 Ibid, 51.

18 "Paul von Hindenburg," Encyclopedia Britannica Online, accessed April 19, 2017, https://www.britannica.com/biography/Paul-von-Hindenburg.

19 "Weimar Germany," The BBC, accessed April 20, 2017, http://www.bbc.co.uk/education/guides/zh9p34j/revision/6.

20 "Erich Ludendorff," Encyclopedia Britannica Online, accessed April 19, 2017, https://www.britannica.com/biography/Erich-Ludendorff.

21 "90 Years Ago: The End of German Hyperinflation," Mises Institute, accessed April 20, 2017, https://mises.org/library/90-years-ago-end-german-hyperinflation.

22 For more information on this, see the introduction to Ursula Meyer's biography, Part of the Family - Volume 1, 119.

23 "Erich Ludendorff," Encyclopedia Britannica Online, accessed April 19, 2017, https://www.britannica.com/biography/Erich-Ludendorff.

[24] William Shirer, The Rise and Fall of the Third Reich (New York: Simon and Schuster, 1960), 138.

[25] Eric Roman, *Austria-Hungary & the Successor States* (New York: Facts On File, Inc., 2003), 603.

[26] Rita Glanz, in discussion with the author, April 17, 2016.

[27] Rita Glanz in Kirsten, Hanus, and Anita Grosz, *Kindertransport Memory Quilt* (Kindertransport Association of North America, 2000), 185.

[28] Ibid.

[29] Colin Bicknell, Recording Brother of Coventry Grosvenor Road Ecclesia, e-mail message to author, March 14, 2016.

[30] H. Madeley, "Intelligence," *The Christadelphian*, September 1933, 425.

[31] Rex Sanders, "The Brotherhood Near and Far," *The Christadelphian*, August 1984, 314. Rex Sanders, "The Brotherhood Near and Far," *The Christadelphian*, June 1985, 234.

ERNST BILLIG

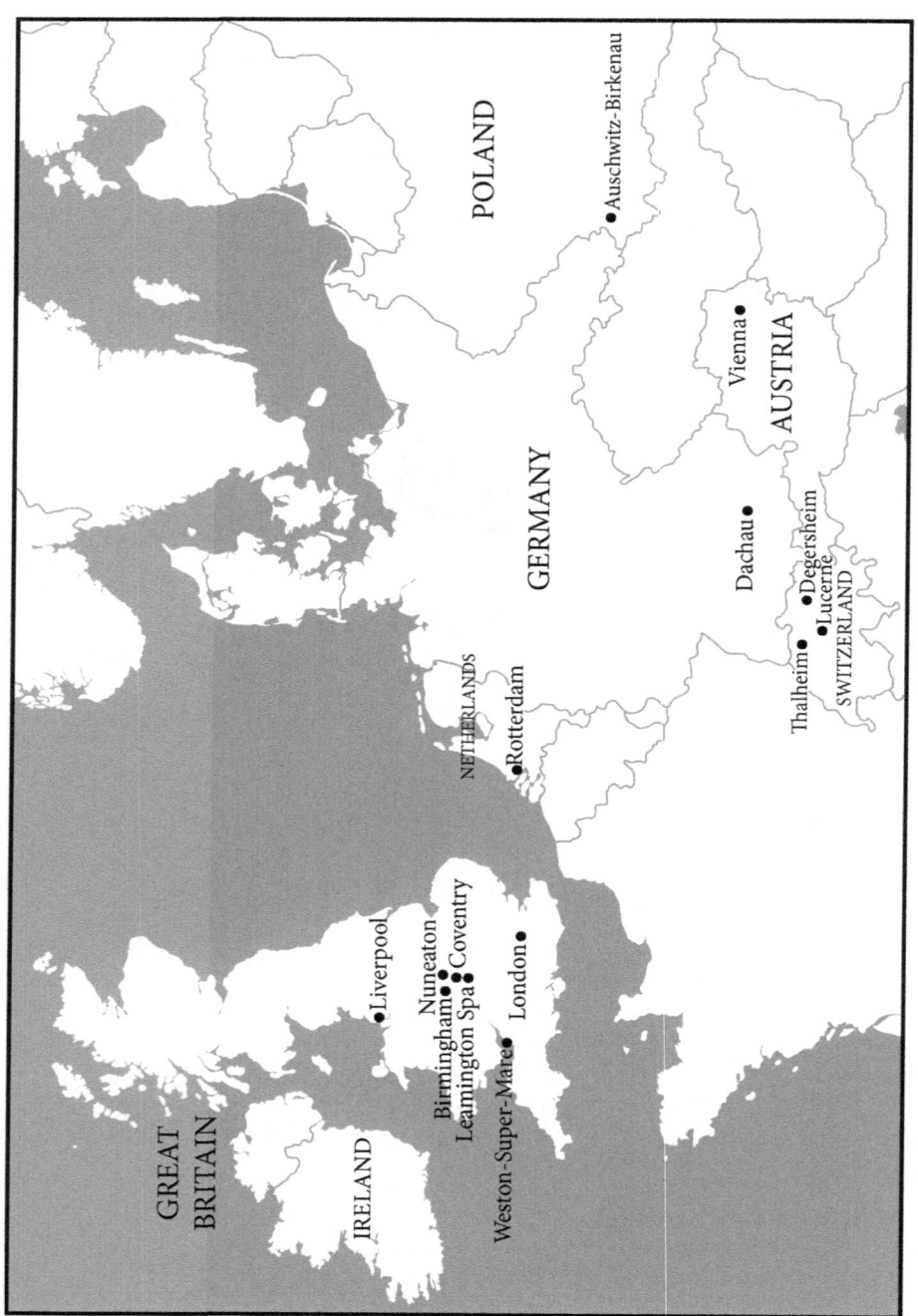

10

ERNST BILLIG

Our synagogue made a trip . . . it was an Eastern Europe tour 10 years ago. One of the places we visited was Auschwitz-Birkenau. I didn't want to, you know. It was an all day thing, so we went in. I wound up going into a room; it was more or less a monument room, a memorial. It was a cage of suitcases, but they were all the same suitcases. The only difference was brown and black, but they were all these large suitcases. The kids who went out [of Europe on the Kindertransport] had different sizes, backpacks, black, little suitcases, big suitcases, but these were big brown suitcases. That was the suitcase I had. That hit me right between the eyes—finding my suitcase in that death house . . . It just hit me really hard.[1]

When Ernst Billig was born in 1935, Hitler had already been the chancellor of Germany for more than two years—and in those two years, he had taken direct action against the Jews. April 1, 1933, had seen the nationwide boycott of Jewish-owned businesses,[2] and in the same month, multiple laws were passed that removed Jews from public life. The "Law for the Restoration of the Professional Civil Service," passed on April 7, 1933, removed Jews and "politically unreliable" civil servants from serving the state. Another law curtailed the number of Jewish students allowed in the country's schools and universities. Another limited the number of Jews allowed in the medical and legal professions. As time went on, further restrictions were passed. Jewish tax consultants lost their licenses, Jewish actors were forbidden to act, either on stage or on the screen, and municipalities added their own various restrictions.[3]

At that point, no one was certain where all this would end. In the 25-point "Party Program" of the Nazis, delivered in a speech in February 1920, Hitler had declared that Nazi policy proscribed Jews from holding German citizenship—and that any further immigration of non-citizens should be prevented. All non-Germans who had indeed immigrated to Germany since August 2, 1914, were to be expelled from the Reich.[4] For Jews, it appeared that Hitler and his party were advocating Jews' expulsion—and the restrictions against them in 1933 and 1934 certainly reinforced that view. They were being removed from society.

But at the same time, just two years after the party program had indicated that the Nazis would attempt to push all Jews out of Germany, Hitler made another speech that discussed the fate of the Jews. This rhetoric was even more menacing. Robert Wistrich, in his book *Antisemitism: The Longest Hatred*, wrote: "In 1922 he declared that if he gained power 'the annihilation of the Jews will be my first and foremost task', and spoke of public hangings that would go on 'until the last Jew in Munich is obliterated' and all of Germany would be cleansed."[5]

Thus, the signs were in conflict. At one point, it appeared that Hitler would attempt to expel all Jews from Germany. Other times, it seemed that he would seek to effect their complete destruction.

For many who did not want to believe—or could not bring themselves to believe—the latter, 1935 would likely have confirmed that Hitler was following the party's points. Within these it was determined that Jews would no longer be given Reich citizenship. And on September 15, 1935, the Reichstag passed the Reich Citizenship Law, part of what came to be known as the Nuremberg Laws. This in essence deprived all Jews of German citizenship and of any civil and political rights.[6] On November 14, 1935, this law was clarified—making it unambiguous that the Jews had lost their citizenship: "A Jew cannot be a citizen of the Reich. He cannot exercise the right to vote on political matters; he cannot hold public office."[7]

At that point, Jews in Germany became stateless. They belonged to no country and no longer had a national identity.

Yet, if one did not want to believe that humanity, or even the "civilized world," could fall so far as to attempt the complete eradication of a group of people, there were signs that perhaps could indicate that the government would slowly attempt to simply remove the Jews from Germany. And perhaps one of the most clear indicators that Hitler appeared to be following his 25 party points appeared in 1935, just months after Ernst Billig was born.

But Ernst was born in Austria.

Perhaps because Hitler was in Germany, not in Austria, that separation provided some solace or perceived barrier. Yet, if it was true that Hitler was following the 25 points, then the Jews in Austria did in fact need to be concerned—because the first of the 25 points stated the Nazis' intention with Austria: "We demand the unification of all Germans in the Greater Germany."[8] Hitler elaborated on this point in *Mein Kampf*:

> German-Austria must return to the great German mother country, and not because of any economic considerations. No, and again no: even if such a union were unimportant from an economic point of view;

yes, even if it were harmful, it must nevertheless take place. One blood demands one Reich.[9]

Though one could possibly convince him or herself otherwise, for Jews living in either Germany or Austria in 1935, the future looked grim—and even terrifyingly short. It was, much more than the 1920s had been, a tumultuous time in which to be born.

Beginnings

Ernst Billig came into this world on March 30, 1935. He was born in Vienna, Austria, to Abisch Billig (b. January 7, 1892) and Cheine Gittel Billig (b. December 15, 1900), who were both originally from the large Jewish community in Brody, Poland, but who had immigrated to Vienna after World War 1, along with a number of their siblings.[10] Ernst was their second child, and his sister, Rita (b. March 18, 1933), was two years older.

Vienna was a city composed of 23 districts, and Ernst spent the first few years of his life in District 9, Alsergrund. Though it is the ninth district, with the way in which the districts are numbered, Alsergrund lies immediately north of the city's central district, the Old Town, known as Innere Stadt. This district is connected with many well-known names: it was in this ninth district that Franz Schubert was born,[11] where Sigmund Freud had his apartment and office,[12] and where Beethoven, with his fist clenched and raised in opposition to a powerful spring thunderstorm, breathed his last.[13] Alsergrund was also home to a strong center of Jewish life in the 1930s; aside from Leopoldstadt, Vienna's second district, Alsergrund had the highest percentage of Jewish residents of Vienna's districts. It was in Alsergrund that most of the Jewish population fell into the middle and professional classes—many were doctors, lawyers, and businessmen—in contrast to the

Abisch Billig.

Jewish residents of Leopoldstadt, most of whom were immigrants. Consequently, Alsergrund became the district to which some Jews specifically moved to escape the conservative and traditional Jewish life of Leopoldstadt, and instead to embrace the more acculturated life of the Viennese non-Jews.[14] However, Ernst recalls that his family did not partake in this trend—they lived in Alsergrund, yet he believes that they were practicing Orthodox Jews at that time.[15]

Nevertheless, it seems there was no synagogue in Alsergrund—and the nearest major synagogue was in Leopoldstadt (one district to the east of Alsergrund), the Leopoldstäter Tempel. This house of worship became known as the "Great Synagogue of Vienna" and was where many of the Viennese Jewish community's events took place.[16] This is likely the synagogue Ernst's family attended. It was the largest synagogue in Vienna, with seating for 2,000. However, even before the events of *Kristallnacht*, in October 1938, the synagogue had been the victim of arson, but the fire was extinguished. Yet, it would only survive for another few days:

> At 6 am on the morning of November 10, 1938, the Gestapo took over the Jewish community's library in the south wing of the synagogue building. A short time later the synagogue's interior was set on fire, and was vandalized by organized SS units and civilians who had rushed to the scene. The fire brigade could not reach the burning building, because civilians had formed a human chain around it, to prevent any attempt to extinguish the blaze. By 10:02 am the Leopoldstadt Temple had burned to the ground. The ruins of the synagogue were cleared in 1941 and the ground was flattened in 1951.[17]

Ernst lived through all of this, and it took place less than two miles from his home.

However, Ernst's family did not simply live in Alsergrund. Though Alsergrund itself was one of the districts of Vienna, it too was divided into various sections, called *Bezirksteile*. Alsergrund has seven of these *Bezirksteile*: Althangrund, Roßau, Alservorstadt, Michelbeuern, Himmelpfortgrund, and Thurygrund I and II.[18] Ernst Billig spent the first years of his life at Roßauer Lände 35a, an apartment overlooking a small canal that had been carved out of the Danube—and part of the second suburb of Alsergrund, Roßau. In that suburb, approximately 1,600 feet from Ernst's home, was the Friedhof Roßau, one of Vienna's oldest Jewish cemeteries, with gravestones dating back to the 1540s. Even then—before it was desecrated by the Nazis—the cemetery spoke of dark days for the Jewish people: it was there that Samuel Oppenheimer, one of the first Jews to be allowed back into Vienna after the 1670 expulsion by Emperor Leopold I, was buried.[19] During the Nazi occupation, many of the old gravestones were hidden to save them from destruction—and only discovered many years later, as the Jews who had hidden them were subsequently murdered by the Nazis.[20] Furthermore, also only about 1,600 feet from Ernst's apartment was Servitengasse—another strong manifestation of the Jewish presence in the Roßau suburb of Alsergrund.[21] Servitengasse was a street in the suburb where, in March 1938, Jews owned 12 of the 24 apartment houses, along with 61 of the 111 shops. It is recorded that 377 Jews lived there—more than half of the estimated 680 residents. Out of those 377, it is known that 133 of them were deported to concentration camps or ghettos.[22]

But Ernst does not remember the rescuing of the headstones in the Jewish cemetery, nor does he remember the deportation of Servitengasse's Jewish residents. Ernst fled Roßau, in Alsergrund, in Vienna, in 1939, before any of that had occurred.

Yet, even that which he lived through he does not remember. On March 12, 1938, German troops entered Austria, fulfilling Hitler's maniacal desire to unite Germany and Austria. This was the *Anschluss*, and it changed the course of Ernst's life completely. By then though, Ernst was only two years old—so the dramatic events of the German and Austrian union entirely escaped his notice, aside from perhaps a few questions he might have asked, in his toddler voice, about some of the changes in the city.

Kristallnacht occurred only eight months after the *Anschluss*. Ernst's family, as did so many in Vienna, suffered. *Kristallnacht*, and the events surrounding it, also was a major turning point in Ernst's life—but again, he would not remember it.

It isn't because he didn't live through the *Anschluss* or *Kristallnacht* that Ernst Billig does not remember the events leading up to the Holocaust. It is because as he experienced those events, he was too young to know what they actually meant. As such, not only does he not remember the significant events that led up to the destruction of European Jewry, but also he holds no memory whatsoever of his life in Vienna before the war.[23] He does not remember any stories, he does not remember any places, and he does not remember anything that took place—except for one thing. He remembers getting a physical examination before he left the country.[24] Other than that, nothing. Everything he knows today of his life in mainland Europe has been pieced together from documents, photographs, and what was told to him by others.

After *Kristallnacht,* Ernst lived in Vienna for another few months. Then he and his sister, Rita, were put on the Kindertransport—leaving everything they had once known. Ernst was four years old—too young to have even begun kindergarten.

The Kindertransport

It was July 12, 1939. Ernst was accompanied by his sister and his big brown suitcase—the one that was identical to the suitcases Ernst eventually saw at Auschwitz after the war. The suitcase contained clothes, some silverware, and Ernst's teddy bear. His name was written on the outside in bold white letters: "Ernsti Billig".

The Billigs' housekeeper took Ernst and Rita to the train station, because their mother, who typically went by Gustie, was too ill to leave the house (more on her sickness to follow). As such, even before the children boarded the train, Gustie had already said goodbye to her two most precious possessions.

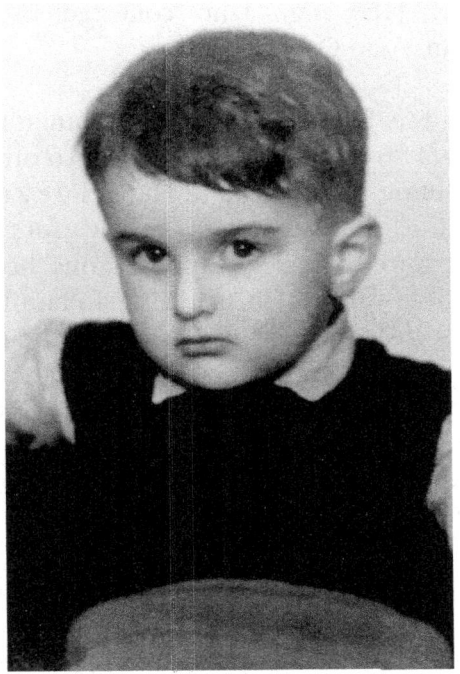

Ernst Billig's passport photo, taken around 1939.

As Ernst and Rita left the house, Gustie wondered when she would see her two babies, her seven-year-old and her four-year-old, again.

But Ernst, again due to his youth at the time, does not remember the parting.

Arrival

Ernst and Rita likely traveled from Vienna to Holland. From Holland, they crossed the channel to England, where they eventually were taken to Liverpool Street Station in London. There they were met by two Christadelphians whose names might be familiar to readers of the first volume of *Part of the Family*: "The man who collected us was . . . a Christadelphian, Alan Overton."[25]

The other man was Sidney Laxon. The two men met Ernst and Rita at Liverpool Street Station, as well as two other children—Suse Herz (Volume 1, story 9) and Hannelore Zack. The six of them boarded a train together, bound for Coventry. In Coventry, they were first taken to the Laxons' home, and from there, they went to various Christadelphian families. Suse went to the Parrys, Ernst to the Moores, Rita to the Morgans, and Hannelore, first to the Calcotts and later to the Dodds. Ernst and Rita did not live together in the same home with the same family, but they did live in the same area and attended the same meetings on Sundays with their Christadelphian families, so they saw each other frequently.

For Ernst, the entire experience consisted of one major change after the last, and with the resilience that only comes from being a young child, he was able to adapt. Ernst has strong memories of this period and these people, and they are not memories of trauma and loneliness. Instead, these powerful memories overflow with positivity. In discussing his arrival and the first time he met Alan Overton, Ernst's thoughts wandered to his memories of Mr. Overton in general:

> Uncle Alan . . . he was a great man. I remember, going back to 1946, it was very emotional for me, just saying goodbye to him, I remember. I had seen him many times, and I remember '46, I was 11, saying goodbye to him. I remember he gave me a gift of five pounds, which was a huge amount of money at that time. He was really one of the righteous, really amazing guy. When I went back in 1962, the first time I went back was 1962, I went to visit him in Rugby, and I imagine you got this from other people too, right?

> . . . he meant so much to everybody I think, all the kinder that were in Coventry . . .

> Alan Overton was responsible for hundreds of kids, such as myself and Rita . . . . He located homes, a hostel for example. And a bunch of stuff he did. They required a 50-pound repatriation fee, which was a huge amount of money. And he did all this. He was just a shopkeeper. I think it was Rugby dry goods . . . he was truly one of the righteous.[26]

The Christadelphians

And it wasn't just Uncle Alan whom Ernst felt this way about. His Christadelphian foster family was composed of just two people: Harold and Marjorie Moore. At that point, they were a young couple with no children.

Ernst was treated as their child.

He described the time and his feelings about it, which he could remember vividly:

> It was amazing. To me, I mean they became my—it was almost like a biological connection—family . . . . You asked me how they treated me; they treated me like I was their very own. And they used to, my sister, she'd come over from the Morgans and, for example, we went on different vacations to the sea side. I think once we went to Weston-Super-Mare [a seaside town about two hours southwest of their home] . . . it was very, very good . . . . The closest family I think I ever experienced were those seven years with the Moores in England. It was an incredible time for me.[27]

Ernst lived with the Moores for seven years, describing himself as an "only child,"[28] for the first six, until 1945, when the Moores had a son of their own, named Howard. During that time, Ernst developed a strong affection for the couple who had rescued him from the terror of the Nazis and had opened up their home to him. He lovingly referred to Harold as "Unc," short for uncle, and eventually—after he found out about the death of his own mother in Vienna in 1940, when he was just five years old—asked Marjorie whether he could begin calling her "mum."[29] From that point on, Marjorie Moore was "mum."

As their son, Ernst joined the Moores in their Christadelphian lives. Although he did all the same things any young person growing up in a Christadelphian home as the biological child

Ernst and Henry Moore.

Ernst and the Moores.

of a Christadelphian would do, he was very clear that he did not feel as though he had been pushed to join the community:

> I never felt pressured to become a Christadelphian. However, I participated in the family's daily Bible readings and memorized my Bible verse ('proofs') for weekly Sunday school. I also attended the Sunday meetings at the Grosvenor Road Ecclesia. However, while in England, I always thought of myself as a 'Jewish refugee.' In the US, after the war, I became immersed in Judaism, particularly after the revealing of the horrors of the Holocaust.[30]

Even after leaving the Moores and coming to the United States, Ernst and Rita, at 11 and 13 years old, respectively, continued to do their Christadelphian "daily Bible readings" together for the first few months.[31]

But Ernst stated that he indeed thought of himself as a Jewish refugee, and the Moores made attempts to help him maintain his Jewish identity. Ernst recalls being enrolled in Jewish correspondence lessons, and he can distinctly remember being given *matzah* in connection with Passover—this was his first experience, at least that he remembers, of any type of Jewish ritual.[32]

Despite the differences of culture, language, and religion, Ernst cannot but speak highly of his time with the Moores and of Christadelphians in general: "I owe so much to the Christadelphians. It's hard not to think back with very warm feelings for them and all they did for me and my sister during those years."[33]

He became part of their family—they loved him, and he loved them.

The War Years

During the war, Harold, as a Christadelphian, was a conscientious objector. He worked at a Harper's green grocer and was also a stretcher-bearer during the Blitz and the air raids. Living through war would have certainly been hard—yet Ernst does not recall experiencing anything unduly difficult during the time. Again, in his mind, his time spent with the Moores was extremely positive—even the privations of war did not seem to change this perception:

> My stay with the Moores (1939–1946) was stress free and in many a sense idyllic. Although food rationing was strict, we never seemed to want for anything. We grew a lot of our own vegetables and fruit and raised poultry, so we always had fresh eggs. My sister lived close enough so we were always in touch.[34]

Rita, living with the Morgans, was at 12 Gypsy Lane, Nuneaton, and the Moores lived at 29 Briton Road, Coventry. The two homes were approximately eight miles apart.

Ernst Billig, Marjorie Moore, and Rita Billig.

Perhaps out of all his experiences in the Moore family, the most traumatic was the Coventry Blitz. It was November 14 and 15, 1940, and the German air force launched its most brutal bombardment of a British city since the war had begun in September 1939. Four hundred and forty-nine German bombers dropped 30,000 incendiary bombs. Five hundred and

The Moores' house on Briton Road in Coventry. Henry Moore is standing outside, and the paper in the window is a flyer for the latest Christadelphian Bible talk.

sixty-eight people were killed, 71 factories were damaged, and 41,500 homes were damaged.[35] The Moores' house was one of them, but thankfully the damage was not beyond repair: "The most momentous early event for me was the Coventry blitz of November 1940. I spent the blitz in an outside air raid shelter. The next morning, all of our ceilings were down, and several windows blown out, but no major damage."[36]

While Ernst lived with the Moores, he was happy. Although life was difficult during the war, he did not feel want but rather felt cherished, valued, and loved. The difficulties in his life were tempered by the care shown to him by those around him and by the care that had been shown to him by his parents when they said goodbye to him and put him on a train to safety.

Ernst's Family

On November 9–10, 1938, *Kristallnacht,* Abisch Billig realized that his future in Vienna was being erased. That night, the Gestapo came to the Billig household. The tragedy was immediate—when the Gestapo entered the house, Gustie Billig fainted.[37]

But they were not looking for Gustie.

The Gestapo found Abisch and took him to the police station to be interviewed. The interview concluded with a straightforward message: Abisch was not welcome in Austria—and he must leave immediately.[38]

Astonishingly, he was released. During *Kristallnacht,* tens of thousands of Jewish men were arrested, and the majority were taken to camps such as Dachau and Buchenwald. Such was not the case for Abisch. He was released, sent home, and expected to vacate Austria.[39]

Abisch was determined to follow the command given to him—lest something worse come upon him and his family. But the matter was complicated by the fact that upon his return home, the family doctor informed Abisch that Gustie had not simply fainted from shock, but that she had suffered a heart attack and her condition would not permit her to emigrate safely.[40]

Because of Gustie's poor health and Abisch's charge to leave Austria immediately, it was determined that Abisch would flee illegally to Switzerland.[41] As Austrian Jews at that point were stateless, he had no visa, nor did he have time to fill out any

Top: Abisch Billig in a Swiss work camp. Abisch is on the front right.
Bottom: Abisch Billig in a Swiss work camp.

necessary paperwork to immigrate legally. If he were able to stay in Switzerland, Abisch would endeavor to make the proper connections to allow his children to flee Austria.[42] His plan was that eventually, when Gustie had recovered and Abish had established himself in Switzerland, he would send for her.[43]

On his last night at home, Abisch tucked the children into bed and said goodbye to his wife. He was gone before Rita and Ernst awoke.[44]

Abisch never saw Gustie again because she never recovered. And on October 7, 1940, she passed away: not at home and not at a Nazi camp, but at Währinger Gürtel 97,[45] the Rothschild Hospital. It was located in Währing (Vienna's 18th district), on the inner border between Alsergrund and Währing, named after Baron Anselm von Rothschild, and served as the Jewish hospital of Vienna until it was closed by the Nazis in 1943.[46] Her death certificate does not state her cause of death. She was only 39 years old.

Abisch, however, survived.

He was able to enter Switzerland, without a visa. There he was interned by the Swiss—but internment in a Swiss camp was much better than was internment in any kind of Nazi camp. Descriptions of the treatment in the Swiss camps vary; many say that the camps were unnecessarily cruel;[47] others, however, felt as though they were treated with respect.[48] Abisch described his experience in the following way:

> The camps were just Summer emergency camps, but we lived there in 20-degree-below weather. . . . Switzerland meant safety, and I owe the Swiss my life . . . but it was hard. I worked on the streets and

roads and dug stones from the mountain. . . . The hope of seeing my children was all that kept me alive.[49]

In 1940, when Gustie passed away, Abisch was a prisoner in the Felsberg internment camp, near Lucerne.[50] But in 1941, Abisch's identity card states that he was then imprisoned in the Thalheim internment camp.[51] Hence, it appears he was imprisoned in at least two Swiss interment centers.

Abisch survived this internment—waiting for the day he would again see his children.

But Abisch Billig was not the only member of his family who was living in Vienna in 1938. Therefore, when the horror of the *Anschluss* and of *Kristallnacht* descended upon Austrian Jewry, more than just Ernst's nuclear family was affected. Abisch's brother in law, Fritz Schattner, was one among many arrested on *Kristallnacht* and sent to Dachau. However, despite being sent to the infamous camp, Fritz was released. Eventually, he and his wife, Abisch's sister, Nesche, were able to escape Europe and set up a home in the United States, around 1940. Such was the case for two other branches of the family—in desperate attempts to flee Austria, Ernst's aunts and uncles scattered around the Western Hemisphere:

> There was an aunt Gustie and her husband, Heinrich, who made it to Mexico . . . . There was an uncle, you'd be surprised, uncle Adolf, [and] his wife, aunt Maria, and their two young sons, Erich and Robert. And they were able to get to the Dominican Republic, which along with . . . the UK was a haven for Jewish immigrants.

Despite the four branches of Ernst's family that survived, many family members did not: "It was a terrible thing after the war, looking at the different lists to see who made it out. None of my people did. None of my family made it out. Except the [four] that I mentioned."[52]

Yet Ernst and his family were the fortunate ones: *some* members survived. Many families were were wiped out entirely.

After the War

In 1946, Ernst and Rita were contacted by aunt Nesche, who had been able, with her husband, Fritz (although now called Philip), to immigrate to the United States. They lived in

Aunt Nesche and uncle Fritz.

Ernst and Rita Billig with Suse Rosenstock in front of the SS Drottningholm just before they left for New York, 1946.

Birmingham, Alabama—and wanted Ernst and Rita to come to live with them.

As such, on May 4, 1946, Ernst and Rita boarded the *SS Drottningholm* in Liverpool, bound for New York.[53] At 11 years old, Ernst went from Coventry, England, to Birmingham, Alabama—from a continent in which antisemitism had caused unimaginable tragedy for his family to a state in which race relations remained a struggle.

> I was interested in race relations in 1946. It was a shock to me to see how black people were treated and regarded in Alabama relative to the UK . . . it's hard to overcome that, the racism that's indigenous, or endemic to that part of the country, the Deep South. It's really deep rooted. I remember I had a good friend in England, he was from South Africa, a black kid, I mean, he was just one of us . . . there was no such thing in Alabama, in Birmingham.[54]

In moving to the United States, however, Ernst had to undergo more than one culture shock. It was in Alabama, living with his aunt and uncle, that he, in earnest, had his first experience with Judaism:

> When I came over to America, the first thing, the first Jewish thing . . . they had me go to Hebrew school and learn the Mourner's *Kaddish*, that's the prayer for the dead. They wanted me to say *Kaddish* for my mother on . . . the anniversary of her death. I did that. I went to Hebrew school and eventually I was bar mitzvahed in 1948 . . . when I was 13.[55]

Even the environment was different: their first summer in Alabama was stiflingly hot, so many of the families in Alabama kept their children indoors. Ernst was used to playing outside with other children, and he spent his first summer cooped up. This kind of weather did not represent an auspicious start to a new country for an 11-year-old boy.

However, Ernst and Rita were about to experience an even larger shock than those resulting from the myriad cultural and environmental changes: Abisch Billig had survived—and he was coming to the United States to be with his children.

Reunion

He had lived for the moment. He had willed himself to survive the Swiss camps to see Ernst and Rita's faces again.

In 1947, eight years after he had tucked his children into their beds and then disappeared, Abisch Billig traveled from Degersheim, Switzerland,[56] to Rotterdam, Holland, and boarded the *SS Noordam,* bound for New York. It was February 15, 1947.[57] The last time Abisch had seen his little boy, Ernst had only been four years old. Now he was one month away from turning twelve. Rita had only been six. Now she was almost fourteen.

Throughout the voyage over the Atlantic, Abisch rehearsed what he would say to his children. What *would* he say? What would *you* say to your adolescent children, from whom you had been separated, who had been raised with people you had never met—yet whom you loved for how they had treated those so dear to you—who spoke a different language, and had grown used to English and American culture, while you had lived in Swiss internment camps, willing yourself to live for this very moment? What would you say?

Abisch had thought it through. He put together the best greeting he could come up with, in the English that he had been teaching himself in any free time he could muster. Over and over, on the ship, he practiced his greeting. He then practiced it on the train from New York to Birmingham. He was going to say things perfectly—get every word right, every intonation, and every syllable. He was going to show them how much he loved them and how much it meant to see them again.

And when he saw Ernst and Rita, his son and his daughter, at the train station in Birmingham, on February 25, 1947, what he had planned and what he had rehearsed no longer mattered. It all left him, and he flung his arms around his children, weeping, gasping, and uttering "Liebchen, Liebchen," "Darling, darling."[58]

This was why he had survived.

Later Years

Ernst continued living in Alabama with Aunt Nesche and Uncle Philip until 1956. Abisch, however, made his home in New York, where he remarried in 1954, and was eventually joined by Rita, who found life in Alabama to be difficult.

In 1956, Ernst enrolled at Northwestern University, where he eventually earned a PhD in chemistry. He went on to do postdoctoral work at Columbia University.

Many years later, in 1986, his life once again changed dramatically. That year, he met Nancy Scher, a Jewish American, who, two years later in 1988, became his wife. At the time, Nancy already had three children—and Ernst has taken those children as his own.

Conclusion

Over the years, Ernst did not lose contact with the Moores. He was like their child—their affection for him did not diminish, nor did his affection for them. Ernst recalled the way Marjorie, or "mum," never forgot a birthday, despite the fact that he lived on another continent:

> Every year she'd bake me a birthday cake . . . she'd send it over . . . English lady, English cooking: marzipan over the fruitcake with icing. Marzipan took six weeks by boat from England to the US . . . . It was like a rock when it got here. It was just the thought. She was so, I mean so wonderful, like a true parent. She'd do this for me for so many years, and she'd never forget my birthday. And, you know, we'd correspond.[59]

Ernst and Nancy Billig, 2016.

Ernst Billig and Rita Glanz, 2016.

In 1962, 16 years after he had left England, and over 10 birthday cakes later, Ernst traveled to England to visit the Moores. He returned in 1968. In 1974, they came to the United States to visit him—and on that trip, he brought them to a Christadelphian ecclesia in New Jersey, where he introduced them to everyone and told the story of what they had done for him. In 1989, he went to London for the 50th Kindertransport reunion and visited them then—also introducing them to Nancy. In 1999, for the 60th reunion of the Kindertransport, Ernst and Nancy again went to England—this time bringing their three children. By that point, Harold and Marjorie were living in the Christadelphian Care Home in Leamington Spa—and Ernst and Nancy returned to see them a few more times until the time of their deaths.

The last time Ernst saw the Moores, he spoke words to them that any son would say to his parents. It was over 60 years since he had first met them, but his feelings for them had not changed. "I love you," he said.

And when asked what he would say to the Moores again if he could see them one more time, without hesitation, Ernst's responded with the same words: "I love you."[60]

Such are his feelings for the couple who brought a little four-year-old boy into their family and treated him as their own.

---

[1] Ernst Billig, in discussion with the author, April 14, 2016.

[2] "1933: Key Dates," *United States Holocaust Memorial Museum*, accessed March 28, 2017, https://www.ushmm.org/wlc/en/article.php?ModuleId=10007499.

[3] "Anti-Jewish Legislation in Prewar Germany," *United States Holocaust Memorial Museum*, accessed March 28, 2017, https://www.ushmm.org/wlc/en/article.php?ModuleId=10005681.

[4] "The Program of the NSDAP," *Yale Law School*, accessed April 28, 2017, http://avalon.law.yale.edu/imt/1708-ps.asp.

[5] Robert Wistrich, *Antisemitism - The Longest Hatred* (New York: Schocken Books, 1991), 66.

[6] "The Reich Citizenship Law," in *The Jew in the Modern World*, ed. Paul Mendes-Flohr and Jehuda Reinharz (Oxford: Oxford University Press, 2011), 731.

[7] "First Decree to the Reich Citizenship Law," in *The Jew in the Modern World*, ed. Paul Mendes-Flohr and Jehuda Reinharz (Oxford: Oxford University Press, 2011), 732.

[8] "The Program of the NSDAP," *Yale Law School*, accessed April 28, 2017, http://avalon.law.yale.edu/imt/1708-ps.asp.

[9] Adolf Hitler, *Mein Kampf* (Boston: Houghton Mifflin, 1971), 3.

[10] Ernst Billig, in discussion with the author, April 14, 2016.

[11] Anthony Haywood and Caroline Sieg, *Vienna* (Melbourne: Lonely Planet, 2010), 99.

[12] Ibid, 98.

[13] Joseph Kerman, *The Beethoven Quartets* (New York: W. W. Norton & Company, 1979), 350.

[14] Kate Melchoir, "Site 8A: Introduction to Jewish Life in Alsergrund," *The Vienna Project: Jewish Communities of Leopoldstadt and Alsergrund*, 2014, http://theviennaproject.org/wp-content/uploads/2014/09/Jewish-Communities-Worksheets-without-Questions.pdf.

[15] Ernst Billig, in discussion with the author, April 14, 2016.

[16] Kate Melchoir, "Site 1B: Leopoldstäter Tempel/Leopoldstadt Temple," *The Vienna Project: Jewish Communities of Leopoldstadt and Alsergrund*, 2014, http://theviennaproject.org/wp-content/uploads/2014/09/Jewish-Communities-Worksheets-without-Questions.pdf.

[17] "Der Leopoldstädter Tempel, Tempelgasse 5 - 2nd District Leopoldstadt" *Synagogue Memorial "Beit Ashkenaz,"* accessed March 29, 2017, http://www.austriansynagogues.com/index.php/archive?pid=58&sid=127:der-leopoldstaedter-tempel-tempelgasse-5-2nd-district-leopoldstadt.

[18] "Alsergrund und siene Bezirksteile," Wien.at, accessed March 29, 2017, https://www.wien.gv.at/bezirke/alsergrund/geschichte-kultur/bezirksteile.html.

[19] Rob Humphreys, *The Rough Guide to Vienna* (London: Rough Guides, 2011), 203.

[20] Kate Melchoir, "Site 10: Friedhof Seegasse/Cemetary Seegasse," *The Vienna Project: Jewish Communities of Leopoldstadt and Alsergrund*, 2014, http://theviennaproject.org/wp-content/uploads/2014/09/Jewish-Communities-Worksheets-without-Questions.pdf.

[21] Kate Melchoir, "Site 8B: Gedenksymbol: Schlüssel gegen das Vergessen/Memorial: Keys against Forgetting," *The Vienna Project: Jewish Communities of Leopoldstadt and Alsergrund*, 2014, http://theviennaproject.org/wp-content/uploads/2014/09/Jewish-Communities-Worksheets-without-Questions.pdf.

[22] "Servitengasse 1938 - The Fate of Those Who Disappeared," *Servitengasse 1938*, accessed March 29, 2017, http://redirect.servitengasse1938.at/page12/files/Servitengasse%20english.pdf

[23] Ernst Billig, e-mail message to author on December 18, 2016.

[24] Ernst Billig, in discussion with the author, April 14, 2016.

[25] Ibid.

[26] Ibid.

[27] Ibid.

[28] Ernst Billig, e-mail message to author on December 18, 2016.

[29] Ibid.

[30] Ernst Billig, e-mail message to author on December 18, 2016.

[31] Ernst Billig, in discussion with the author, April 14, 2016.

[32] Ibid.

[33] Ibid.

[34] Ernst Billig, e-mail message to author on December 18, 2016.

[35] Jennifer Harby, "The Coventry Blitz: 'Hysteria, terror and neurosis,'" *BBC*, November 13, 2015, http://www.bbc.com/news/uk-england-coventry-warwickshire-34746691.

[36] Ernst Billig, e-mail message to author on December 18, 2016.

[37] Jane Aldridge, "Dreams of Horror-Filled Years Come True As Nazi Prisoner Is Reunited With Family," *The Birmingham Post* (Birmingham, AL), February 26, 1947.

[38] Ibid.

[39] Ibid.

[40] Ibid.

[41] Ibid.

[42] Ernst Billig, in discussion with the author, April 14, 2016.

[43] Jane Aldridge, "Dreams of Horror-Filled Years Come True As Nazi Prisoner Is Reunited With Family," *The Birmingham Post* (Birmingham, AL), February 26, 1947.

[44] Ibid.

[45] Cheine Gittel Billig's Death Certificate. Copy in possession of the author.

[46] "Rothschild Hospital," *Top Health Clinics,* accessed March 31, 2017, http://www.tophealthclinics.com/clinic/919849078079887/Rothschild+Hospital.

[47] David Cay Johnston, "Jews Remember Forced Labor Camps in Wartime Swiss Refuge," *The New York Times* (New York, NY), January 15, 1998.

"Swiss put Jews in labor camps, British documentary contends," *The Jewish News of Northern California,* January 9, 1998, http://www.jweekly.com/1998/01/09/swiss-put-jews-in-labor-camps-british-documentary-contends/.

[48] Robert Scheinberg, "Controversy erupts over Swiss WWII labor camps," *Jewish Telegraphic Agency,* February 12, 1999. http://www.jta.org/1999/02/12/life-religion/features/controversy-erupts-over-swiss-wwii-labor-camps.

[49] Abisch Billig, quoted in Jane Aldridge, "Dreams of Horror-Filled Years Come True As Nazi Prisoner Is Reunited With Family," *The Birmingham Post* (Birmingham, AL), February 26, 1947.

[50] Cheine Gittel Billig's Death Certificate. Copy in possession of the author.

[51] Personalausweis für Auslander, Abisch Billig, 1941. Copy in possession of the author.

[52] Ernst Billig, in discussion with the author, April 14, 2016.

[53] Ship manifest of the *SS Drottningholm*, departing Liverpool for New York, May 4, 1946.

[54] Ernst Billig, in discussion with the author, April 14, 2016.

[55] Ibid.

[56] Abisch Billig's Declaration of Intention for the United States, April 9, 1947. Copy in possession of the author.

[57] Ship manifest of the *SS Noordam*, departing Rotterdam for New York, February 15, 1947. Copy in possession of the author.

[58] Abisch Billig, quoted in Jane Aldridge, "Dreams of Horror-Filled Years Come True As Nazi Prisoner Is Reunited With Family," *The Birmingham Post* (Birmingham, AL), February 26, 1947.

[59] Ernst Billig, in discussion with the author, April 14, 2016.

[60] Ibid.

APPENDIX

PRIMARY SOURCE ARTICLES ABOUT ELPIS LODGE

The Birmingham Post
The Coventry Standard
The Jewish Chronicle
The Christadelphian Magazine
The Christadelphian Children's Magazine

THE BIRMINGHAM POST

Transcript © 'Trinity Mirror'. Reproduced with the kind permission of The British Newspaper Archive (www.britishnewspaperarchive.co.uk).

December 15, 1939
"Birmingham Council for Refugees"*

The constitution of the new Birmingham Council for Refugees, the organisation which replaces the Birmingham Co-ordinating Committee for Refugees and the Birmingham Jewish Refugee Committee, was approved at a meeting of the Council last night. The Lord Mayor presided.

It was stated the Christadelphian Central Ecclesia of Birmingham had offered to provide a hostel to give accommodation for about twenty young men.

Mr. G. Philip Achurch moved the approval of the constitution. He said the outbreak of war between the Allies and Germany raised a number of new and difficult problems. From the beginning, it was clear that, for the time being at any rate, a suspension of immigration and in some cases a retraction in the work of the Birmingham Council for Refugees was unavoidable. The comprehensive report of the Council required only a little imagination to realise the strain which had been imposed upon all those who had been working for the Council. It was impossible to review all that had been done without paying tribute to those who bore the heat and burden of the day before the formation of the Council, a few weeks prior to the beginning of hostilities.

Comment was made in the report upon an agreement between the Birmingham Co-ordinating Committee for Refugees and the Birmingham Jewish Refugee Committee, of which that Birmingham Council for Refugees is the outcome. It has been felt that there was much work and many problems common to both parties, which could be better dealt with by one organisation. Once the principle was agreed upon to unite, the willingness to co-operate which was shown by representatives of Birmingham Jewry, under the chairmanship of Mr. Oscar Deutsch, would linger in the memory of those who took part in the negotiations.

Agreement Justified

From the experience of the last few months he could say that this agreement to work together had been amply justified. A committee is to be formed to help financially the recently established Polish Relief Fund, and later on its efforts would be supplemented by the proceeds of a flag day provisionally arranged for March 30.

They could now face a future, full as it might well be of anxieties and difficulties, with confidence and determination to do their part in bearing the cruel burdens of those who for the most part had been the victims of Nazi oppression.

Mr. A. Blanckensee, who seconded, said the new constitution was the expression of the goodwill and co-operation of men and women of all denominations to do what they could as a single body in an attempt at opposing the forces of evil which unfortunately were so prevalent in the world to-day. The constitution welded together organisations which had been trying to help those who, unfortunately, were born in lands less happy than Britain.

The Lord Mayor, who proposed the election of Mr. G. Philip Achurch as chairman of the Council, said Birmingham was a hospitable city and it was anxious to retain that reputation. Britain was prepared to take its share in looking after those who had suffered by events on the Continent. This could not be done without support and if, as Lord Mayor, he could be of assistance to the Council in furthering its interests, he hoped that those associated with the organisation would not fail to approach him him [sic] and ask him for help in any direction. The work of dealing with the refugees was now united and in that unity there should be strength. He paid a tribute to the efforts of Mr. Achurch, who had taken a large part in forming the United Council.

The motion was carried.

Christadelphian Ecclesia's Offer

The Rev. Dr. A. Cohen, Chief Minister of the Hebrew Congregation, said that up to November, 1938, the burden of looking after the refugees was being born by the Jewish community. An entirely new situation was created thirteen months ago, when the problem grew to such dimensions that Lord Baldwin made his clarion call to the Christian world. That met with a magnificent response in Birmingham. Once of the religious bodies which had been active and prominent in its work to relieve the refugees had been the Christadelphian Central Ecclesial of Birmingham. During the last thirteen months this Ecclesia had raised regular collections and had thus made a contribution of tremendous value. Not satisfied with this, the Ecclesia had now come forward with a wonderful proposal. It offered to acquire commodious premises in Birmingham, equip and maintain the place, so that there could be brought into the city about twenty young men who were in what one might call a temporary clearing house. The great value of this offer would be that, in addition to looking after the physical care of the young men, it would be possible to find employment for them after they had been given training in useful handicraft work. That would be accomplished without imperiling the earnings of British boys. He wished to express profound thanks to the members of the Ecclesia. Control of the hostel would be in the hands of the Jewish community under the final supervision of that Council.

Mr. H. W. Gosling submitted the annual report.

*A shortened form of this article also appeared in the Birmingham Mail, December 15, 1939.

APPENDIX - ELPIS LODGE - *THE BIRMINGHAM POST*

April 22, 1940
"Elpis Lodge – 'Abode of Hope'"

Elpis Lodge (a name signifying "Abode of Hope") was opened in Gough Road, Edgbaston, yesterday, for the reception of twenty Jewish refugee boys from the Continent. It has been bought and equipped, and will be maintained by voluntary contributions from members of Birmingham and Coventry Christadelphian Ecclesias. The first contingent of fifteen boys will arrive on May 1 and will be cared for and educated by two wardens, Dr. A. Hirsch and his wife. Dr. Hirsch was headmaster of a school of 700 boys in Frankfurt before he and his family were driven out of Germany by the Nazi persecution.

Yesterday Mr. L. L. Jacobs, who is eighty-nine and a past president of the Birmingham Hebrew Congregation, handed the key of the Home to Mr. Benjamin Walker, treasurer of Birmingham Central Christadelphian Ecclesia. Mr. Walker declared Elpis Lodge open and handed it over to the care of the Representative Council for Birmingham Jewry.

Dr. A. Cohen, minister of Birmingham Hebrew congregation, conducted a short dedication service. He said that the occasion of the opening of the Home fell very appropriately on the eve of the Jewish Passover. That festival called to mind the first attempt to enslave and annihilate the Children of Israel. The Home brought to mind the latest of the long series of similar attempts; but, if the parallel were pushed farther, there was one noteworthy point of difference. When the Israelites left Egypt and set out on their journey through the wilderness, in their helpless state they were attacked by the Amalekites. But when the victims of Nazi oppression were driven from the land of their birth and adoption the Amalekites were few, and there was around throughout the world a measure of sympathy and helpful kindness that must linger in the memory of all of them.

Christian Support Appreciated

> The Jewish community, true to its tradition, rallied to the help of its stricken brethren, but the problem was too gigantic, the numbers too vast, to be dealt with by our efforts alone, and we can never appreciate sufficiently the manner in which the Christian world rallied to our support. Among those not of our own people, conspicuous in their sympathy and endeavour to be helpful, was the community of Christadelphians. This is by no means the first occasion when they have shown their interest in the welfare and fate of the Jewish people. For long years they have contributed generously to our efforts to re-establish the Jewish people in their homeland. Therefore we appreciate to the full the magnificent act of generosity which is finding expression in this hostel for refugee boys. We feel that a sacred trust has been committed to us, and we shall endeavour to discharge it faithfully.

They must care physically for these boys, who had suffered privations, and train them in a livelihood. Another aspect was even more important. It would be realized that Jewish boys and girls who had been subjected to bestial cruelty might have their minds scarred and their souls embittered by what they had gone through. So far as was possible, the effects of that ill-treatment must be eradicated from their natures. As Israel was told of old, that, in spite of the treatment at the hands of the Egyptians, "Thou must not abhor the Egyptians," so they must teach these boys that they had seen only one side of the world. They must be told that, though they might have suffered simply because they were Jews, through the kindness of others who also were not Jews they were being given in the Home a chance to live in the future.

APPENDIX - ELPIS LODGE - *THE BIRMINGHAM POST*

Mr. S. J. Levi, chairman of the Trustee and Management Committee, outlined the history of the scheme, and asked Mr. E. W. Newman (Birmingham Christadelphian Ecclesia) and Mr. S. Laxon (Coventry Ecclesia) to accept replicas of the key of the Home. Both made short speeches in reply.

Mr. Newman mentioned that all contributions made by members of the Christadelphian community were anonymous. He said that they had received a small brown paper packet by registered post. It was found to contain an anonymous gift of £350 in notes for the Lodge.

Dr. Hirsch and Mr. G. Philip Achurch, chairman of the Birmingham Council for Refugees, made short speeches.

THE COVENTRY STANDARD

Transcript © 'Trinity Mirror'. Reproduced with the kind permission of The British Newspaper Archive (www.britishnewspaperarchive.co.uk).

April 27, 1940
"Hostel for Jewish Boys"

An anonymous gift of £350—sent in notes—was one of the gifts which made possible the opening on Sunday of the Birmingham Hostel for Jewish Boys at Elpis Lodge—meaning "The Abode of Hope"—in Gough Road, Edgbaston.

The hostel, which will house 20 boys, has been purchased and equipped, and will be maintained by voluntary contributions of the Birmingham and Coventry Christadelphian Ecclesias.

The £350 was received wrapped in a brown paper packet at the office of a Christadelphian magazine. Accompanying the gift was a note explaining that the money had been saved by the donor, who was "overjoyed to think that God has permitted me to help in our hostel for His afflicted people."

It was pointed out that all gifts by Christadelphians are anonymous.

THE JEWISH CHRONICLE

Transcript © 'The Jewish Chronicle'. Reproduced with the kind permission of *The Jewish Chronicle* (www.thejc.com).

May 3, 1940
"Christadelphians' Fine Gesture"
[From our Correspondent]

Christadelphians have again demonstrated their sympathy for Jewish victims of persecutions. It has this time taken the form of a hostel which the Birmingham and Coventry Ecclesias have given for Jewish refugee boys in Birmingham. The opening ceremony, which took place recently, was followed by a dedication service conducted by the Rev. W. Lewi and the Rev. S. I. Solomons. The Rev. Dr. A. Cohen delivered an address.

"For long years," said Dr. Cohen, "the Christadelphians have contributed generously to our efforts to re-establish the Jewish people in their Homeland. We appreciate to the full the magnificent act of generosity which is finding expression in this hostel for refugee boys. We feel that a sacred trust has been committed to us, and we shall endeavour to discharge it faithfully."

Mr. E. W. Newman (Birmingham Christadelphian Ecciesia) and Mr. S. Laxon (Coventry Ecclesia) accepted replicas of the key of the Home from Mr. S. J. Levi, Chairman of the Trustee and Management Committee.

Anonymous Gift of £350

Mr. Newman mentioned that all contributions made by members of the Christadelphian Community were anonymous. They had received a small brown paper packet by registered post, which was found to contain an anonymous gift of £350 in notes for the Hostel.

It was in October last that the Representative Council of Birmingham Jewry, of which Mr. Oscar Deutsch is the Chairman, was approached by Mr. Newman and Mr. Mr. [sic] Laxon with the offer to purchase, equip, and maintain, a hostel for twenty Jewish refugeee [sic] trainee boys, and to hand over the Hostel when completed to a Jewish Committee to be administered as an Orthodox Jewish Home. They were desirous of not merely caring for the physical welfare of the boys but of providing facilities for their moral and cultural education too. The offer was gratefully accepted and the necessary Trustee and Management Committees for its administration were appointed, Mr. S. J. Levi being elected Chairman, Mr. E. W. Newman Hon. Treasurer, and Mr. S. Marks Hon. Secretary. A suitable house was purchased at Gough Road, Edgbaston, where certain alterations have been made, and the furnishings and equipment installed. The Hostel has been named Elpis Lodge (The Abode of Hope).

Dr. Albert Hirsch and his wife have been appointed Wardens. Dr. Hirsch it a refugee; he was driven out of Germany in August last and was headmaster of the Philanthropic School, Frankfort, which accommodated 700 boys.

APPENDIX - ELPIS LODGE - *THE JEWISH CHRONICLE*

August 30, 1940
"Birmingham Refugee Hostel"
[From our Correspondent]

It is now four months since the Hostel for Jewish Refugee Boys was opened, through the generosity of the local Christadelphian Ecclesia, at Gough Road, Edgbaston, Birmingham. A report just issued by Mr. S. J. Levi, Chairman of the Management Committee, shows the fine work the Hostel is performing. It says, in part:

> On May 1, the first batch of boys arrived, having been selected by Dr. and Mrs. Hirsch, the Wardens, who had, accompanied by the Chairman, visited London and Ipswich for that purpose. The first sixteen boys were soon settled in suitable trainee jobs and I am pleased to say that they have for the most part given complete satisfaction, and are happy in their work. The boys receive cultural education from Dr. Hirsch, and English education from Mr. J. L. Cresswell, a secondary school teacher introduced by Dr. Cohen.
>
> It is too early yet to ascertain exactly the cost of running the Home. I may state, however, that the whole of the financial expenditure, both on the equipment and maintenance of the Home, is being borne by the Christadelphian Ecclesia, of which Mr. Newman is Treasurer. I have no reason to doubt that they will be able to maintain the Home for an indefinite period, in the same manner as they have started. No reasonable expense has been spared by them as far as maintenance is concerned, the provision of good substantial food together with some items which may be looked upon as luxuries, is one of the features of the catering.

As soon as they are placed in trainee jobs, the boys receive wages of from 15s. to 20s. per week, out of which a certain proportion is allocated to them for pocket money and daily expenses, another portion for savings, which is invested in National Savings Certificates (a War Savings Group having been established). A portion goes to the Home for their maintenance and a further allocation for renewal of clothing, etc. The health of the boys has been uniformly good and it has not been necessary up to the present to make use of the room provided for sickness.

I am sorry to say that on July 4, three boys who had become 16 years of age were interned and we are now in communication with them in the Isle of Man. Subsequently five more boys were received from Bloomsbury House to fill the vacancies, and the Home is now complete with 19 boys, all of whom are under 16 years of age.

THE CHRISTADELPHIAN MAGAZINE

Transcript © 'The Christadelphian Magazine and Publishing Association'. Reproduced with the kind permission of The Christadelphian Magazine and Publishing Association (www.thechristadelphian.com).

July 1939
Volume 76, Number 901, 318-319.
"Jewish Relief Problems: How can We Help?"
John Carter

The following paragraph is from a recent address by Mr. Neville Laski, K.C., delivered at the invitation of the Coventry ecclesia, and it shews the plight and shame of the Jewish people, and particularly of their children.

> There are cruelties unbelievable within the concentration camps and in the streets of Vienna and Berlin. You do not know a thousandth part of the humiliation, physical and spiritual, which has been heaped upon these people, but the worst of all is the searing of the souls of little children. These children are made to sit apart from others, and to listen to lessons where the racial doctrines of the German people are taught. When play time comes they have to stand apart. They are spat upon and humiliated. What is going to be the future of these children? If they remain there they are going to have a lasting impression on their minds which the future will not eradicate. We have felt so strongly that as the future lies with our children, so does the future of these people lie with their children too, and that is why so much of an endeavour has been made to get them out of this hell to the happy haven of England.

Our interest in Israel springs from our knowledge of God's purpose with them. In fact, for the time being Gentile believers have taken their place as branches which have been grafted into the Abrahamic olive tree. But God's gifts and callings are not subject to any change of mind. Israel is still the chosen nation. Since the past and future of this people (of whom as concerning the flesh Christ came, as Paul remarks) touches our faith so closely, we are naturally sympathetic to their needs at the present time. But the practical question is how best to give effect to this desire to help them.

The Arranging Brethren of the Central Ecclesia have had the matter under consideration. A circular was sent to each family in the ecclesia explaining the need and asking if any could give hospitality to a child, or if regular contributions could be given. The difficulties of taking a child into the home are many, but some are willing. But a greater opening for helping is by contribution. An extra collection is being taken each Sunday, and the liberal response has enabled the Arranging Brethren to promise such regular financial support as will enable the Co-ordinating Committee for Jewish Relief to proceed with equipping a hostel. The Coventry ecclesia is proceeding with a similar scheme.

It has been suggested that many ecclesias in towns where there are not many Jews and where there are not the opportunities for placing trainees may yet wish to help, but have not the same opportunity as exists in a city like Birmingham; and many a small ecclesia may desire to help but is not able to give on a scale to be of value locally. It is here where collective effort finds the way.

If any ecclesias are desirous of making regular monthly contributions to be devoted to running hostels, and to providing help in any other way necessary, we are willing to receive such sums, in addition to contributions for Jewish Relief in general.

The Arranging Brethren are willing that such help should be used to extend their own efforts, since Birmingham is in many ways a suitable centre for such work. But if there is a generous response and there are similar schemes in other places, the contributions could be disbursed through more than one channel. By this arrangement a small ecclesia may make regular contributions, however small, which, though they could not be put to satisfactory use locally, may, when added to other contributions, be of very practical value in providing the means for a refuge for some of Jacob's sons.

A considerable number of brethren and sisters are taking Jewish Refugee girls into their homes, and a few are taking Refugee boys. The need of the boys is most urgent, in view of the attitude of the German Government towards them; hence the emphasis in this article upon the desirability of assisting in the establishment of hostels, where Refugee boys can be brought under the direct influence of the Jewish people, and brought up as Jews.

A considerable need also exists for the exercise of temporary hospitality to older Jewish people, whose time limit in Germany and other countries is expired, and who are due to emigrate shortly afterwards to America and elsewhere. There is often an anxious period of a few weeks or months between these two dates, and to such refugees as find themselves so placed, temporary hospitality is often an urgent necessity. Here is a sphere in which some may feel able to help.

Those who have the leisure can also be of considerable assistance in finding trainee positions for Jewish refugee boys.

Any communications on these matters, if addressed to the office, will be forwarded to the appropriate quarter.

The ecclesias have already generously helped to the extent of £1,250, which has been sent to Lord Baldwin's Fund. By the scheme outlined above, we are able to control into what particular channels our help is directed. We thank all who have so splendidly helped before, and commend this method of still further assisting.

APPENDIX - ELPIS LODGE - *THE CHRISTADELPHIAN MAGAZINE*

December 1939
Volume 76, Number 906, 556.
"Jewish Refugee Problems"
John Carter

In the July issue of this magazine (page 318) we wrote of the plight and shame of the Jewish people, of the natural sympathy of the brotherhood towards Israel in their time of need, and of endeavours which were being made to give practical expression to this sympathy. The sufferings of Israel at the present time are truly appalling, and when we have done all that can be done to mitigate these sufferings, it is only a small fraction of what is needed. Those who have come into actual contact with the misery which has been created by Jewish persecution in Germany and elsewhere realise this the more keenly. Nevertheless, the fact that this is so should not deter us from doing what we can. Rather should it spur us on to greater effort.

Reference was also made to the extra weekly collection which was being taken each Sunday at the Birmingham Central Ecclesia, and to the fact that the liberal response had enabled the arranging brethren to promise such regular financial support to the local Co-ordination Committee for relief of refugees as would enable them to proceed with the establishment of a Hostel for the reception of Jewish boys. Many Jewish girls have been taken into Christadelphian homes, but only a few Jewish boys. The need of the boys is the most urgent.

It was also mentioned that the Coventry Ecclesia was proceeding with a scheme for the establishment of a Hostel for Jewish boys in Coventry.

Both these schemes were hindered by the outbreak of war. The Coventry brethren also found that on account of the small

Jewish population in Coventry and the absence of religious, social, and educational institutions amongst them, a Hostel in Coventry suffered certain disadvantages which would not be experienced in Birmingham, where there is a larger Jewish population and where Jewish life is therefore more organised and tolerable.

We are pleased now to be able to state that as a result of discussions which have taken place with members of the Representative Council of Birmingham Jewry, it has been found possible to proceed immediately with the establishment of a Hostel for the reception of twenty Jewish boys. The Birmingham Ecclesia, in association with the Coventry Ecclesia, has undertaken to provide the necessary finance for the maintenance of the Hostel and the Representative Council of Birmingham Jewry has undertaken the responsibility for its management and administration. They have received an offer of a suitable house, furnished and rent free, capable of accommodating at least thirty Jewish boys.

In our July issue we suggested that ecclesias in towns where there are not many Jews, and where the same opportunity therefore does not exist as in a city like Birmingham, may yet wish to help, and that the Central Ecclesia was willing that such help should be used to extend its efforts. We stated also that if any ecclesias were desirous of making regular contributions to this end, we were willing to receive such sums. We take this opportunity of repeating this, and also of stating our willingness to receive contributions, whether regular or otherwise, from individual brethren and sisters. If the response is sufficient, it may be possible to arrange for the reception of a larger number of boys than is at present contemplated.

It might be thought that as the outbreak of war has put a stop to the influx of Jewish refugees into this country, the need for further efforts to relieve them has ceased. This is not so. There are several centres up and down the country at which Jewish boys and girls are housed in temporary quarters awaiting accommodation of more permanent character. To relieve this pressure is a worthy object. To do so will remove a great deal of anxiety from those who have undertaken the responsibility for the care of these boys and girls in circumstances of grave difficulty.

It should be noted that the Hostel to be established in Birmingham will be supported entirely from Christadelphian sources and that it will be kept separate and distinct from other Hostels. It is therefore our Hostel. Here, then, is an opportunity for collective effort.

January 1940
Volume 77, Number 907, 42.
"The Jewish Boys' Hostel"
John Carter

The arrangements for a hostel in Birmingham are proceeding. Plans are drawn for the necessary structural alterations to adapt the house which has been placed rent free at the disposal of the Committee. It is hoped to be able to give more particulars next month.

A small brown paper packet which came to this office by registered post contained £350 in notes. A brief note enclosed read: "I have saved £350, and I am overjoyed to think that God has chosen me to help in 'Our Hostel' for his afflicted yet chosen People." It bore no signature.

Not only ourselves but the Jews associated with this work will be deeply touched by this gift. Every effort will be made to see that it is used to best advantage, and some account of the progress of the hostel and the way in which this and other gifts are used will be made from time to time in these pages.

February 1940
Volume 77, Number 908, 86.
"Jews and the Birmingham Hostel"
John Carter

Some unsought but not unkindly publicity has come to the Christadelphian community through Jewish appreciation of Birmingham Central Ecclesia's offer to provide a hostel for about twenty young refugees. Reference to it was given prominence in a report in the *Birmingham Post* of December 15th of the first meeting of the Birmingham Council for Refugees, an organisation which replaces the Birmingham Co-ordinating Committee for Refugees and the Birmingham Jewish Refugee Committee.

The Rev. Dr. A. Cohen, Chief Minister of the Hebrew Congregation, said:

> One of the religious bodies which had been active and prominent in its work to relieve the refugees had been the Christadelphian Central Ecclesia of Birmingham. During the last thirteen months this Ecclesia had raised regular collections and had thus made a contribution of tremendous value. Not satisfied with this, the Ecclesia had now come forward with a wonderful proposal. It offered to acquire commodious premises in Birmingham, equip and maintain the place, so that there could be brought into the city about twenty young men who were in what one might call a temporary clearing house. The great value of this offer would be that, in addition to looking after the physical care of the young men, it would be possible to find employment for them after they had been given training in useful handicraft work. That would be accomplished without imperilling the earnings of British boys. He wished to express profound thanks to

the members of the Ecclesia. Control of the hostel would be in the hands of the Jewish community under the final supervision of that Council.

April 1940
Volume 77, Number 910, 183.
"The Hostel for Jewish Refugee Boys"
John Carter

After overcoming many difficulties, a house has been secured and is now being altered to meet the needs of its new use. The wardens have been appointed and are in attendance supervising the alterations. The Jewish Committee who are co-operating with the scheme, desire to open the Hostel for the Passover. We hope to give full particulars next month.

The following letter has been sent to bro. E. W. Newman, who is acting as Treasurer to the Hostel:

> 15th March, 1940.
>
> Dear bro. Newman,—
> I am sending the enclosed cheque for £500 to you as treasurer of the Hostel which is being opened by the joint efforts of the Birmingham Central and Coventry ecclesias, with the contributions of others sent to the office of *The Christadelphian*.
>
> This amount includes the anonymous gift of £350, to which previous reference has been made in *The Christadelphian*.
>
> Several ecclesias are sending regular contributions, and I will pass on to you such amounts at intervals to be arranged.
>
> With greetings,
> Faithfully your brother,
> John Carter.

Part of the Family - Volume 2

Bro. E. W. Newman,
68 Gillhurst Road,
Harborne,
Birmingham.

June 1940
Volume 77, Number 912, 258-260.
"An Abode of Hope"
John Carter

Elpis Lodge, 117 Gough Road, Edgbaston, the Birmingham Hostel for Jewish Refugee Boys, was opened on Sunday, April 21st, 1940, by bro. Benjamin Walker, in the presence of a number of Jews associated with the care of refugees and of brethren and sisters who had been invited.

The Hostel has been provided by the Birmingham (Central) and Coventry ecclesias, with contributions from many other brethren and sisters, sent through *The Christadelphian*. It is to take about twenty boys of from 14 to 15½, who will be trained to useful occupations, and will be educated and cared for in an atmosphere of Orthodox Jewry by the warden and his wife, Dr. and Mrs. Hirsch. While the management of the Hostel has been handed over to Birmingham Jewry, the funds for maintenance will be provided by Christadelphians.

The key with which the hostel was opened was handed to bro. Walker by Mr. I. L. Jacobs, the doyen of the Birmingham Hebrew Congregation, who is in his 89th year. "You and your association," he said, "have done exceedingly good work. I hope you may have the blessing of the Almighty to continue it for many years to come".

Bro. Walker, after opening the door, presented the key to the Warden, and handed over the Hostel to the care of the Representative Council for Birmingham Jewry and the Council for Refugees.

A service of dedication was conducted by Rabbi Dr. Cohen, assisted by the Revs. S. I. Solomons and W. Lewi. Psalms 30,

146 and 121, and portions of Job 29, Isaiah 58 and Proverbs 3 were read.

Dr. Cohen, in an address, said the opening of that home fell very appropriately on the eve of the Jewish Passover. That festival called to mind the first attempt to enslave and annihilate the Children of Israel. The home presented to their minds the latest of a long series of similar attempts. One noteworthy point of difference must strike them. When the Israelites left Egypt to start on their journey through the wilderness, they were in their helpless state attacked by the Amalekites. When the victims of Nazi oppression were driven from the land of their birth or their adoption, the Amalekites were few, and there was aroused throughout the world a measure of sympathy and helpful kindness which must linger in the memory of all of them. The Jewish Community, true to its tradition, rallied to the help of their stricken brethren to the utmost of their means; but the problem was too gigantic and the numbers too vast to be dealt with by them alone.

"We can never appreciate sufficiently", said Dr. Cohen, "the manner in which the Christian world rallied to our support. Among those not of our own people who were conspicuous in their sympathy and their endeavour to be helpful was the community of the Christadelphians. This is not by any means the first occasion on which they have shown their interest in the welfare and fate of the Jewish people. For long years they have contributed generously to our efforts to re-establish the Jewish people in their homeland; and therefore we appreciate to the full the magnificent act of generosity which has found its expression in this Hostel for Refugee Boys. We of the Jewish Community feel that a sacred trust has been committed to us, a trust we shall endeavour to discharge faithfully to the utmost of our ability".

Their task was two-fold. The first was to care physically for the boys who were brought there, to mend so far as they could the ravages of privation to which these boys had been subjected, to build up their bodies and train them in a livelihood so that they might look forward to an independent future.

The other task was even more important. Those who had any understanding of human psychology must realise that these Jewish boys and girls who had been subjected to such bestial cruelty for the past seven years, might have their minds scarred and their souls embittered by what they had gone through. "These who are put into our charge must, so far as we can, have the effects of this ill-treatment eradicated from their minds", said Dr. Cohen. "Just as Israel of old was told that in spite of what they had received at the hands of the Egyptians, 'Thou shalt not abhor an Egyptian', so we must teach these boys that they have only seen one side of the world, and that there is a higher and better side. They may have suffered at the hands of those who were not of their own people, simply and solely because they are Jews, but we shall tell them that in this Home, through the kindness and sympathy of those who also are not of our own race, they are being given a chance to live as self-supporting men in the future.

> The name which has been given to this house, Elpis Lodge, signifies the Abode of Hope, and above all I do hope our generous Christadelphian friends will have there ward for their act of generosity; that the boys, when they leave these portals after being in our charge, will go forth in the world imbued and enlightened with the hope of a better future.

The service concluded with a beautiful prayer for the reign and righteousness of God.

Several speeches followed. Mr. S. J. Levi, Chairman of the Trustee and Management Committee of the Hostel, said that was a unique event not only in Birmingham Jewry but in Anglo-Jewry. In October last Mr. Newman, representing the Birmingham Christadelphian ecclesia, and Mr. Laxon, the Coventry ecclesia, came voluntarily to the Representative Council of Birmingham Jewry with an offer to purchase, equip and maintain a hostel for twenty Jewish refugee boys, and told them that on completion they would hand it over to be administered as an Orthodox Jewish Hostel. They had found a more than suitable home for it; he thought that they would agree they had found something of a palace.

He believed also that they had found absolutely suitable wardens in Dr. and Mrs. Hirsch. Dr. Hirsch was a doctor of philosophy, and before he and his wife and family were driven from Germany by Nazi persecution, he was headmaster in Frankfurt for two years of a school of 700 boys. He felt they could confidently hand over their charges to their care, in the assurance that they would maintain the ideals for which that Home was being established.

In the task of transforming that old house to its new use they had been helped by the vision and inspiration of their friend, Mr. Laxon. The various members of the Management Committee had been efficient and willing helpers; and he must especially mention the work done by Mrs. Newman. They had selected fifteen boys who they thought would be suitable for that Home, limiting the receiving age from 14 to 15½. They would come in on May 1. Lady Reading was extremely interested in the movement, and it would not be surprising if one day she came to Birmingham to see for herself what they were doing.

On behalf of the Management Committee, Mr. Levi presented bro. E. W. Newman and bro. S. Laxon with golden replicas of the key with which the Hostel was opened.

Bro. Laxon, in reply, explained the grounds of Christadelphian interest in Jewish affairs. They considered friendship for the Jews a privilege not only for the nation which showed it but for the individual who promoted it. The faith of Christadelphians was rooted in the Law which Jesus said he came not to destroy but to fulfil.

Bro. Newman also replied, explaining that the contributions of Christadelphians were made anonymously, and quoting the note in the January issue of *The Christadelphian* recording the receipt of a packet containing £350 for that Hostel. He referred to the willing spirit of co-operation with which they were met by the neighbours on either side of that house, and also expressed appreciation of the builders who had carried out the alterations.

Dr. Hirsch said the boys of 14 who would come to that home had lived half their lifetime in anxiety. They had not known freedom until they received the hospitality of kind men and women in this country. In that Home of Hope they would learn that they would not be friendless; and they would learn also the certainty that the Jewish faith would never die.

Mr. G. Philip Achurch, M.B.E. (Chairman of the Birmingham Council for Refugees), read the following letter which he had received from the General Secretary of the Movement for the Care of Children from Germany, Ltd.: "... I write to say that the Constitution of the New Hostel at Gough Road, Edgbaston, is a very satisfactory document from the point of the Movement. The existence of this Hostel will fulfil a long-felt want. We have experienced great difficulties in finding both homes and suitable employment for Orthodox

Jewish refugee boys. I will be much obliged if you will kindly convey the thanks of the Executive Committee of the Movement for the Care of Children from Germany to the Christadelphian ecclesias of Birmingham and Coventry for their generosity in undertaking the support of the Hostel and to the Representative Council of Birmingham Jewry for the arrangements they have made for launching the scheme, and last but not least, our thanks are due to your Council which has piloted the undertaking".

The visitors inspected the house, and admired the well-equipped kitchen, the excellent bathrooms, and the light, airy bedrooms with comfortable-looking beds well spaced. The garden proved an astonishing little Eden in the midst of Birmingham: fine trees of many years' growth are perfectly planned to give an effect of perspective; there is a long stretch of green lawn, a rockery, and a vegetable plot with fruit trees.

The boys duly arrived on May 1, and are settling happily into their new surroundings.

July 1940
Volume 77, Number 913, 332.
"The Jews and Palestine"

A letter in *The Jewish Chronicle* mentions that the committee of the Birmingham Jewish Refugee Boys' Hostel has arranged for copies of the Bible Readers' Bulletin, which contains a calendar for regular reading, to be sent regularly to Elpis Lodge.

July 1940
Volume 77, Number 913, 334-335.
Birmingham Refugee Boys' Hostel

The sixteen boys at Elpis Lodge, the Birmingham Hostel for Jewish Refugee Boys, are settling down into a happy community, healthy and full of good spirits. All have been found work: four in jewellery, three as tailors; and the occupations of others include tool maker, upholsterer, garage hand, electrician, wood-worker, baker, etc. One boy is a junior clerk to a firm of chartered accountants, and is studying to take his matriculation.

In placing the boys in the trades they are now learning, Dr. Hirsch (the Warden) has been at pains to find out their natural aptitudes, and has taken into account their family history. Some of the Viennese families, for instance, have been tailors for generations, and one boy's grandfather is a tailor's cutter of considerable repute in Vienna. The father of the boy who is doing wood-work is a turner of chessmen. The boy learning upholstery hopes some day to join his brother, who is an upholsterer in the Argentine.

Many of them can tell of scattered and broken families. A boy who is very keen on his work in learning jewellery has his father in Shanghai and his mother in London; another boy's father is in Ireland, while his mother and sister are still on the Continent; another has a sister working as children's nurse in a Palestine colony; and yet another's father is in U.S.A. and his mother in the Reich.

Many have lost their fathers, as even before the Nazi regime the mortality among male Jews in Germany was very high in the post-war period. The resulting lack of parental control, and the loss of all home life in the last twelve or fourteen months, has made all the more necessary the influence they are now receiving at the Hostel. Regulations are strict, but Dr. and Mrs. Hirsch are doing their utmost to create the atmosphere of a family, and to build up the moral background of the boys in an environment of orthodox Jewry. It is an interesting experience to hear the boys chant their Grace in Hebrew, antiphonally, after a meal. Their principle service is at the commencement of the Sabbath on Friday nights, and afterwards Dr. Hirsch talks to them on the Synagogue lesson for the day.

Standards of culture are not forgotten in their general training, and Dr. Hirsch aims at raising their taste above the level of the cinema, and laying some foundation for future appreciation of "things lovely and of good report".

The hostel is now well provided with games. It is a tribute both to the control exercised and to the boys' response to it that a neighbour, who was at first a little dubious at the scheme in a residential district, has now very kindly given a table tennis set.

One boy who became 16 since arriving at the hostel has been granted his "C." certificate. The boys' greatest hardship under the new aliens restrictions is that they have had to be deprived of their bicycles.

August 1940
Volume 77, Number 914, 383.
"Refugee Boys' Hostel"
John Carter

Three boys from Elpis Lodge, the Birmingham Jewish Refugee Boys' Hostel, have been interned. They had become 16, and held "C" certificates, but suffered in the general tightening of restrictions on aliens. They have written that they are well and happy.

Five more boys are coming to the Hostel from Wellingford, near Oxford, where they have been at a farming school.

October 1940
Volume 77, Number 916, 480.
"The Refugee Boys' Hostel"
John Carter

Seventeen boys are now living at the Birmingham Hostel for Jewish Refugee Boys. Three were interned, but one has been released and has come back to the Hostel. One boy has left to join his father in Ireland with the hope of shortly emigrating to America; and one has gone to join a sister in London. It is probable that the number of boys will shortly be made up again to 20 or 21.

A shorthand class has been started, in addition to the other cultural activities of the hostel. Eight or nine boys who volunteered form a keen-witted and enthusiastic class, and the study is of incidental help in improving their knowledge of English.

January 1941
Volume 78, Number 919, 39.
"Elpis Lodge: Six Months' Work Reviewed"
E. W. Newman

Bro. E. W. Newman, who acts as treasurer to the Birmingham Hostel, has sent the following report:

> Dear Bro. Carter,—The Hostel for Jewish refugee boys was opened on May 1, and as it has now been in existence for more than six months a brief review of its activities may interest all who have contributed to its welfare.
>
> The steady financial support of the Hostel by the brethren and sisters of the Birmingham Central, the Coventry and other ecclesias and also by readers of the Magazine not only at home but abroad, has been most gratifying, and testifies to the fact that the interest in Jewry which has always been associated with Christadelphian outlook upon the world is undiminished.
>
> Under the care of Dr. and Mrs. Hirsch the twenty boys accommodated at the Hostel have found a peaceful and orderly home in which the things of the mind we well as of the body have opportunity for development. There have of course been "incidents". With twenty boys so diverse in upbringing and experience it would have been surprising if nothing had happened. The conduct of the boys, however, has been generally excellent. Recently I received a letter from one of the neighbours, an elderly gentlemen who was somewhat dismayed at the prospect of having so many boys next door to him. He wrote: "I met Dr. Hirsch to-day and was pleased to know he seems quite satisfied with the

way the boys are getting on. We could not wish for pleasanter neighbours."

The boys are of course under discipline, which is not rigorous, but contributes to the smooth running of the Home. Evening classes in English, English literature and history are held at the Hostel under the direction of a qualified teacher, and every effort is made to encourage each boy to speak fluent English. In addition, some of the boys are learning shorthand, bro. L. G. Sargent having devoted himself to the task of teaching this subject. Also, Dr. Hirsch himself regularly instructs the boys in Old Testament history, and the subsequent history of the Jews.

No difficulty has been experienced in securing employment for all the boys. Each boy makes a weekly contribution of one-half of his earnings towards his maintenance. He is allowed to retain one-fourth for pocket money and the balance is saved for him. Some of the boys whose parents are alive and who are in need send small contributions to them from time to time.

I would like to make brief reference to the House itself and to the standard of living which exists in it. A remark made at the opening of the Hostel has given rise to the suggestion that the Hostel is a somewhat luxurious place. It was referred to as a palace, and the garden was likened to Eden. These are figures of speech not to be taken too literally. The house is old. So is the garden. The presence of an old cedar lends dignity to the garden, and there is a rockery which has been beautiful, and could be made so again. The house itself is very simple in design inside and out. There is nothing palatial about it, and in its furnishing and equipment it resembles a hospital. Any suggestion of luxury is completely absent. The same can be said of the food. The living is frugal. This may be judged from the fact that for the first six months the average cost of food, toilet and cleaning materials per person in the Hostel was 10s. 11d. per week. The average cost of running the Hostel, including the remuneration of Dr. and Mrs. Hirsch, the domestic staff, rates, lighting, heating and cleaning and all other outgoings was 29s. per week per boy, which was reduced to 24s. 6d. per week by the boys' contributions towards their maintenance. These figures will indicate that the Hostel is run on the simplest lines well fitted for the objects in view.

Gifts which have been greatly appreciated have been sent to the Hostel by sisters in Glasgow and Huddersfield. The gifts included knitted bedspreads and socks.

The Hostel is successfully fulfilling the objects expressed by Dr. Cohen when it was opened. These boys are being given a chance to live as self-supporting men in the future. Though they have suffered at the hands of those who were not of their own people, the effects of ill-treatment are being eradicated from their minds, and their embittered souls are responding to kindness and sympathy. One of the injunctions of the Mosaic Law was: "Thou shalt not abhor an Egyptian". This was surely a very remarkable injunction bearing in mind the treatment Israel had received at Egyptian hands.

I ought to add to this brief review a reference to the possible departure of Dr. and Mrs. Hirsch. Before leaving Germany over two years ago, they had applied to the U.S.A. for permission to emigrate there. After this long delay, permission has been granted. Though very loath to go, they feel they ought to do so for the sake of their two young children. If they do go, I can only express the hope that whoever may be appointed to take their place will be able to continue the conduct of the Home in the same spirit and with the same efficiency.

Faithfully your brother,
E. W. Newman.

June 1942
Volume 79, Number 936, 230.
"Refugee Boys' Hostel"
John Carter

The Birmingham Hostel for Jewish Refugee Boys has now been in existence for two years, and of the first batch who came on May 1, 1940, eleven are still residing at the Hostel. Others have left on becoming self-supporting, or have joined their parents in this country or elsewhere. The maximum number of 19 boys is still maintained. All are employed, and they are in the following trades: two garage hands, two jewellers, two carpenters, one draughtsman, three tailors, one electrician, one furrier, one plumber's mate, one optician, one assistant at a School Laboratory, one upholsterer, two clerks, one office boy. The educational purpose in the Hostel has remained; but consideration has been given to special training. Seven boys attend classes in Woodwork, and 13 boys the classes in Physical Training. Dr. Hirsch (the Warden) gives lessons in French. Two boys attend classes in mathematics, mechanics, and physics at the Technical College, one boy is taking a Correspondence Course of the School of Opticians, two tailors take a private course in cloth-cutting. One boy, who is a musical enthusiast with very definite classical tastes, is having lessons on the violin.

On Friday evenings Dr. Hirsch gives a talk on Jewish themes. Jewish holidays are strictly observed.

Only two boys now in the hostel have their parents in England. The parents of one boy were able to leave Germany during the war, and are now in U.S.A. All the others get only rare Red Cross letters from their parents who are still in Germany, Austria, Shanghai or in German-occupied countries.

APPENDIX - ELPIS LODGE - *THE CHRISTADELPHIAN MAGAZINE*

September 1943
Volume 80, Number 951, 166.
"Hostel for Jewish Refugee Boys: Elpis Lodge"
E. W. Newman

Dear Bro. Carter,

The hostel completed its third year on April 30, 1943. It may therefore be well, through the medium of the magazine, if you will permit it, to review very briefly its circumstances and say a word about its finance.

First, you will recollect that this hostel began with the gift from anonymous donors of a house equipped and furnished to make it suitable for its purpose and that the local Jews undertook to manage it, the Birmingham (Central) and Coventry ecclesias and yourself on behalf of other ecclesias and readers of The Christadelphian agreeing to provide the necessary funds. The need for accommodation for refugee boys was at that time of the utmost urgency. The equipment of a hostel was simple in character, no place being given for anything of luxury. The same simplicity of living was also adopted from the start, and is still maintained. This fact is reflected in the costs. The all-in maintenance cost per head, including the salary of the warden and his wife and the necessary assistance for them, also lighting, heating, cleaning, and all other expense incurred in running the hostel, has been:—First year, £1 8s. 11d. per week; second year, £1 8s. 9d. per week; third year, £1 9s. 8d. per week. The cost of food per head has been:—First year, 11s. 1d. per week; second year, 10s. 11d. per week; third year, 10s. 8d. per week. Bearing in mind the rising cost of living, the maintenance of so constant a level of expenditure speaks well for the carefulness exercised by the wardens (Dr. and Mrs. Hirsch) throughout this difficult period.

The work of the wardens is supported by the management committee which was appointed by the Representative Council for Birmingham Jewry, upon whom devolves, as already stated, the responsibility for the conduct of the hostel.

It has been their endeavour throughout to accommodate twenty boys. Some of the boys who entered the hostel at the first have reached 18, and those who have become self-supporting have been transferred to other quarters. This has made room for younger boys from time to time. It should be said in this connection that care is exercised in the choice of occupation, which in war time is specially necessary. The endeavour has been always to equip each boy for his future, and not to think of immediate gain. Nevertheless, the earnings of the boys enable them to bear an increasing proportion of the running costs of the hostel.

Through the administration of this hostel, these boys, cruelly deprived of their parents, have been brought up during a critical period in their lives in a well-ordered and healthy environment, and it may encourage all those who have contributed and continue to contribute to its maintenance to know what success has attended the efforts which have been made. To have delivered these boys from the terrors which have overtaken Jewry on the Continent and to have made it possible for them to grow up in the peaceful atmosphere of Elpis Lodge is something for which all will surely feel thankful. And this thankfulness is felt, and will continue to be felt, by every boy who has thus come under its influence.

Faithfully your brother,
E. W. Newman.

November 1945
Volume 82, Number 977, 129.
"The Ecclesial Visitor - Elpis Lodge"
John Carter

In May last, the Hostel for Jewish Refugee boys entered its sixth year. The hostel was established in 1940 when the need for providing homes for boys rescued from Nazi persecution was desperate, and the torment of German Jewry during the war years has served to emphasize the value of what has been accomplished at Elpis Lodge, though quite overshadowed by the vastness of the need as a whole.

The Jewish boys who came to this country prior to the outbreak of war have grown up. Most of them, including those who entered the hostel in 1940, have become self-supporting. Earlier this year a number of boys were due to leave the hostel, and the number of Jewish refugee boys still in this country in need of the care and accommodation which Elpis Lodge was designed to give has rapidly diminished.

Discussions as to the future of the hostel have therefore taken place with the Representative Council for Birmingham Jewry and the Refugee Children's Movement in London, and it has been agreed that as the objects for which the Hostel was established have been fulfilled, the financial obligations which the Birmingham Central ecclesia, the Coventry ecclesia, and contributors through the Christadelphian Magazine undertook, and have continued to meet, could now be terminated.

Letters of appreciation of what has been done during the five years of the hostel's existence have been received from the Representative Council of Birmingham Jewry, and from the Refugee Children's Movement. We have also received a letter from Dr. Hirsch who, with Mrs. Hirsch, have acted as

Wardens of the hostel, and have contributed so much to its success. His letter reviews what has been done, and we therefore quote it here. Dr. Hirsch says:

> On this occasion I would like to express our heartiest thanks to you personally as well as to the subscribers of *The Christadelphian* and *The Path* for their continuous interest and their spiritual and material help. You have been so closely connected from the beginning with the magnanimous foundation of 'Elpis Lodge' that it will hardly be necessary to give you any details. Still I would like to say that you have enabled 48 boys, most of whom are to be regarded as orphans, to be properly trained in a trade or employment best suited for them, that you have given them the opportunity of being instructed in the English language, of being introduced into the cultural life of this country and educated in the religion of their parents. I need not say how much we were pleased about articles in *The Christadelphian* and *The Path* concerned with 'Elpis Lodge' and how often we ourselves found consolation and encouragement in your magazines. We are very grateful indeed for all your good work which we highly appreciate. I am sure that every boy who has been educated in 'Elpis Lodge' will keep his gratitude for his lifetime.

We venture to think that the brethren and sisters who have contributed to the maintenance of the hostel will be gratified to read what Dr. Hirsch says. They will feel that at a time when Israel's need was so great, the establishment and maintenance of this hostel out of funds contributed solely by Christadelphians has thoroughly justified itself.

When all obligations have been met, there will remain in the hands of bro. E. W. Newman, the treasurer of the hostel, a sum of £275 or thereabouts. It is proposed to remit this balance, together with other sums which come into our hands, to the Chief Rabbi's United Appeal Fund, and The Women's Appeal for Jewish Women and Children, for the relief of Jews on the Continent and in or near Palestine. These are the two funds to which the Birmingham Central ecclesia and ourselves have been sending contributions.

As regards the future of Elpis Lodge, the Refugee Children's Movement desiring that the hostel should continue to serve the needs of refugees in this country by an extension of its objects to cases of special need, the providers of the hostel and its equipment (who it will be recalled were private brethren) have placed it at the disposal of the Movement for objects which may be deemed appropriate. But the full financial responsibility for the hostel now rests upon the Refugee Children's Movement.

August 1946
Volume 83, Number 986, 125-126.
"The Ecclesial Visitor - Jewish Relief Notes"
John Carter

When the work of providing a home for Jewish refugee boys at Elpis Lodge came to an end, there was a balance in the treasurer's hands. all accounts have now been cleared, and the balance of £274 7s. 8d. has been passed to us to include with other contributions to forward to the Chief Rabbi's Fund, and the Women and Children's Fund. A sum of £250 has been sent to each of these funds.

A letter was received some months ago by bro. E. W. Newman from one of the boys who had lived at Elpis Lodge, and who had arrived in Palestine. He says:

> Now I have the opportunity to thank you for everything you have done for me. All the happy years I spent at the Hostel under the able guidance of Dr. and Mrs. Hirsch I must admit there was little we went without. In all the ways in which you helped us, I do not think there could have been a better place in a foreign country, except being together with our families.
>
> My father is very sorry he cannot add a few lines, as he does not speak any English, but he will always be grateful to you for having made a man out of me. You can imagine how he felt when he saw me after seven years' separation. I left at the age of eleven and then return a full grown youth of eighteen. I will never be able to thank you enough for what you have done for me.

The Jew moves from one storm-tossed place to another to find trouble as his lot. Palestine appeared to be a haven of rest, yet it is becoming the centre of trouble. "No ease" and no rest, trembling of heart and sorrow of mind—these were to be the results of disobedience (Deut. 28: 65). "O Israel, return unto the Lord thy God; for thou hast fallen by thine iniquity ... I will heal their backsliding. I will love them freely: for mine anger is turned away from him ... who is wise, and he shall understand these things?" (Hos. 14).

THE CHRISTADELPHIAN CHILDREN'S MAGAZINE

Transcript © 'The Christadelphian Magazine and Publishing Association'. Reproduced with the kind permission of The Christadelphian Magazine and Publishing Association (www.thechristadelphian.com).

1940
Volume III, Fourth Series, 136-137.
"With Refugee Boys"
L. G. Sargent

"Would you like to see those rings?"

I fancied that the boy who spoke had been lurking in the corner of a passage way to see that I did not forget a promise. He dashed upstairs to his bed room, and returned with half-a-dozen or more rings be had been making for practice in cheap metal.

One was in a twisted cable design. Others were made to hold gems, and the boy explained the method of fixing the stones in place. There were several ingenious designs, and one which consisted of two circlets of metal held together with tiny pierced metal beads.

"That," he said, "had to be soldered nine times." There was a touch of pride in the emphasis on the "nine."

A clever-fingered Jewish refugee boy, he is living at the Birmingham hostel, and is learning jewellery.

All at Work

The 16 boys at the hostel have settled down into a happy community, well, and in good spirits. All of them have been found work. One boy is a junior clerk to a firm of accountants, four are learning jewellery, and four tailoring. Among the others there is a wood-worker (whose father is a turner of chessmen), a tool maker, an upholsterer, a garage-hand, an electrician, a baker, and so on. One or two are working in offices.

Under the guidance of one of the members of the Birmingham Christadelphian Ecclesia, they have set to work in the garden of Elpis Lodge (the hostel), and have got it in good order, growing vegetables and fruit.

Broken Families

Only when they speak of their fathers and mothers or other members of their families do the boys show the note of sadness that is at the back of their minds. Many have parents still in lands which the Germans control; and those families which have escaped are scattered all over the world.

One boy's father in is Shanghai and his mother in London.

The prophet Isaiah, speaking of the regathering of Israel, says: "Behold, these shall come from far : and, lo, these from the north and from the west; and these from the land of Sinim (China)." Is. 49 :12.

Let us hope that the fulfilment of that prophecy will come soon, and will mean a happy reunion in the land of Israel for this boy and his parents.

1940
Volume III, Fourth Series, 166-167.
"Hostel Boys and their Work"
L. G. Sargent

What sort of people are the boys of Elpis Lodge and those who look after them? All who have read from time to time about the Birmingham Hostel for Jewish Refugee Boys will be interested in the photograph which shows the Wardens (Dr. and Mrs. Hirsch) with the boys [note that Rudi Hart is standing second from the right, and Heinz Weiss, Ben Weiss's older brother, is sitting in the bottom right corner]. Three of those shown in the group have since been interned; one has now been released. Several new boys have come since the photograph was taken, and there are now 20 in the hostel.

All but one or two of the latest arrivals are in work, and two boys have written to tell us something of what they are doing. One who is In a vacuum cleaner shop says:

> To-day I sold my first vacuum- cleaner . . . I, of course, started with cleaning the carpet and emptying the paper-baskets, which I am naturally still doing. But as I can see in this job an opportunity of learning selling and repairing cleaners, I don't mind that. Although we are doing quite good business, the war affects our trade just as well as anything else. As we can still get cylinder-machines, which are made out of tin, we are getting shorter of upright, revolving-brush machines, because their aluminium is now helping to win the war.

Making Rings

A boy who is learning jewellery work describes a day in the workshop as follows:

My work is roughly parted in two. One is the rough work and forming the ring. The second is to get the ring ready to polish it. I am mostly doing the second one, whist my master is doing the first one. At about nine we start to work full speed, that means serious, and more work than talk. . . . Now how a diamond ring is made. There are two important parts: the claw and the shank. The claw holds the stone. It is made out of white gold and the top is platinum because it is not so hard. This claw is soldered on the backwire which is always the same metal as the shank and the back wire is fixed on to the shank. The second part is to take all scratches out and make it nice and neat. I like the work very much, but still the last two hours go so slow that I am glad to break off in the evening. We have to clear up the shop very decently because no gold must be lost or wasted, and so it is always half-past-six when I come home. As soon as I arrive the first words are, "Any post ?" If yes, "Good"; if no, "What a pity". Then we have supper and afterwards we play games or so till about ten, when we go to bed.

One of the latest activities at the Hostel is a weekly shorthand class attended by ten boys, who show keen interest in the study.

January 1942
Volume 5, Fourth Series, 92.
"Refugee Boys' Work"
L. G. Sargent

The Jewish refugee boys at Elpis Lodge, Birmingham, recently showed what they could do by a small exhibition. Coming to the hostel after they leave school, they live together there while they go out to work. The Warden (Dr. Hirsch) has done his best to find them occupations which suit them, and in which they can be trained for useful crafts, and that he has succeeded was shown by the examples of the work they are doing. One boy had upholstered two easy chairs in a way which showed sound craftsmanship. A lad who is training as a furrier had made a fur tie in baby sealskin. Two who are jewellers had made some neat tie pins and cuff-links. A garage hand had made a letter-rack from scrap metal as an example of his hobby of metal work. A woodworker also showed an example of his craft.

Engineer's Draughtsman

A very interesting exhibit was a set of engineering drawings and prints. The youth who made them wrote an account of his first job, selling vacuum cleaners, which appeared in *The Children's Magazine*. He afterwards became an electrician; and then by hard study he fitted himself to go into the drawing office of an engineering works, where he now is. He feels that now he has found the work for which he really has aptitude, and he is very keen and happy. To show the kind of work he does, he had taken the stamp used for embossing the address of Elpis Lodge on notepaper, and made a set of detailed drawings of it with prints such as could be passed into an engineering shop for the article to be made.

The hostel has now been running for over two years, and everyone who has taken an interest in it will be glad to know that the boys have settled down so well. It is good to know that those who have come out of such unhappy surroundings in Central Europe have been able to find a place in English life, and to learn trades which will enable them to lead a happy and useful existence.

Glossary

The definitions below were taken, with permission, from the Echoes and Reflections glossary of terms. *For the full glossary, see http://echoesandreflections.org/the-lessons/glossary.*

antisemitism
Prejudice or discrimination against Jews. Antisemitism can be based on hatred against Jews because of their religious beliefs or their group membership (ethnicity), but also on the erroneous belief that Jews are a race. Nazi antisemitism was racial in nature; Jews were viewed as racially inferior to Aryans and destructive of the world order. —**antisemitic** *adj.*

Aryan
A rather ambiguous term the Nazis primarily applied to people of Northern European racial background. Although never defined, in April 1933, the Nazis defined "non-Aryans" as individuals who had a parent or grandparent who was Jewish.

Auschwitz (ow sch vits), Auschwitz camp complex (Auschwitz I, Auschwitz II-Birkenau, Auschwitz III-Monowitz)

Auschwitz I was the first and main camp of the Auschwitz camp complex. Established near the town of Oswiecim in Polish Upper Silesia, it was 37 miles west of Cracow and located in a former Polish military compound. On April 27, 1940, Heinrich Himmler ordered the establishment of a concentration camp at the site. Construction began in May 1940 and the officially reported date of the camp's opening was May 20, 1940. The first prisoners were Germans and Poles, sent from Sachsenhausen and Tarnow. By March 1941, prisoner ranks had swelled to 11,000. Primarily a concentration camp serving penal functions, Auschwitz I included a crematorium and, in late summer 1941, the camp briefly operated an experimental gas chamber. From 1940 to 1942, prisoners were primarily Polish political, civic, and spiritual leaders, the intelligentsia, and members of the resistance. Beginning in 1942, some of the Jews deported to Auschwitz were admitted to this main camp. Auschwitz I was also a testing ground for SS physicians carrying out inhumane and pseudoscientific medical experiments in the camp "hospital" (Block 10). Near the hospital was the Death Wall (a.k.a. "Black Wall") where thousands of prisoners were shot. Auschwitz I expanded rapidly and by late 1941 held 18,000 prisoners; by 1943 it held approximately 30,000 inmates. The evacuation

Glossary

from the camp started on January 18, 1945. On January 27, 1945, Soviet troops liberated 1,200 prisoners at Auschwitz I.

During his March 1, 1941 visit to Auschwitz I, Heinrich Himmler ordered an expansion of the camp. In October 1941, 10,000 Soviet POWs began the construction of Auschwitz II-Birkenau. The site of the camp was near the Polish village of Brzezinka which was emptied of its Polish population for the project. Overcrowding in Auschwitz I, caused by the arrival of Soviet prisoners of war in late 1941, forced the acceleration of the camp's construction. The first sections of Auschwitz II-Birkenau were completed in 1942. When construction was complete, the camp had nine sections separated by electrified barbed-wire fences. Originally intended as a camp for 100,000 Soviet POWs, Auschwitz II-Birkenau's main function became the murder of European Jews. The insecticide Zyklon B was used in the camp's gas chambers. The first provisional gas chambers were judged inadequate for the scale of gassing planned. Four large gas chamber and crematoria facilities became operational between March and June 1943. When all four were operational, Auschwitz II-Birkenau possessed an unsurpassed capacity for mass murder and body disposal. Gassing operations continued until November 1944. The pace of deportations increased in the spring of 1944 after the German occupation of Hungary. The Hungarian Jewish community was by then the largest remaining Jewish community in German-controlled Europe. Between April and November 1944 Auschwitz received more Jewish deportees than it had in the previous two years. During the initial selection, newly arrived prisoners were declared fit or unfit for forced labor by SS physicians or other camp officials. Most were sent immediately to the gas chambers. On January 27, 1945, the Auschwitz camp complex was liberated by Soviet forces; at Auschwitz II-Birkenau 5,800 prisoners remained alive. During the course of its existence, prisoners in the camp represented many categories including political prisoners, Poles, criminals, Jews, Soviet POWs, and Sinti-Roma. It is estimated that between 1.1 and 1.6 million predominantly Jewish men, women, and children were murdered at Auschwitz, nearly all of them in the gas chambers at Auschwitz II-Birkenau.

Auschwitz III-Monowitz, also called Buna, was located near the Polish town of Monowice and was the last of three Auschwitz camps established in the vicinity of Oswiecim. Construction began in late 1941 and the camp opened in 1942. Auschwitz III-Monowitz was a massive slave-labor camp that supplied workers for the large chemical and synthetic-rubber works of IG Farbenindustrie's Buna Werke. By summer 1944, the prisoner population rose to over 10,000 not including the prisoners of its forty subcamps. Due to conditions in the camp, the average life span of prisoners was three to four months and even less in the subcamps. Over 30,000 prisoners died in Auschwitz III-Monowitz during its existence. The evacuation of Auschwitz III-Monowitz and its subsidiary camps began on January 18, 1945, and the prisoners were sent to the camp at Gleiwitz. On January 27, 1945, when Soviet forces liberated Auschwitz, there were only 600 remaining prisoners at Auschwitz III-Monowitz.

boycott
To abstain from using, buying, or dealing with a business as an expression of protest or disfavor or as a means of coercion.

Brownshirts (SA, Sturmabteilung <shturm ap tile ung>, **Storm Troopers)**
The Nazi militia created in 1921 that helped the Nazi Party come to power but was eclipsed by the SS in 1934; known as "Brownshirts" because of the color of the uniform.

Buchenwald (boo khen vald)
A concentration camp established in 1937 near Weimar, Germany. While it was primarily a labor camp in the German concentration camp system and not an extermination center, thousands died there from exposure, over-work, and execution. Many Jews from other camps were forcibly marched there by the Nazis in early 1945.

cantor
A role (traditionally held by a man) within formal Jewish religious worship which employs elaborate musical chanting while leading a congregation in prayer.

Chanukah *or* **Hanukkah**
An eight-day holiday that celebrates the unlikely victory of the Israelites, led by the Maccabees, against Greek Assyrian persecution and religious oppression in the Land of Israel in the second century B.C.E. In addition to marking a military victory against religious oppression and the subsequent rededication of the Temple in Jerusalem, Chanukah recognizes a miracle in that a single flask of oil used to light the Temple menorah lasted for eight days.

Christianity
A monotheistic system of beliefs and practices based on the Old Testament and the teachings of Jesus as embodied in the New Testament and emphasizing the role of Jesus as savior.

Glossary

concentration camp
Camps established by the Nazi regime, which eventually became a major instrument of terror, control, punishment, and killing performed through both deliberate means as well as attrition by hunger and/or disease.

D-Day (Invasion of Normandy)
The name associated with June 6, 1944 when some 160,000 American, British, and Canadian forces landed on five beaches along a 50-mile stretch of the heavily fortified coast of France's Normandy region. The invasion was one of the largest amphibious military assaults in history.

Dachau (dak how)
Dachau was a concentration camp located near Munich, Bavaria. The opening of Dachau was announced at a press conference by Heinrich Himmler on March 20, 1933. The first group of prisoners, consisting mainly of Communists and Social Democrats, were brought to Dachau on March 22, 1933. During the camp's 12-year existence, the prisoner population included, among others, political opponents, criminals, Sinti and Roma, Jews, homosexuals, Jehovah's Witnesses, and members of the Catholic clergy. During World War II, Dachau and its system of subcamps was principally responsible for furnishing slave labor to the armament industries. Over 200,000 prisoners were incarcerated at Dachau during its existence. American forces liberated Dachau on April 29, 1945. They found box cars near the camp filled with bodies in an advanced state of decomposition. These were prisoners who were brought to Dachau from other camps towards the end of the war. In the main camp, American forces liberated approximately 30,000 prisoners.

deportation
Removal of people from their areas of residency for purposes of resettlement elsewhere. With regard to the Jews of Europe during the Holocaust, deportation by the Nazis meant removal to another city, ghetto, concentration camp, or extermination center.

Euthanasia Program
Referring to the Nazi order for the deliberate extermination of German people institutionalized with physical, mental, and emotional disabilities, carried out as a measure to prevent contamination of the Nazi-defined Aryan race. The Euthanasia Program began in 1939, with German non-Jews as the first victims.

Glossary

extermination camp *also called* **death camp**
A Nazi facility where victims were killed on a mass industrialized scale and their bodies burned or buried in mass graves. The Nazis operated six extermination camps: Auschwitz-Birkenau, Belzec, Chelmno, Majdanek, Sobibor, and Treblinka.

"Final Solution of the Jewish Question" ("Final Solution")
A Nazi code phrase referring to their systematic plan to murder every Jewish man, woman, and child in Europe.

Gentile
Someone who is not of the Jewish faith; most often referring to a Christian.

Gestapo (gesh tah poh)
The Nazi Secret State Police who were directly involved in implementing the murder of Jews and other Nazi victims during the Holocaust.

ghetto
Sections of towns and cities that the German occupation authorities and their allies used to concentrate, exploit, and starve regional Jewish populations.

Great Depression
The economic crisis beginning with the stock market crash in the United States in 1929 and continuing through the 1930s; a worldwide economic downturn resulted.

Hitler Youth (Hitlerjugend <hit ler yoo gent>)
The Nazi Party's compulsory (after 1939) youth movement, which emphasized physical training, Nazi ideology, and absolute obedience to Hitler and the Nazi Party. Youth were subject to intensive propaganda regarding racial and national superiority.

Holocaust
The murder of approximately six million Jews by the Nazis and their collaborators. Sinti-Roma, Poles, people with physical and mental disabilities, homosexuals, Jehovah's Witnesses, Soviet prisoners of war, and political dissidents were also targeted by the Nazis.

Jewish Badge
Symbol that Jews were forced to wear during the Holocaust so they could be identified as Jews. The Germans used the Jewish Badge, often in the

form of a yellow Star of David, to harass and isolate the Jews, thereby creating a wide rift between Jews and the rest of the population.

Judaism
A religion developed among the ancient Hebrews and characterized by belief in one God who has revealed himself to Abraham, Moses, and the Hebrew prophets and by a religious life in accordance with Scriptures and rabbinic traditions.

Kindertransport
A rescue operation carried out primarily by British organizations for Jewish children from Greater Germany, following the *Kristallnacht Pogrom*. The British government allowed 10,000 children to enter Great Britain.

kosher
Food that is permissible to eat under Jewish dietary laws; can also describe any other ritual object that is fit for use according to Jewish law.

Kristallnacht (kris tahl nakht) **Pogrom**
An organized pogrom against Jews in Germany and Austria on November 9–10, 1938. *Kristallnacht* is also known as the "Night of Broken Glass," or "Crystal Night." Orchestrated by the Nazis in retaliation for the assassination of a German embassy official in Paris by a seventeen-year-old Jewish youth named Herchel Grynzspan, 1,400 synagogues and 7,000 businesses were destroyed, almost 100 Jews were killed, and 30,000 were arrested and sent to concentration camps. German Jews were subsequently held financially responsible for the destruction wrought upon their property during this *pogrom*. (See also **pogram**.)

League of Nations
An intergovernmental organization founded as a result of the Paris Peace Conference that ended World War I. It was the first international organization whose principal mission was to maintain world peace.

Nazi
Short for Nationalsozialistische deutsche Arbeiter-Partei (N.S.D.A.P.), the German national socialist political party that emerged in Munich after World War I. The party was taken over by Adolf Hitler in the early 1920s. The swastika was the party symbol.

Glossary

Nazi ideology *or* **Nazi racial ideology**
The Nazi system of beliefs, based on a racial view of the world. According to Nazi ideology, the Nordic Aryan Germans were the "master race." Other races were inferior to them and the Jews were considered to be the "anti-race," the exact opposite of the Germans, and an evil and destructive race. Germans were said to be the natural rulers of the world and, in order to achieve that position, influence of the Jews needed to be ended. Thus, racial antisemitism and solving the so-called "Jewish Question" lay at the heart of Nazi ideology, as did the desire for more territory or *Lebensraum* (living space).

Palestine
The Roman term for what is now Israel; the name used by the British during World War II to denote the area they held under a League of Nations mandate.

Passover
The celebration of the Jewish people's freedom from Egyptian bondage that took place approximately 3,500 years ago, as told in the first fifteen chapters of the biblical Book of Exodus. The celebration is organized into a feast called the Passover *Seder*. The word *"seder"* means "order" or "procedure" in Hebrew and refers to the order of historical events recalled in the Passover meal as well as the meal itself.

pogrom
Originally a Russian word meaning "devastation" used to describe organized, large-scale acts of violence against Jewish communities, especially the kind instigated by the authorities in Czarist Russia.

refugee
One who flees or is deported in search of safety, as in times of war, political oppression, or religious persecution.

Reich (rye ch), **Third Reich**
The official name of the Nazi regime; ruled from 1933 to 1945 under the command of Adolf Hitler. Historically, the First Reich was the medieval Holy Roman Empire, which lasted until 1806. The Second Reich included the German Empire from 1871–1918.

SA (See **Brownshirts.**)

Glossary

SS, Schutzstaffel (shoe ts shtah fel)
Originally organized as Hitler's personal bodyguard, the SS was transformed into a giant organization under Heinrich Himmler. Although various SS units were assigned to the battlefield, the organization is best known for carrying out the destruction of European Jewry.

Shoah (sho ah)
A Hebrew word meaning "catastrophe," referring to the Holocaust.

survivor
Within the context of the Holocaust, a survivor is someone who escaped death at the hands of the Nazis and their collaborators.

swastika
An ancient Eastern symbol appropriated by the Nazis as their emblem.

Theresienstadt
A ghetto in Theresienstadt (Terezin), a town in Northwestern Czechoslovakia, where the Jews of Bohemia and Moravia, elderly Jews and persons of "special merit" in the Reich, and several thousand Jews from the Netherlands and Denmark were interned. Although in practice the ghetto, run by the SS, served as a transit camp for Jews en route to extermination camps, it was also presented as a "model Jewish settlement" for propaganda purposes.

Treaty of Versailles (ver sigh)
A peace treaty that was signed at the end of World War I in Versailles, France.

Treblinka (tre blink a)
The Treblinka death camp was built in a thinly populated area four kilometers from the village and train station of Treblinka, Poland. The camp was established as a part of Aktion Reinhard in 1942. The first transports arrived from the Warsaw ghetto in July 1942. Between July 23 and September 21, 1942, 254,000 Jews from Warsaw and 112,000 from other places in the Warsaw district were murdered at Treblinka II. From mid-November 1942 until January 1943, transports to Treblinka II came primarily from Bialystok. Some transports of Jews from the Warsaw ghetto were sent to Treblinka II in the second half of January 1943. It is estimated that around 900,000 Jews were murdered in Treblinka between July 1942 and March 1943.

Glossary

In March 1943, an operation was launched to burn the bodies of the victims in order to obliterate traces of the killing. An uprising in the camp took place on August 2, 1943. About 850 inmates were at the camp during the uprising. A number of prisoners managed to escape, but only about 150-200 evaded capture but many of them did not survive the war. It is estimated that around 70 prisoners from Treblinka were alive at the end of World War II. The last transports to Treblinka II came from the Bialystok ghetto on August 18 and 19, 1943. In November 1943 about thirty Jewish prisoners remained in Treblinka II. They were all shot before the German and Ukrainian staff left the site of the dismantled camp.

Warsaw ghetto
The Warsaw ghetto was officially established on October 2, 1940 and sealed on November 16, 1940. At one point, the ghetto held over 500,000 Jews. The first wave of mass deportations took place between July 22, 1942 and September 12, 1942. A second wave of deportations, meant to clear the ghetto, began January 18, 1943 but was suspended after four days due to armed resistance. The Warsaw Ghetto Uprising began on April 19, 1943, in response to renewed efforts to deport the remaining Jews and was led by the commander of the Zydowska Organizacja Bojowa (Z.O.B.), Mordecai Anielewicz. The Germans declared the ghetto liquidated on May 16, 1943, although fighting continued after that date and some Jews remained in bunkers within the razed ghetto area until at least January 1944.

Weimar (vi mahr) **Republic**
The period of German history from 1919 to 1933; named after the city of Weimar, where a national assembly convened to produce a new constitution after the German monarchy was abolished following the nation's defeat in World War I. The first attempt at establishing a democracy in Germany was a time of great tension and conflict, and it ultimately failed with the ascent of Adolf Hitler and the Nazi Party in 1933.

Yad Vashem
The Holocaust Martyrs' and Heroes' Remembrance Authority in Jerusalem. The name Yad Vashem is taken from an Old Testament passage: *"I will build for them a name and a memorial."* (Isaiah 56:5).

Bibliography

The following are the sources that were consulted for each section of the book.

Part I

A Distinct Community

Aarons, Mark, and John Loftus. *Unholy Trinity*. New York: St. Martin's Griffin, 1998.

Batiste, Deborah, Kaye, Ephraim, and Claudia Wiedeman. "Meet the Team Behind Echoes and Reflections." *Echoes and Reflections*. September 1, 2014. http://echoesandreflections.org/uncategorized/meet-the-team/.

"Birmingham Refugee Hostel - Christadelphians' Continued Generosity." *The Jewish Chronicle* (London, UK), August 1940.

Carter, John. "An Abode of Hope." *The Christadelphian*, June 1940.

Carter, John. "Christadelphians and Jewish Relief." *The Christadelphian*, August 1943.

"Christadelphians' Fine Gesture - Hostel for Birmingham Refugees." *The Jewish Chronicle* (London, UK), May 1940.

Cornwell, John. *Hitler's Pope*. New York: Penguin Putnam, 1999.

Cymet, David. *History vs. Apologetics: The Holocaust, the Third Reich, and the Catholic Church*. Lanham: Lexington Books, 2012.

"Ecclesial Notes." *The Fraternal Visitor*, January 1935.

"From Across the Seas." *The Fraternal Visitor*, July 1939.

"From Across the Seas." *The Fraternal Visitor*, August 1939.

Gray, Michael. *Teaching the Holocaust: Practical Approaches for Ages 11-18*. Abingdon: Routledge, 2015.

Bibliography

G.S.S. "News of the Brethren in Germany." *The Fraternal Visitor*, December 1945.

"Intelligence." *The Christadelphian*, August 1941.

Jackman, Graham. "'Ich Kann Nicht Zwei Herren Dienen': Conscientious Objectors and Nazi 'Militärjustiz' The Undocumented Cases of Three Brothers." *German Life and Letters* 64, no. 2 (2011): 188–216.

"Jewish Tribute to Bro. Walker." *The Christadelphian*, June 1940.

Joint, Guy. "Ecclesial Notes." *The Fraternal Visitor*, October 1937.

Kotzin, Chana Revell, "Christian Responses in Britain to Jewish Refugees in Europe: 1933–1939." doctoral thesis, University of Southampton, 2000.

Lipstadt, Deborah. *Beyond Belief: The American Press and the Holocaust*. New York: The Free Press, 1986.

Mansfield, H.P. "Debtors to Israel." *Logos Magazine*, December 1943.

"Martin Niemöller: 'First They Came for the Socialists...'" *United States Holocaust Memorial Museum*. Accessed June 9, 2017. https://www.ushmm.org/wlc/en/article.php?ModuleId=10007392.

"Obituary - Bro. J.M. Thomas, Llanelly." *The Christadelphian*, June 1940.

Owen, Stanley. *Into All the World*. Glasgow: Self-Published, 1998.

Phayer, Michael. *The Catholic Church and the Holocaust, 1930-1965*. Bloomington: Indiana University Press, 2000.

Ramsden, L.A. "From Across the Seas." *The Fraternal Visitor*, August 1937.

"Sachsenhausen (Oranienburg): History & Overview." *Jewish Virtual Library*. Accessed June 9, 2017. http://www.jewishvirtuallibrary.org/history-and-overview-of-sachsenhausen-oranienburg-concentration-camp.

Bibliography

"Sachsenhausen." *United States Holocaust Memorial Museum.* Accessed June 9, 2017. https://www.ushmm.org/wlc/en/article.php?ModuleId=10005538.

Schulweis, Harold. *Voices and Views: A History of the Holocaust,* Edited by Deborah Dwork. New York: The Jewish Foundation for the Righteous, 2002.

S.H.R. "The Work of the Truth in Germany." *The Fraternal Visitor,* September 1934.

"The German Church and the Nazi State." *United States Holocaust Memorial Museum.* Accessed February 28, 2017. http://www.ushmm.org/wlc/en/article.php?ModuleId=10005206.

"The Jews and Palestine." *The Christadelphian,* November 1941.

Turner, Barry. *…And the Policeman Smiled.* London: Bloomsbury, 1990.

"Wannsee Protocol, January 20, 1942." *Yale Law School.* Accessed April 30, 2017. http://avalon.law.yale.edu/imt/wannsee.asp.

Wyman, David. *The Abandonment of the Jews.* New York: Pantheon Books, 1984.

Zucotti, Susan. *Under His Very Windows.* New Haven: Yale University Press, 2000.

Part II

Netty Gladstone's Biography

"1940: Belgium Surrenders Unconditionally." *History.com.* Accessed April 28, 2017. http://www.history.com/this-day-in-history/belgium-surrenders-unconditionally.

Bradsher, Greg. *Hitler's Final Words.* Washington D. C.: Prologue Magazine, 2015.

Bibliography

"Drancy." *United States Holocaust Memorial Museum.* Accessed April 28, 2017.
https://www.ushmm.org/wlc/en/article.php?ModuleId=10005215.

"Joseph Goebbels." *History.com.* Accessed April 28, 2017.
http://www.history.com/topics/world-war-ii/joseph-goebbels.

"Joseph Goebbels." *Jewish Virtual Library.* Accessed April 28, 2017.
http://www.jewishvirtuallibrary.org/jsource/Holocaust/goebbels.html.

"Joseph Goebbels: On the 'Big Lie.'" *Jewish Virtual Library.* Accessed April 28, 2017,
http://www.jewishvirtuallibrary.org/jsource/Holocaust/goebbelslie.html.

"German Invasion of Western Europe, May 1940." *United States Holocaust Memorial Museum.* Accessed April 28, 2017.
https://www.ushmm.org/wlc/en/article.php?ModuleId=10005181.

Moore, Robert. *Refugees from Nazi Germany in the Netherlands 1933-1940.* Dordrecht: Martinus Nijhoff, 1986.

"Nazi Transit Camps: Rivesaltes." *Jewish Virtual Library.* Accessed April 28, 2017.
http://www.jewishvirtuallibrary.org/jsource/Holocaust/Rivesaltes.html.

"Reich Fascist Convicted." *The New York Times* (New York, NY), September 2, 1930.

"The Man Behind Hitler." *PBS,org.* Accessed April 28, 2017.
http://www.pbs.org/wgbh//amex/goebbels/filmmore/pt.html.

"The Netherlands." *United States Holocaust Museum and Memorial.* Accessed April 28, 2017.
https://www.ushmm.org/wlc/en/article.php?ModuleId=10005436.

"The Nuremberg Race Laws." *United States Holocaust Memorial Museum.* Accessed April 28, 2017.
https://www.ushmm.org/outreach/en/article.php?ModuleId=10007695.

Bibliography

Rudi Hart's Biography

"Adolf Hitler: Speech at the Berlin Sports Palace." *Jewish Virtual Library.* January 30, 1941. http://www.jewishvirtuallibrary.org/hitler-speech-at-the-berlin-sports-palace-january-30-1941.

"Average Weather in Kaliningrad Russia." *Weather Spark.* Accessed June 5, 2017. https://weatherspark.com/y/86511/Average-Weather-in-Kaliningrad-Russia.

"Average Weather in Mayen Germany." *Weather Spark.* Accessed June 5, 2017. https://weatherspark.com/y/57723/Average-Weather-in-Mayen-Germany.

Average Weather in Warendorf Germany." *Weather Spark.* Accessed June 5, 2017. https://weatherspark.com/y/58173/Average-Weather-in-Warendorf-Germany.

"Birmingham Refugee Boys' Hostel." *The Christadelphian,* July 1940.

"Deportations to Killing Centers." *United States Holocaust Memorial Museum.* Accessed June 7, 2017. https://www.ushmm.org/wlc/en/article.php?ModuleId=10005372.

"East Prussia." *Encyclopedia Britannica Online.* Accessed May 30, 2017. https://www.britannica.com/place/East-Prussia.

"Flossenbürg." *United States Holocaust Memorial Museum.* Accessed June 6, 2017. https://www.ushmm.org/wlc/en/article.php?ModuleId=10005537.

Frank, Anne. *The Diary of a Young Girl.* Seattle: Kindle, 2015.

Frank, Hans. "We Must Finish with the Jews," in *The Jew in the Modern World.* Edited by Paul Mendes-Flohr and Jehuda Reinharz. Oxford: Oxford University Press, 2011.

"Gedenkbuch - Opfer Der Verfolgung Der Juden Unter Der Nationalsozialistischen Gewaltherrschaft in Deutschland 1933-1945." *Das*

Bibliography

Bundesarchiv. Accessed June 5, 2017, https://www.bundesarchiv.de/gedenkbuch/en861212.

"Gedenkbuch - Opfer Der Verfolgung Der Juden Unter Der Nationalsozialistischen Gewaltherrschaft in Deutschland 1933-1945," *Das Bundesarchiv.* Accessed June 5, 2017. https://www.bundesarchiv.de/gedenkbuch/en861241.

"Gedenkbuch - Opfer Der Verfolgung Der Juden Unter Der Nationalsozialistischen Gewaltherrschaft in Deutschland 1933-1945." *Das Bundesarchiv.* Accessed June 5, 2017. https://www.bundesarchiv.de/gedenkbuch/en861242.

Hart, Kitty. *Return to Auschwitz.* New York: Atheneum, 1982.

Josephs, Zoë. *Survivors: Jewish Refugees in Birmingham.* West Midlands: The Birmingham Jewish History Research Group, 1988.

"Kovno." *United States Holocaust Memorial Museum.* Accessed June 6, 2017. https://www.ushmm.org/wlc/en/article.php?ModuleId=10005174.

Messent, Maureen. "Saved from Hell." *Birmingham Mail* (Birmingham, UK), May 8, 2000.

Newman, E. W. "Elpis Lodge: Six Months' Work Reviewed." *The Christadelphian*, January 1941.

"Polish Corridor." *Encyclopedia Britannica Online.* Accessed May 30, 2017. https://www.britannica.com/place/Polish-Corridor.

William Shirer. *The Rise and Fall of the Third Reich.* New York: Simon and Schuster, 1960.

"Zinten," in *The Encyclopedia of Jewish Life Before and During the Holocaust.* Edited by Shmuel Spector and Geoffrey Wigoder. Jerusalem: Yad Vashem, 2001.

"Zinten," in *The London General Gazetteer, or Geographical Dictionary, Volume III.* London: William Baynes and Son, 1825.

Susan Clapper's Biography

Bibliography

Baumel-Schwartz, Judith Tydor. *Never Look Back: The Jewish Refugee Children in Great Britain, 1938-1945*. West Lafayette: Purdue University Press, 2012.

"Buchenwald." *United States Holocaust Memorial Museum*. Accessed April 27, 2017. http://www.ushmm.org/wlc/en/article.php?ModuleId=10005198.

Clapper, Susan. *USC Shoah Foundation Institute Testimony of Susan Clapper*. USC Shoah Foundation Interview, November 23, 1995.

"Durban's Own Kinder." *Ha Shalom*, February 1995.

"Gedenkbuch - Opfer Der Verfolgung Der Juden Unter Der Nationalsozialistischen Gewaltherrschaft in Deutschland 1933-1945." *Das Bundesarchiv*. Accessed April 27, 2017. http://www.bundesarchiv.de/gedenkbuch/de854544.

"Gedenkbuch - Opfer Der Verfolgung Der Juden Unter Der Nationalsozialistischen Gewaltherrschaft in Deutschland 1933-1945." *Das Bundesarchiv*. Accessed April 27, 2017. http://www.bundesarchiv.de/gedenkbuch/de854552.

"Gedenkbuch - Opfer Der Verfolgung Der Juden Unter Der Nationalsozialistischen Gewaltherrschaft in Deutschland 1933-1945." *Das Bundesarchiv*. Accessed April 27, 2017. http://www.bundesarchiv.de/gedenkbuch/de854556.

"Gedenkbuch - Opfer Der Verfolgung Der Juden Unter Der Nationalsozialistischen Gewaltherrschaft in Deutschland 1933-1945." *Das Bundesarchiv*. Accessed April 27, 2017. http://www.bundesarchiv.de/gedenkbuch/de854559.

Hayes, W. H. "Intelligence." *The Christadelphian*, July 1947.

Mühlberger, Detlef. *Hitler's Voice: The Völkischer Beobachter 1920–1923*. Bern: Peter Lang, 2004.

Nyomarkay, Joseph. *Charisma and Factionalism in the Nazi Party*. Minneapolis: University of Minnesota Press, 1967.

Bibliography

"Ravensbrück." *United States Holocaust Memorial Museum.* Accessed April 27, 2017. https://www.ushmm.org/wlc/en/article.php?ModuleId=10005199.

"Riga." *United States Holocaust Memorial Museum.* Accessed April 27, 2017. http://www.ushmm.org/wlc/en/article.php?ModuleId=10005463.

Shirer, William. *The Rise and Fall of the Third Reich.* New York: Simon and Schuster, 1960.

Thompson, Dorothy. "As to Werfel." *The New York Times* (New York, NY), January 24, 1926.

Tudor, Allen. "Touching Reunion for Hilda, 100, from Jewish girl, 13, she saved from Hitler's grasp." *Herald Express* (Devon, UK), not dated.

Rudi Weil's Biography

"Anschluss." *United States Holocaust Memorial Museum.* Accessed March 23, 2017. https://www.ushmm.org/research/research-in-collections/search-the-collections/bibliography/anschluss.

Barnett, Ruth. "Therapeutic Aspects of Working Through the Trauma of the Kindertransport Experience," in *The Kindertransport to Britain 1938/1939: New Perspectives.* Edited by Andrea Hammel and Bea Lewkowicz. Amsterdam: Rodopi, 2012.

Brown, Mary Elizabeth. "Laura Fermi (1907–1977): Illustrious Immigrants," in *The Making of Modern Immigration: An Encyclopedia of People and Ideas,* edited by Patrick J. Hayes. Santa Barbara: ABC-CLIO, 2012.

"Ebrei stranieri internati in Italia durante il periodo bellico." *Anna Pizzuti.* Accessed March 24, 2017. http://www.annapizzuti.it/database/ricerca.php?a=view&recid=8840.

Emmanuel, Muriel and Vera Gissing. *Nicholas Winton and the Rescued Generation.* London: Vallentine Mitchell, 2002.

Bibliography

Feisst, Sabine. *Schoenberg's New World: The American Years*. Oxford: Oxford University Press, 2011.

"Ferramonti di Tarsia." *Yad Vashem*. Accessed March 24, 2017. http://www.yadvashem.org/odot_pdf/Microsoft%20Word%20-%205847.pdf.

"France." *United States Holocaust Memorial Museum*. Accessed March 24, 2017. https://www.ushmm.org/wlc/en/article.php?ModuleId=10005429.

"Hermine Weil." *Geni*. Accessed March 23, 2017. https://www.geni.com/people/Hermine-Weil/6000000010722407518?through=6000000010722093906.

"Kindertransport, 1938–1940." *United States Holocaust Memorial Museum*. Accessed March 23, 2017. https://www.ushmm.org/wlc/en/article.php?ModuleId=10005260.

Kranjc, Gregor Joseph. "On the Periphery - Jews, Slovenes, and the Memory of the Holocaust," in *Bringing the Dark Past to Light: The Reception of the Holocaust in Postcommunist Europe*. Edited by John-Paul Himka and Joanna Beata Michlic. Lincoln: University of Nebraska Press, 2013.

Ladson, C. A. "The Jews and Zionism." *The Christadelphian,* April 1938.

Lavsky, Hagit. *The Creation of the German-Jewish Diaspora: Interwar German-Jewish Immigration to Palestine, the USA, and England*. Berlin and Jerusalem: De Gruyter and Magnes, 2017.

L. G. Hathaway. "Intelligence." *The Christadelphian*. June 1940.

L. G. Hathaway. "Intelligence." *The Christadelphian*, September 1938.

Lichtblau, Albert. "Austria," in *The Greater German Reich and the Jews: Nazi Persecution Policies in the Annexed Territories 1935–1945*. Edited by Wolf Gruner and Jörg Osterloh. Translated by Bernard Heise. New York: Berghahn, 2015.

"Life in Ferramonti." *Italy and the Holocaust Foundation*. Accessed March 24, 2017.

Bibliography

http://www.italyandtheholocaust.org/places-life-in-Life-In-Ferramonti-2.aspx.

Pauley, Bruce. "The Austrian Nazi Party before 1938," in *Conquering the Past: Austrian Nazism Yesterday and Today,* edited by. F. Parkinson. Detroit: Wayne State University Press, 1989.

Rees, Laurence. *Hitler's Charisma: Leading Millions into the Abyss.* New York: Vintage Books, 2014.

"Rudolf Weil." *Geni.* Accessed March 23, 2017.
https://www.geni.com/people/Rudolf-Weil/6000000010722093906.

"Schmalzhofgasse 3 (Synagogue association) - 6th district Mariahilf / Neubau." *Synagogue Memorial "Beit Ashkenaz."* Accessed March 23, 2017.
http://www.austriansynagogues.com/index.php/archive?sid=119:schmalzhofgasse-3-synagogue-association-6th-district-mariahilf-neubau.

"Search Burial Records." *Montefiore Cemetery Co.* Accessed April 28, 2017.
http://www.montefiore.us/search.asp?pname=W.

Siemens, Daniel. *The Making of a Nazi Hero: The Murder and Myth of Horst Wessel.* Translated by David Burnett. London: I. B. Tauris, 2013.

Shirer, William. *The Rise and Fall of the Third Reich.* New York: Simon and Schuster, 1960.

Steinberg, Phyllis. "Vienna Welcomes Jews to Its Community," *Jewish Journal,* October 10, 2014.
http://boston.forward.com/articles/185696/vienna-welcomes-jews-to-its-community/.

"The Laws of Jewish Names." *Chabad.org.* Accessed March 23, 2017.
http://www.chabad.org/library/article_cdo/aid/1158837/jewish/The-Laws-of-Jewish-Names.htm

"Vienna." *United States Holocaust Memorial Museum.* Accessed March 22, 2017.
https://www.ushmm.org/wlc/en/article.php?ModuleId=10005452.

Bibliography

"Virtual Jewish World: Lodz, Poland." *Jewish Virtual Library*. Accessed March 22, 2017. http://www.jewishvirtuallibrary.org/lodz-poland-jewish-history-tour.

"Virtual Jewish World: Vienna, Austria." *Jewish Virtual Library*. Accessed March 22, 2017. http://www.jewishvirtuallibrary.org/vienna-austria-jewish-history-tour.

"Warsaw." *YIVO Institute for Jewish Research*. Accessed March 22, 2017. http://www.yivoencyclopedia.org/article.aspx/Warsaw.

Woods, Sarah. *National Geographic Traveler: Vienna*. Washington, D. C.: National Geographic, 2012.

Wyman, David. *The Abandonment of the Jews*. New York: Pantheon, 1984.

"Yugoslavia." *United States Holocaust Memorial Museum*. Accessed March 24, 2017. https://www.ushmm.org/wlc/en/article.php?ModuleId=10007886.

Zucotti, Susan. *Under His Very Windows*. New Haven: Yale University Press, 2000.

Inge Beacham's Biography

"Antisemitic Legislation 1933–1939." *United States Holocaust Memorial Museum*. Accessed April 28, 2017. https://www.ushmm.org/wlc/en/article.php?ModuleId=10007901.

Beacham, Inge. "Inge," in *Living Stones: Ordinary people - Extraordinary stories*. Birmingham: The Christadelphian Sunday School Union, 2015.

"Boycott of Jewish Businesses." *United States Holocaust Memorial Museum*. Accessed April 28, 2017. https://www.ushmm.org/wlc/en/article.php?ModuleId=10005678.

Fryer, G. T. "Intelligence." *The Christadelphian*, May 1947.

Bibliography

"German Jews' Passports Declared Invalid." *United States Holocaust Memorial Museum.* Accessed June 2, 2017. https://www.ushmm.org/learn/timeline-of-events/1933-1938/reich-ministry-of-the-interior-invalidates-all-german-passports-held-by-jew.

"Law on Alteration of Family and Personal Names." *United States Holocaust Memorial Museum.* Accessed April 28, 2017, https://www.ushmm.org/learn/timeline-of-events/1933-1938/law-on-alteration-of-family-and-personal-names.

Rimer, Sara. "Reunion Recalls School for Jews in Nazi Germany." *The New York Times* (New York, NY), November 11, 1985. http://www.nytimes.com/1985/11/11/nyregion/reunion-recalls-school-for-jews-in-nazi-germany.html.

"Timeline of Events." *United States Holocaust Memorial Museum.* Accessed April 28, 2017. https://www.ushmm.org/learn/timeline-of-events/1933-1938/hitler-appointed-chancellor.

Ben Weiss's Biography

Abrahamson, Günther. "Günther Abrahamson," in *I Came Alone: the Stories of the Kindertransports.* Edited by Bertha Leverton and Shmuel Lowensohn. Sussex: The Book Guild Ltd., 1990.

Berton, Pierre. *The Great Depression: 1929–1939.* Toronto: Anchor Canada, 2001.

Carter, John. "An Abode of Hope." *The Christadelphian,* June 1940.

Carter, John. "Refugee Boys' Hostel." *The Christadelphian,* June 1942.

Carter, John. "Birmingham Refugee Boys' Hostel." *The Christadelphian,* July 1940.

"Dachau." *United States Holocaust Memorial Museum.* Accessed April 28, 2017. https://www.ushmm.org/wlc/en/article.php?ModuleId=10005214.

Bibliography

"Datei:Stolperstein Fehrbelliner Str 20 (Mitte) Max Wisen.jpg." *Wikipedia.* Accessed April 28, 2017. https://de.wikipedia.org/wiki/Datei:Stolperstein_Fehrbelliner_Str_20_(Mitte)_Max_Wisen.jpg.

"Gedenkbuch - Opfer Der Verfolgung Der Juden Unter Der Nationalsozialistischen Gewaltherrschaft in Deutschland 1933-1945." *Das Bundesarchiv.* Accessed April 28, 2017. http://www.bundesarchiv.de/gedenkbuch/de1180821.

"Gedenkbuch - Opfer Der Verfolgung Der Juden Unter Der Nationalsozialistischen Gewaltherrschaft in Deutschland 1933-1945." *Das Bundesarchiv.* Accessed April 28, 2017. http://www.bundesarchiv.de/gedenkbuch/de1180822.

"German Wartime Expansion." *United States Holocaust Memorial Museum.* Accessed April 28, 2017. https://www.ushmm.org/wlc/en/article.php?ModuleId=10005481.

Goldstein, Susy, Gina Hamilton, and Wendy Share. *Ten Marks and a Train Ticket.* Toronto: The League for Human Rights of B'nai Brith Canada, 2008.

"Gustav Stresemann." *Encyclopedia Britannica Online.* Accessed April 28, 2017. https://www.britannica.com/biography/Gustav-Stresemann.

Hillman, Herman in *Memories of Liberation.* Edited by Violet Zeitlin. Philadelphia: Gratz College.

Kreutzmüller, Christoph. *Jewish Book Council.* March 11, 2016. http://www.jewishbookcouncil.org/_blog/The_ProsenPeople/post/max-wisens-tailor-shop.

"Oct. 28–29, 1929: Stock Crash." *The Wall Street Journal* (New York, NY), October 27, 2014. http://blogs.wsj.com/wsj125/2014/10/27/oct-28-29-1929-stock-crash/.

Shirer, William. *The Rise and Fall of the Third Reich.* New York: Simon and Schuster, 1960.

Turner, Barry. . . . *And the Policeman Smiled.* London: Bloomsbury, 1990.

Bibliography

Max Harper's Biography

"Aryanization." *Yad Vashem.* Accessed April 6, 2017. http://www.yadvashem.org/odot_pdf/Microsoft%20Word%20-%205775.pdf.

Carter, John. "The Ecclesial Visitor." *The Christadelphian,* August 1946.

Carter, John. "The Ecclesial Visitor." *The Christadelphian,* November 1945.

"Gedenkbuch - Opfer Der Verfolgung Der Juden Unter Der Nationalsozialistischen Gewaltherrschaft in Deutschland 1933-1945." *Das Bundesarchiv.* Accessed April 7, 2017. https://www.bundesarchiv.de/gedenkbuch/en902033.

"Gedenkbuch - Opfer Der Verfolgung Der Juden Unter Der Nationalsozialistischen Gewaltherrschaft in Deutschland 1933-1945." *Das Bundesarchiv.* Accessed April 7, 2017. https://www.bundesarchiv.de/gedenkbuch/en902036.

"Gedenkbuch - Opfer Der Verfolgung Der Juden Unter Der Nationalsozialistischen Gewaltherrschaft in Deutschland 1933–1945." *Das Bundesarchiv.* Accessed April 7, 2017. https://www.bundesarchiv.de/gedenkbuch/en932655.

"Gedenkbuch - Opfer Der Verfolgung Der Juden Unter Der Nationalsozialistischen Gewaltherrschaft in Deutschland 1933-1945." *Das Bundesarchiv.* Accessed April 7, 2017. https://www.bundesarchiv.de/gedenkbuch/en932657.

"Germany: Hamburg." *Jewish Virtual Library.* Accessed April 6, 2017. http://www.jewishvirtuallibrary.org/hamburg.

"Hamburg." *Yad Vashem.* Accessed April 6, 2017. http://www.yadvashem.org/odot_pdf/Microsoft%20Word%20-%206350.pdf.

"Hamburg - 11a Rutschbahn, Alte und Neue Klaus Synagogue." *Synagogue Memorial "Beit Ashkenaz."* Accessed April 6, 2017. http://germansynagogues.com/index.php/synagogues-and-commun

Bibliography

ities?pid=58&sid=603:hamburg-11a-rutschbahn-alte-und-neue-klaus-synagogue.

"Hamburg - 8 Bornplatz (Rotherbaum Locality)." *Synagogue Memorial "Beit Ashkenaz."* Accessed April 6, 2017. http://germansynagogues.com/index.php/synagogues-and-communities?pid=58&sid=601:hamburg-8-bornplatz-rotherbaum-locality.

"Hamburg - Introduction." *Synagogue Memorial "Beit Ashkenaz."* Accessed April 7, 2017. http://germansynagogues.com/index.php/synagogues-and-communities?pid=58&sid=599:hamburg-introduction.

Hoffman, Peter. *German Resistance to Hitler*. Cambridge: Harvard University Press, 1988.

Kaplan, Chaim. "Scroll of Agony," in *The Literature of Destruction*. Edited by David Roskies. Philadelphia: The Jewish Publication Society.

Koenigsbuch, Rolf S. Personal Experiences. Weiner Library P II.a. No. 175.

"Last Letters from the Lodz (Lodsch) Ghetto." *JewishGen*. Accessed April 28, 2017. http://www.jewishgen.org/databases/jgdetail_2.php.

"Lodz." *United States Holocaust Memorial Museum*. Accessed April 7, 2017. https://www.ushmm.org/wlc/en/article.php?ModuleId=10005071.

"Lodz." *YIVO Institute for Jewish Research*. Accessed April 7, 2017. http://www.yivoencyclopedia.org/article.aspx/%C5%81odz.

"Port of Hamburg." *Port of Hamburg*. Accessed April 6, 2017. https://www.hafen-hamburg.de/.

Rosen, Jacob. "The Search for Koenigsbuch on the Internet." *Sharsheret Hadorot,* August 2005.

Shirer, William. *The Rise and Fall of the Third Reich*. New York: Simon and Schuster, 1960.

Bibliography

"The Jewish Traveler: Hamburg." *Hadassah Magazine,* November 2008. http://www.hadassahmagazine.org/2008/11/29/jewish-traveler-hamburg/.

Rita Devletian's Biography

"Adolf Hitler: Early Years, 1889–1913." *United States Holocaust Memorial Museum.* Accessed April 28, 2017. https://www.ushmm.org/wlc/en/article.php?ModuleId=10007430.

"Adolf Hitler and World War I: 1913–1919." *United States Holocaust Memorial Museum.* Accessed April 28, 2017. https://www.ushmm.org/wlc/en/article.php?ModuleId=10007431.

"Antisemitic Legislation 1933–1939." *United States Holocaust Memorial Museum.* Accessed April 28, 2017. https://www.ushmm.org/wlc/en/article.php?ModuleId=10007901.

"Citizenship for Hitler." *The New York Times* (New York, NY), July 15, 1930.

Devletian, Rita. "Biography," typescript.

"Fascists Glorify Pan-German Ideal." *The New York Times* (New York, NY), September 15, 1930.

"German Citizenship Acquired by Hitler." *The New York Times* (New York, NY), February 26, 1932.

Shirer, William. *The Rise and Fall of the Third Reich.* New York: Simon and Schuster, 1960.

Rita Glanz's Biography

"90 Years Ago: The End of German Hyperinflation." *Mises Institute.* Accessed April 20, 2017. https://mises.org/library/90-years-ago-end-german-hyperinflation.

"Adolf Hitler Wounded in British Gas Attack." *History.com.* Accessed April 19, 2017. http://www.history.com/this-day-in-history/adolf-hitler-wounded-in-british-gas-attack.

Bibliography

Dwork, Deborah and Robert Jan van Pelt. *Holocaust - A History*. New York: W. W. Norton & Company, 2002.

"Erich Ludendorff." *Encyclopedia Britannica Online*. Accessed April 19, 2017. https://www.britannica.com/biography/Erich-Ludendorff.

Grosz, Kirsten, Hanus, and Anita. *Kindertransport Memory Quilt*. Kindertransport Association of North America, 2000.

Hitler, Adolf. *Mein Kampf*. Boston: Houghton Mifflin, 1971.

Madeley, H. "Intelligence." *The Christadelphian*, September 1933.

"Marshal." *Encyclopedia Britannica Online*. Accessed April 19, 2017. https://www.britannica.com/topic/marshal.

"Paul von Hindenburg." *Encyclopedia Britannica Online*. Accessed April 19, 2017. https://www.britannica.com/biography/Paul-von-Hindenburg.

Roman, Eric. *Austria-Hungary & the Successor States*. New York: Facts On File, Inc., 2003.

Sanders, Rex. "The Brotherhood Near and Far." *The Christadelphian*, August 1984.

Sanders, Rex. "The Brotherhood Near and Far." *The Christadelphian*, June 1985.

Shirer, William. *The Rise and Fall of the Third Reich*. New York: Simon and Schuster, 1960.

"Terms of the Armistice with Germany." *The National Archives*. Accessed April 19, 2017. http://www.nationalarchives.gov.uk/pathways/firstworldwar/transcripts/aftermath/armistice_terms.htm.

"Weimar Germany." *The BBC*. Accessed April 20, 2017. http://www.bbc.co.uk/education/guides/zh9p34j/revision/6.

Ernst Billig's Biography

Bibliography

"1933: Key Dates." *United States Holocaust Memorial Museum*. Accessed March 28, 2017. https://www.ushmm.org/wlc/en/article.php?ModuleId=10007499.

Aldridge, Jane. "Dreams of Horror-Filled Years Come True As Nazi Prisoner Is Reunited With Family." *The Birmingham Post* (Birmingham, AL), February 26, 1947.

"Alsergrund und siene Bezirksteile." Wien.at. Accessed March 29, 2017. https://www.wien.gv.at/bezirke/alsergrund/geschichte-kultur/bezirksteile.html.

"Anti-Jewish Legislation in Prewar Germany." *United States Holocaust Memorial Museum*. Accessed March 28, 2017. https://www.ushmm.org/wlc/en/article.php?ModuleId=10005681.

"Der Leopoldstädter Tempel, Tempelgasse 5 - 2nd District Leopoldstadt." *Synagogue Memorial "Beit Ashkenaz."* Accessed March 29, 2017. http://www.austriansynagogues.com/index.php/archive?pid=58&sid=127:der-leopoldstaedter-tempel-tempelgasse-5-2nd-district-leopoldstadt.

"First Decree to the Reich Citizenship Law." in *The Jew in the Modern World*. Edited by Paul Mendes-Flohr and Jehuda Reinharz. Oxford: Oxford University Press, 2011.

Harby, Jennifer. "The Coventry Blitz: 'Hysteria, terror and neurosis.'" *BBC*. November 13, 2015. http://www.bbc.com/news/uk-england-coventry-warwickshire-34746691.

Haywood, Anthony and Caroline Sieg. *Vienna*. Melbourne: Lonely Planet, 2010.

Hitler, Adolf. *Mein Kampf*. Boston: Houghton Mifflin, 1971.

Humphreys, Rob. *The Rough Guide to Vienna*. London: Rough Guides, 2011.

Bibliography

Johnston, David Cay. "Jews Remember Forced Labor Camps in Wartime Swiss Refuge." *The New York Times* (New York, NY), January 15, 1998.

Kerman, Joseph. *The Beethoven Quartets*. New York: W. W. Norton & Company, 1979.

Melchoir, Kate. "Site 10: Friedhof Seegasse/Cemetary Seegasse." *The Vienna Project: Jewish Communities of Leopoldstadt and Alsergrund.* 2014. http://theviennaproject.org/wp-content/uploads/2014/09/Jewish-Communities-Worksheets-without-Questions.pdf.

Melchoir, Kate. "Site 1B: Leopoldstäter Tempel/Leopoldstadt Temple." *The Vienna Project: Jewish Communities of Leopoldstadt and Alsergrund.* 2014. http://theviennaproject.org/wp-content/uploads/2014/09/Jewish-Communities-Worksheets-without-Questions.pdf.

Melchoir, Kate. "Site 8A: Introduction to Jewish Life in Alsergrund." *The Vienna Project: Jewish Communities of Leopoldstadt and Alsergrund.* 2014. http://theviennaproject.org/wp-content/uploads/2014/09/Jewish-Communities-Worksheets-without-Questions.pdf.

Melchoir, Kate. "Site 8B: Gedenksymbol: Schlüssel gegen das Vergessen/Memorial: Keys against Forgetting." *The Vienna Project: Jewish Communities of Leopoldstadt and Alsergrund.* 2014. http://theviennaproject.org/wp-content/uploads/2014/09/Jewish-Communities-Worksheets-without-Questions.pdf.

"Rothschild Hospital." *Top Health Clinics.* Accessed March 31, 2017. http://www.tophealthclinics.com/clinic/919849078079887/Rothschild+Hospital.

Scheinberg, Robert. "Controversy erupts over Swiss WWII labor camps." *Jewish Telegraphic Agency.* February 12, 1999. http://www.jta.org/1999/02/12/life-religion/features/controversy-erupts-over-swiss-wwii-labor-camps.

"Servitengasse 1938 - The Fate of Those Who Disappeared." *Servitengasse 1938.* Accessed March 29, 2017.

Bibliography

http://redirect.servitengasse1938.at/page12/files/Servitengasse%20english.pdf

"Swiss put Jews in labor camps, British documentary contends." *The Jewish News of Northern California.* January 9, 1998. http://www.jweekly.com/1998/01/09/swiss-put-jews-in-labor-camps-british-documentary-contends/.

"The Program of the NSDAP." *Yale Law School.* Accessed April 28, 2017. http://avalon.law.yale.edu/imt/1708-ps.asp.

"The Reich Citizenship Law," in *The Jew in the Modern World.* Edited by Paul Mendes-Flohr and Jehuda Reinharz. Oxford: Oxford University Press, 2011.

Wistrich, Robert. *Antisemitism - The Longest Hatred.* New York: Schocken Books, 1991.

Glossary

Excerpted with permission from the Glossary in *Echoes and Reflections Teacher's Resource Guide* (New York: Anti-Defamation League, 2005, 2014), www.echoesandreflections.org. All rights reserved.

Acknowledgements

The biographies contained in this book were written together with the Kinder and their families, as well as the Christadelphian foster families. It has been an honor to hear your stories, and to be taken back in time, as it were, to witness faith in action. Thank you for allowing me to be a part of sharing these memories.

Thank you specifically to Netty Gladstone, along with Molly Lawrence and Sarah Tibbs; Peter and Moira Hart; Michael Clapper, along with Clive and Ruth Bennet and Ursula Meyer and family; Fay Weil, along with Dottie and Stephen Ford; Inge Beacham, along with Sarah Watts and Bob Beacham; Ben and Rita Weiss, along with Wendy Share; Max and Ada Harper, along with Megan Harper, Jacob Rosen, and Fritz Neubauer; Rita Devletian, along with Adrian Kriss and Rachel Newman; Rita Glanz, along with Jill Glanz; Ernst and Nancy Billig, along with Corina Midgett.

The book is the second in the *Part of the Family* series. The number of people who have approached me and offered words of encouragement has simply been astounding. At times, my desire to keep writing about such dark times has flagged—but your support has helped to provide additional motivation. Thank you for your kind words, they have been invaluable.

Thank you to Heather Rothman, who served as the main editor for the entirety of both *Part of the Family* books. Thanks also goes to Pat Hampson, Gordon Hensley, Rebecca Laben, Jeff Lange, Bethany Robinson, Felicity Robinson, Rachel Robinson, who together, proofread the book multiple times. Dr. Stephen Snobelen read through the manuscript, providing a further round of editing as well as insight. Jason Robinson designed the cover.

Acknowledgments

Graham Jackman's assistance has been much appreciated. He translated a number of the letters out of German and into English, and gave feedback about the section of the introduction about German Christadelphians. Jenny Levin translated documents out of both Polish and German.

My family has been immensely supportive throughout all of this, and it is hoped that the stories contained herein may be inspiring to my children once they are of age both to read them, and to read in general. My wife has given of herself to further this project—both in allowing me the time to work on it, in providing feedback throughout, and in designing the maps for the chapters.

Above all, thanks goes to God and His son, the Lord Jesus Christ, who together make all things possible. May God's Kingdom come soon, so that suffering and pain will be known no more, and harrowing stories like these will no longer need to be told.

INDEX

Alsergrund, Vienna 340–343, 355
Amsterdam, Netherlands 47, 49, 226, 250
Anschluss 149, 151, 174, 325, 343–344, 356
Antwerp, Belgium 60–61
Argentina 84, 86, 111
Auschwitz extermination camp 51, 62–63, 69, 93, 131, 186, 219–220, 270–271, 302–303, 337, 344

Bad Salzuflen, Germany 123–124, 131, 138
Bages, France 69
Bampton, England 272–273
Barham House, England 88, 90, 92, 231–233, 237
Beacham, Inge 179–197, 290–299, 302–305, 308–309, 312–313
Beer Hall Putsch 122, 147, 286, 323
Belgium 60–62, 213, 319, 323
Berlin, Germany 5, 7, 12–14, 16, 39, 101, 145, 182, 184–186, 189–190, 203–204, 211–213, 216–217, 219–222, 231, 240, 252, 261, 287, 297–298, 302, 313
Bernburg Euthanasia Center 131
Billig, Abisch and Cheine Gittel 340, 344–345, 353–357, 360–361
Billig, Ernst 335–367
Birmingham, England 20–22, 54, 65, 70, 91, 93, 96–98, 100, 102, 104, 106, 110–111, 134, 153–154, 187, 189–190, 193–194, 235–237, 240, 244, 273–274, 298, 303, 310

Birmingham, United States 325, 328–329, 359, 361
Brandenburg, Germany 18
Braunau am Inn, Austria 285
Bruchsal, Germany 12
Brunswick, Germany 287
Brzesko, Poland 252
Buchenwald concentration camp 127, 261, 353
Buenos Aires, Argentina 84, 91

California, United States 72
Canada 276
Carter, John 26, 278
Catholic Church 4–5, 37, 40, 249
Chelmno extermination center 265, 268
Clapper, Michael 126, 133, 138–139
Clapper, Susan 119–141
Claydon, England 88, 90–93, 231
Coventry, England 235, 244, 274, 310, 325, 327–330, 346–347, 351–352, 359

Dachau concentration camp 109, 210–212, 353, 356
Danzig, Free City of 79
Dawes Plan 201, 323
Day, Roland and Kate 187–188, 298
Degersheim, Switzerland 360
Devletian, Rita 283–316
Drancy transit camp 62–63
Durban, South Africa 138

East Prussia, Germany 79–80, 84, 91, 319
Eichmann, Bruno 123, 125, 132
Eichmann, Hans and Gertrud 123–132
Eichmann, Ilse 132
Elpis Lodge, England 20, 24–25, 91–100, 104, 110, 235–237,

Index

240–241, 244, 273–275, 277–278

Felixstowe, England 230–231
Felsberg internment camp 356
Ferramonti di Tarsia concentration camp 159–163
Flossenbürg concentration camp 109
Frank, Anne 106
Frank, Hans 105
Ford, Horace, and Lily 152–156, 163, 166–174
Ford, Stephen 173
Forst, Germany 182, 185, 288, 290–291
Fort Ontario, New York 164–166
France 62, 69, 79, 156–157, 201, 323

Gas chambers 106, 131, 219–220, 265, 302
Gestapo 151, 263, 296, 342, 353
Ghetto 108–109, 131–132, 264–266, 268, 343
Gladstone, Netty 35–75
Glanz, Rita 317–333, 340, 344–347, 349, 351, 355, 357–361, 363
Goebbels, Joseph 37–39
Goldschmidt, Leonore 185, 188, 297
Great Depression 203, 251, 323

Hamburg, Germany 87, 249–251, 254–256, 260, 262–264
Harper, Max 247–282
Hart, Paul and Paula and Kurt 81–88, 95, 101, 103, 108–110
Hart, Peter 88, 113–114
Hart, Rudi 77–118
Hart-Moxon, Kitty 93

Harwich, England 52, 186, 230–232, 298
Hayes, Hilda 128, 132–137
Hayes, Walter and Ethel 134, 136–137
Hindenburg, Paul von 319–324
Hitler Youth 211–212
Holland 47–48, 51, 53, 130, 186, 213–214, 217, 220–232, 238–298, 345, 360
Hook of Holland 229
Hoverd, William and Priscilla 187, 298, 303–314
Hyperinflation 121, 323,

Ipswich, England 52, 88, 93, 231
Italy 4, 111, 158–163

Jasenovac concentration camp 5
Jerred, Eardley and Edna 54–72

Kent, England 309
Kleve, Germany 220_221
Kornevo, Russia 80
Koenigsbuch, Aron and Elisabetha 252–270
Koenigsbuch, Rolf 247–282
Königsberg, East Prussia 80, 86–87
Kovno ghetto 108–109
Kristallnacht 14, 46, 84, 126–128, 152, 174, 184–185, 190, 208, 211, 253–254, 260–262, 295, 300, 342–344, 353, 356
Kupperman, Suger Anber and Zara 39–47, 51, 59–63, 69–70

Lawrence, Molly 55–56, 58, 63, 65–66, 71–72
Laxon, Sydney 236, 346
Leamington Spa, England 331, 363
Leeds, England 237–238, 240
Leopoldstadt, Vienna 340–342

Index

Levy, Gerhard and Mary 185–186, 288–303
Liverpool, England 359
Liverpool Street Station, London 132, 345–346
Ljubljana, Yugoslavia 158–159, 162
Locarno, Pact of 201–202
Lodz, Poland 145
Lodz ghetto 264–271
London, England 52, 54, 132, 187, 241, 243, 271, 274, 329, 345, 363
Los Angeles, United States 70
Lucerne, Switzerland 356
Ludendorff, Erich 319–323

Mariahilf, Vienna 149
Mayen, Germany 81
Mein Kampf 121, 146, 321–322, 339–340
Merz, Albert 9, 12, 14–19
Merz, August 11, 13
Merz, Rudolf 11–12
Meyer, Ursula 123, 125, 137, 189
Moore, Henry and Marjorie 325, 329, 346–352, 362–364
Morgan, Harry and Freda 325–331, 346–347, 351
Munich, Germany 210, 285–286, 338
Münster, Germany 252

Naples, Italy 111
Netherlands, The 48–49, 227, 270
Newman, E. W. 92, 95, 236, 277
New Jersey, United States 363
New York, United States 68–70, 145, 169–170, 301, 325, 358, 360–361
Nijmegen, Holland 220, 222–224
Norwich, England 92

Nuneaton, England 327, 330–331, 351

Oswego, New York 165
Overton, Alan 153, 346–347

Palestine 22, 145, 158, 184, 229, 270, 277, 294
Paris, France 62
Parry, George and Florrie 346
Philadelphia, United States 166, 169–171
Posen, Prussia 79, 319
Prussia, East 79–80, 84, 91, 319

Ravensbrück concentration camp 131
Red Cross 95, 102–103, 106–110, 219, 233, 243, 268, 299, 303
Rheydt, Germany 37, 39, 47
Rhodesia 137, 139
Riga ghetto 131–132
Rivesaltes transit camp 62–63
Rosenstock, Suse 329, 346, 358
Rotterdam, Netherlands 186, 298, 360
Ruddington, England 190
Rugby, England 153, 346–347

Sachsenhausen concentration camp 13–14, 260–264
Saint-Nazaire, France 156–158
Schattner, Fritz and Nesche 356–357, 361
Smallheath, England 194
Solihull, England 55, 65, 153
South Africa 137–139, 359
Southampton, England 87–88, 169
Stresemann, Gustav 201–203
Stuttgart, Germany 7, 9, 12
Stutthof concentration camp 109
Sudetenland 127

Index

Switzerland 328, 353, 355–356, 360

Thalheim internment camp 356
Theresienstadt ghetto 260,
Thuringia, Germany 287
Torquay, England 137, 139
Toronto, Canada 276
Tunbridge Wells, England 52
Typhus 159

United States 4, 9, 68–70, 121, 151, 164–167, 201, 203, 208, 212, 300–302, 309, 312–313, 325, 327, 356–360, 363
United States Holocaust Memorial Museum 4, 151

Versailles, Treaty of 79, 321
Vichy France 62, 157
Vienna, Austria 92, 145–156, 230, 237, 285, 324–325, 327, 340–345, 348, 353, 355–356

Walker, Charles Curwin 22
Wallingford, England 238
Warendorf, Germany 81
Warsaw, Poland 145, 264
Warsaw ghetto 265
Washington, D.C., United States 301
Waterhouses, England 271–272
Weil, Aranka and Hugo 148–174
Weil, Fay 149, 152, 162, 166, 171–173
Weil, Rudi 143–177
Weimar Republic 122, 146, 201–203, 210, 251, 320–324
Weiss, Ben 199–246
Weiss, Heinz 199–246
Weiss, Max and Golda 203–220, 226–229, 238, 243
Welwyn Garden City, England 271

West Bromwich, England 134
Weston-Super-Mare, England 347
Wijk aan Zee, Holland 224–226
Winton, Nicholas 154

Yugoslavia 158–159

Zinten, East Prussia 80–88

Photographic Credits

Christadelphians and the Jews

Page 9: photograph courtesy of the Christadelphian Magazine and Publishing Association.

Page 20: photograph courtesy of the Christadelphian Magazine and Publishing Association.

All other photographs courtesy of Graham Jackman.

Netty Gladstone's Biography

All photographs courtesy of Netty Gladstone.

Rudi Hart's Biography

All photographs courtesy of Peter and Moira Hart and family.

Susan Clapper's Biography

Page 124: photograph courtesy of Ursula and Max Meyer.

Page 129: photographs ©National Holocaust Centre and Museum, used with permission.

All other photographs courtesy of Clive and Ruth Bennet (née Hayes).

Rudi Weil's Biography

Page 160: photograph courtesy of Ferramonti di Tarsia museum.

Page 161 top: photograph courtesy of Ferramonti di Tarsia museum.

Page 164: COFOSHS, NYSOPRHP: Collections of Fort Ontario State Historic Site, New York State Office of Parks, Recreation, and Historic Preservation. Used with permission.

Photographic Credits

Page 165: COFOSHS, NYSOPRHP: Collections of Fort Ontario State Historic Site, New York State Office of Parks, Recreation, and Historic Preservation. Used with permission.

Page 173: photograph courtesy of Fay Weil.

All other photographs courtesy of Stephen Ford.

Inge Beacham's Biography

Page 182: photograph courtesy of Rita Devletian.

Page 188: photograph courtesy of Rita Devletian.

Page 192 bottom: photograph courtesy of Rachel Newman.

All other photographs courtesy of Inge Beacham and family.

Ben Weiss's Biography

All photographs courtesy of Ben Weiss and family.

Max Harper's Biography

Page 255: photograph from Fred at the German language Wikipedia [GFDL (http://www.gnu.org/copyleft/fdl.html) or CC-BY-SA-3.0 (http://creativecommons.org/licenses/by-sa/3.0/)], from Wikimedia Commons.

Page 256: photograph by unknown; file: James Steakley - Alles begann mit Ansgar. Hamburgs Kirchen im Spiegel der Zeit (Hamburg: Pressestelle des Senats der Freien und Hansestadt Hamburg, 2006), p. 53., Public Domain, https://commons.wikimedia.org/w/index.php?curid=8583007

Page 264: photograph courtesy of Zentralarchiv zur Erforschung der Geschichte der Juden in Deutschland, Heidelberg, Germany Collection: B. 5/1 Abt. IV Nr. 322

Page 269: photograph courtesy of Archiwum Panstwowe v Lodzi.

Page 270: photograph courtesy of Archiwum Panstwowe v Lodzi.

Photographic Credits

All other photographs courtesy of Max Harper and family.

Rita Devletian's Biography

Page 304: photograph courtesy of Rachel Newman.

All other photographs courtesy of Rita Devletian.

Rita Glanz's Biography

All photographs courtesy of Ernst Billig.

Ernst Billig's Biography

All photographs courtesy of Ernst Billig.

Appendix

Page 424: photograph courtesy of the Christadelphian Magazine and Publishing Association.

A Note about the Author

Photograph courtesy of the US Holocaust Memorial Museum.

Photograph courtesy of the US Holocaust Memorial Museum.

A Note About the Author

Jason Hensley, M.A.Ed, is the principal of a small private school in California. At school, he teaches religious studies and a senior-level course on Christianity and the Holocaust. Related to the *Part of the Family* project, he is currently pursuing an M.A. in Holocaust and Genocide studies from Gratz College. He frequently lectures on this and related topics throughout North America. Find him on Facebook, and at iwaspartofthefamily.com

Made in the USA
Middletown, DE
05 November 2022

14189396R00268